Farewell to the 70s

A
Canadian
Salute to a
Confusing
Decade

Farewell to the 70s

Edited by Anna Porter & Marjorie Harris

A Discovery Book

Published by
Thomas Nelson & Sons (Canada) Limited

A Discovery Book
Published in Canada by
Thomas Nelson & Sons (Canada) Limited
81 Curlew Drive
Don Mills, Ontario, Canada
M3A 2R1

ISBN 017-600772-5

All of the cartoons in this book were selected from
research material for a book on the history of
Canadian political cartoons to be published in the fall
of 1979 by McClelland & Stewart. The co-authors
of this book are Peter Desbarats and Terry Mosher.

Designed by David Shaw & Harrison Shannon

Printed and bound in Canada
by John Deyell Company

This book
is dedicated to all
the contributors.

Contents

Editors' Note

The idea for this book was a very simple one. We wanted to remember the 1970s before they slipped away from us. We wanted to do so in the company of some of those people in Canada who put their stamp on it; and others who, as writers and journalists, recorded its passage. In one sense or another, most of these contributors are '70s people: many of them came into their own, others dramatically changed the pattern of their lives, during the decade.

Since these years have been labelled the most narcissistic in our history, we assumed this book would reveal a mass of self-indulgence. We were wrong. As it took shape, the book revealed a sense of joy and optimism on the part of its authors, and beyond that, a great deal of caring about what happened to us all, and a profound concern about the future.

Obviously, no book can be everything to everyone – but what we've tried to do in words and pictures is address ourselves to most things (light and serious) that made an impact on our lives during the past ten years.

Thank you to all our contributors for creating a valuable handbook of the decade – and now – here's looking at the '80s!

Anna Porter
Marjorie Harris

Our Style Was the Man Himself

If there's a word that sums up the style of the 1970s in Ottawa, from the War Measures Act to *Beyond Reason,* the word is *surreal.* So it somehow makes perfect sense that the event that serves as funeral for the decade should have been a wedding.

At this particular wedding, on May 26, 1979, four days after the election, in a set piece in the grand imperial style out of an Anthony Powell novel, U.S. Ambassador Thomas Enders' daughter Alice married Ottawa lawyer Peter Cronyn. Bride and groom, though, were really beside the point. The man who seized the occasion, shaped it to his own purposes from the instant he slipped quietly up the side aisle of Notre Dame basilica with a red rose in the lapel of his frock coat, was Pierre Elliott Trudeau. Afterwards, at the ambassador's residence, he kidded defeated cabinet ministers over champagne. He posed with the bride for photographers. He danced with all the bridesmaids, almost until the last guests left. "He's sending us a message," whispered a woman who was standing next to me. "He is saying, 'You're going to be *sorry.'* "

A christening, rather than a wedding, on a chilly night in November in 1969, serves as my own starting point for the '70s. The world's first domestic communications satellite, which is *our* communications satellite, has just been christened Anik. Its bureaucratic parent, the feisty new Department of Communications – Eric Kierans as minister – is throwing a party. One reason people have been fighting for invitations is that Leonard Cohen is coming. (When Communications organized a public contest to name the satellite – participatory democracy is the new orthodoxy – it asked Cohen to be a judge.) The other reason is that Trudeau is coming. So far, after a year and a half in office, he's been a bit of a disappointment to those who expected Camelot North to rise at 24 Sussex. But this kind of carelessly elegant soirée, at the elegant house of Communications Deputy Minister Allan Gotlieb, elegant food by Sondra Gotlieb eaten off the lap, is the kind of social scenario everyone had been expecting to happen. Trudeau plays his part to the hilt. He brings with him a willowy brunette in a see-through crocheted minidress. "Who is she?" people ask. "She's from Vancouver," someone says. "I think her last name," someone else adds, "is Sinclair."

It's fitting, if a bit frivolous, to bracket the 1970s in Ottawa with a pair of social events that Trudeau dominated. Ottawa style, this last decade, is inescapably intertwined with Trudeauvian style. He recreated the town in his own baffling, contradictory, infuriating, but always compulsively fascinating, image.

It began with a bang. The Philosopher King. As courtiers, in his own words, "New guys, with new ideas." The ideas had names like Access (to power, to information, to cable television systems, to pretty well everything), the Just Society, Democratization and Decentralization. All nicely bolstered with quotes from McLuhan, Marcuse, Roszak and Alvin Toffler. The biggest idea, at the very beginning, was Youth, which had its own committee of countercultural consultants studying it. (A lot of these people eventually turned up on the RCMP's blacklist, and Youth, alas, turned in its final report on the very same day the War Measures Act was declared.)

This was also the era when cabinet memos with titles like "The Priority Problem of Participation" were flying around like confetti. Not to mention flip-charts, decision trees and synectics.

As much as the new ideas, the new guys turned the town on its ear. As early as 1971, the Ottawa man on the Mike Pearson model, the only indigenous folk figure Ottawa had ever produced, was being pushed off centre stage by a new breed of mandarin. These guys were technocrats. Toughminded problem solvers is the description they liked. They talked and wrote a language that owed more to MIT than to Oxbridge. They knew more about Kahn than Kant. They went in for squash at the Skyline Club instead of bridge at the Rideau Club. They put Vasarely on their office walls instead of A.Y. Jackson. The hot shops, in the early 1970s, weren't the old mandarin haunts of Finance, Justice and External Affairs, but activist new branches like Secretary of State (Bernard Ostry, first mandarin in Ottawa to carry a purse; Mike McCabe, first mandarin to go in for shirts open-buttoned to show chest hair), Communications (bushy-tailed types like my husband, Richard Gwyn, in his pre-pundit period, all cock-a-hoop about satellites, wired cities and computers), CRTC (Pierre Juneau, the cabling of Canada, Canadian content).

Above all, there was PCO. Privy Council Office, that is to say, which was and is the prime minister's own department. Trudeau himself had worked there as a bureaucrat in the early 1950s; it was recalled that he used to stand on his head. Now, coming into his own as a consummate bureaucrat, who often went to cabinet meetings knowing more about what was going on in certain departments than the ministers who ran them, Trudeau trebled PCO's size. PCO people were closer to the levers of power than any other bureaucrats in town. They edited, often rewrote from scratch, all policy proposals headed for cabinet. They wrote the minutes of cabinet committee meetings and often interpreted, according to what they knew the man at the top wanted, the actual decisions. Towards the end of the decade, Michael Pitfield, the aloof patrician whom Trudeau named to the top PCO job in 1975, came to terrorize official Ottawa in much the same way that Bismarck once terrorized Europe. Earlier on, though, the style of the new high-flyer was epitomized best by a guy over at Manpower of an entirely different type. His name was Cam Mackie, and journalists quickly tagged him a "guerrilla bureaucrat." Mackie had long, stringy hair, never wore a tie and was the man who'd invented first OFY and later LIP. When interviewed, he would talk a blue streak about "showing people how to make the system work for them." Mackie, like Trudeau before him, liked to stand on his head.

Goodbye, by 1975, to all of that. Trudeau, in the wake of wage and price controls, started talking about "discipline and restraint." Out as hostages-to-headlines in order to sell the government's restraint program to the public went OFY and the Company of Young Canadians. As well, 1975 was the year when it started to become painfully apparent that the new-style technocrats that Trudeau had brought in were making as big a mess of things as any of their duller, more uptight predecessors. Between 1969 and 1975, the number of federal bureaucrats earning $20,000 or more increased by 1,300 percent. In the same period, the number of assistant deputy ministers increased by 95 percent. We'd been promised participatory democracy. What we'd gotten instead was a mixture of the Harvard Business School plus Berkeley in the free speech era. Everyone going around in circles, at $25,000 a year for starters. Auditor-General James McDonnell wasn't amused. The government, he pronounced in 1977, was "out of financial control."

Individually and collectively, this unwieldy new bureaucracy clutched to its bosom a French-language dictionary. Trudeauvian style – next to this first principle, everything else paled into insignificance – was about the French Fact. The good news was that for the first time in our history, francophones could feel on the fringes of being at home in their own national capital. Somehow, despite a lot of good intentions, they and the rest of us never really got together: quite apart from language, there simply weren't enough common reference points, enough shared inside jokes for us to break out of a curious, gentle state of apartheid. Yet more and more often, the petit armée who marched in during the early 1970s, trailing clouds of *Gauloises,* found themselves working at least part of the time in French. Ordering meals in French, as new and much more adventurous restaurants sprouted. Buying groceries at the Dominion and even socks at Simpsons in French.

The bad news was that when it came to anglophone bureaucrats, the whole massive, costly program for making them bilingual turned into a terrible flop. In the beginning it had all seemed so right: a chance to learn a second language and a second culture; a chance to save Confederation; a chance to create a federal bureaucracy that would reflect the kind of nation we are. Yet by 1976, though at any given moment up to 2,400 public servants were sweating their guts out in government language schools, back on the job, less than a third of the graduates ever needed to utter so much as *oui* or *non* in the other official language. Far too many jobs had been classified bilingual, as the panic went down through the bureaucracy that to have any hope of promotion you needed that precious certificate, but no one dared tell Trudeau what was going wrong. "Questioning any aspect of bilingual policy," Erna Paris reported in *Saturday Night*, "is considered in bad taste and is likely to call forth indignant accusations of bigotry."

None of us who lived through the '70s in Ottawa is as optimistic as once we were. We no longer take for granted, for instance, that any of the promises will be kept. For me, the moment when I felt personally betrayed came early in January, 1976, when Trudeau in his famous New Year's message mused about a New Society "where people would come together to share and help each other." A fortnight earlier, he had axed CYC.

And yet. Watching him at the Enders wedding, dancing with the insolent grace of a 20-year-old, I found myself first thinking, and then knowing, that we were indeed going to be sorry. Which in part was a private farewell not so much to the man himself as to the style-of-the-man-himself that a decade ago we were all trying to emulate. Which was also just too much champagne.

Sandra Gwyn, journalist.

The Worst Government Rip-off

The government in 1973 elected to give itself (MPS after six years of service) and 300,000 federal civil servants (at age 55) fully indexed pensions. Incredibly, they passed this Act without bothering to have the cost to the taxpayer calculated. The Act was passed by all parties with unseemly haste. As a result of the public hue and cry, an actuarial firm, Tomenson Alexander Inc., was engaged by the government to do a complete study of the taxpayers' liability. The report indicated that it would cost the rest of us $5.8 billion immediately, if properly handled, plus additional billions as a result of inflation in years to come.

The ironic part of this arrangement is that it's the MPS and top civil servants who control how much inflation there will be.

Can anyone imagine such an enormous self-serving action carried out without any permission from the taxpaying public? This is one of the reasons why there's been a demand in the late '70s for the power of referendum so that people can have the ability to fend off future offences such as this.

Colin Brown, President, National Citizens' Coalition

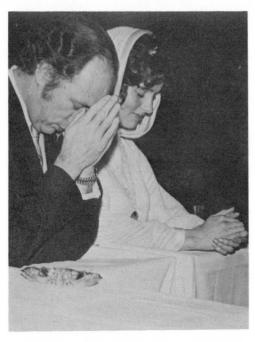

Pierre Trudeau married Margaret Sinclair in 1971 in what was described as the romance of the decade. Schiffer/CP

During the 1972 election Trudeaumania was still with us, the Trudeau romance continued to enchant us all and Justin was becoming the centre of everyone's attention. CP

Trudeau was the first head of state to visit
the People's Republic of China. With
Premier Chou-en-Lai in Peking.
Peter Bregg.

Trudeau travelled to Cuba in 1976 in spite
of the bitter resentment at home about
Castro's African policies. CP

Even in defeat, Trudeau did things with
style—the ever-present flower in his lapel
and the self-effacing grin. CP

After the win—November 15, 1976: René Lévesque led the Parti Québécois to victory in the Quebec provincial election. CP

Quebec:
United We Fall – Divided We Stand?

French-speaking Quebeckers took over Quebec in the '70s. We can now look back on this as a kind of massive *coup d'état* that affected all aspects of life in the province. It was a development of far more importance than the October Crisis of 1970, interpreted by some politicians at the time as an abortive, formal *coup d'état,* or the election of a separatist government in Quebec in November, 1976. Both these political events led people to make alarming predictions about the political future of Quebec, none of which turned out to be true. Instead, French-speaking Quebeckers continued their historic progress toward greater control of their own affairs, as usual in opposition to English-speaking Canadians and in collaboration with them.

As the decade neared its end, there was some hope that in the '80s, the reality of a French-dominated Quebec would be reflected in new forms of political association with the rest of Canada.

That would have seemed a laughably optimistic forecast when the decade opened with the kidnapping of a British diplomat in Montreal, the abduction and murder of a Quebec cabinet minister and the imposition of the War Measures Act suspending many of the basic civil liberties of Canadians. There had never been anything like this in contemporary Canadian experience and it produced many alarming predictions, mainly in English Canada, that we were about to follow other nations down the path of civil unrest toward revolution and anarchy. Even those who believed that the War Measures Act was an exaggerated response to a limited and well-contained terrorist threat in Quebec were concerned that the Act itself would escalate the conflict.

As it turned out, the events of October, 1970, marked not the beginning of a decade of revolution but the end of a decade of violence and civil unrest in Quebec. The psychology of Prime Minister Trudeau's response to the kidnappings of James Cross and Pierre Laporte was correct, no matter how deeply it alarmed defenders of a free society in Canada. Faced with the possibility of serious unrest, with the prospect of becoming another Northern Ireland, French-speaking Quebeckers retreated within the citadel of established order and abandoned their self-proclaimed patriots to the mercies of the police and the courts.

The election of the Parti Québécois in 1976 also was hailed as the beginning of a new era. It soon began to look more like the end product of political events of the previous 15 years, its own future increasingly murky.

The separatist victory was the political expression of the pure, high-minded enthusiasm for self-determination that had animated many of the best people in Quebec for the previous 16 years. Once the separatists came to power, reality started to erode the ideal. The seeds of trouble were sown even before the election when the Parti Québécois, in order to attract the support

New Quebec Liberal Leader Claude Ryan raises his mother's hand on the podium after he was elected leader. CP

of nonseparatists, committed itself to holding a referendum on political sovereignty after the election. As the deadline for holding the referendum approached, it became a source of confusion and controversy within the government. It distracted energy and attention from the essential tasks of administration and preparing for the next Quebec election. These weaknesses became more serious for the Parti Québécois with the emergence of Claude Ryan as leader of the Liberal opposition in the National Assembly, a man the equal of Premier Lévesque in his commitment to Quebec nationalism and perhaps his superior in political organizing ability and tenacity.

As a respectable option for Quebec nationalists in the first election of the '80s, Ryan will stand an excellent chance of bringing the separatist dream of the '60s to a political conclusion, at least for this generation.

The important development in Quebec in the '70s was the battle for supremacy between French and English in Montreal.

In the '60s, many English-speaking Quebeckers supported the efforts of their French-speaking neighbours to improve their status, under the illusion that progress could be painless. It began to hurt in the '70s as people and money from English-speaking Montreal flowed out of the province. The drain had become so severe by the end of the decade that it was decimating the public school system of the English-speaking community, by far the best in the province only 20 years earlier, and creating public debate about the

Tony Jenkins, *The Globe & Mail*, Toronto.

future of such major cultural institutions as McGill University. The city's two English-language daily newspapers appeared to be locked in a battle of attrition to decide which would survive to serve the dwindling community.

The main weapon of the French-speaking community was a restrictive language law that effectively changed the face and character of Montreal in the '70s. The law probably was unnecessary in the sense that social and economic forces already were diminishing the role of the English in the city but there is no doubt that it hastened change, infuriated the English and satisfied some deep need within the French.

The conquest of Montreal symbolized the effective takeover of power at all levels in Quebec by French-speaking Quebeckers and the increasing separation of Quebec from the rest of Canada in terms of language and political and economic ambitions. By the end of the decade, Montreal no longer even pretended to be the nation's leading financial and business centre. It had become the metropolis of a region rather than, as it once had been, of half a continent. More and more of its leaders spoke French as their first language; their perspective on Quebec was both deeper and more limited than the leadership that had been given by the old class of English-speaking entrepreneurs.

At the end of the decade, French-speaking Quebeckers were only starting to appreciate what had happened; English Canada hadn't even begun to grapple seriously with the fact that such a massive change in the leadership of Quebec probably would have to be reflected in the political structure of Confederation. This will be expressed within a few years in political demands by the government in Quebec, no matter who is at the head of it. It is to be hoped that English Canada will be able to welcome this as a chance to enlist the new Quebec as a willing partner in the enterprise of creating a strong federation of distinctive regions within Canada.

Peter Desbarats, author, journalist, television commentator, Ottawa Bureau chief, Global Television Network.

Canada in World Affairs

The reality of Pierre Trudeau and the legacy of Lester B. Pearson dominated Canadian foreign policy and our international relations in the 1970s.

Trudeau shifted some of the Pearsonian foreign policy priorities. But Pearson's basic wisdom about what Canada could accomplish in the world survived amazingly well two decades after he helped define our overseas role.

It was the directions, preferences and charisma of Prime Minister Trudeau that dominated our foreign policy almost, but not quite, to the end of the decade.

On May 22, 1979, he was defeated by the new Conservative Prime Minister Joe Clark, who was very definitely the lesser man at that time in terms of foreign affairs experience.

The era of the Trudeau Doctrine began with Mr. Trudeau's major foreign policy statement of May, 1968, which outlined his altered priorities for Canada in the world.

This document emphasized what he later called "the harmonious environment," with Canada declaring her strong sovereignty rights in our Western Hemisphere, more aid to an always needy Third World, technological breakthroughs like our two Anik communications satellites.

All these would be emphasized before our older priorities, the military role in NATO (North Atlantic Treaty Organization) and our armed forces' peacekeeping functions in unsettled nations of the globe.

But Trudeau did not remove Pearson's underpinnings, as these remained the basis for his shifts of direction. We remained a member nation of NATO, of course, though Trudeau cut our European military commitment in half. We maintained our honest broker role in the United Nations and in global crises with a consistent use of our peacekeeping military arm. At the end of the '70s our armed forces were celebrating 15 continuous years of peacekeeping in an uneasy Cyprus. Even the long and bitter war in Vietnam in which we did not fight saw a Canadian peacekeeping force on ten months' assignment there in 1973 while an Asian peace was arranged elsewhere in Paris.

The first year, 1970, remained the high-water point for foreign policy changes. It was the year of Canada's new White Paper on Foreign Policy. It emphasized trade and aid both with the European Economic Community and the emerging nations over NATO and curiously ignored altogether the very important Canada-U.S. trade relationship.

The Trudeau Doctrine centred on important unilateral pronouncements by Canada in 1970, extended our historic three-mile territorial sea limit to 12 miles and established so-called 100-mile-wide "sanitation zones" around our Arctic islands.

The latter move was cemented in the Arctic Waters Pollution Prevention Bill, passed unanimously by Parliament in June, 1970. It was both environmental and political in nature. It was meant to protect the fragile Arctic environment against pollution by foreign supertankers of the future, but also to say to the Americans that the Northwest Passage is Canadian waters.

On October 13, 1970, Canada recognized the People's Republic of China, using a formula that would be adopted by about 40 other countries who recognized Peking during the '70s.

The prime minister travelled abroad more than any previous Canadian head of government, to Asian nations at the start, including his stellar official visit to China in October, 1973; but also to Russia in 1971; western Europe and the USA in 1974-78; Mexico, Cuba and Venezuela in 1976, where his unique public responses on tour gained for Canada both international fame and notoriety.

Premier Fidel Castro says farewell to his young friend, Michel Charles Emil Trudeau at the end of his 3-day visit to Cuba in 1976. CP

In Russia he actually compared the ruthless KGB (Soviet secret police) to the RCMP. And in Cuba in 1976 he gave a hearty public *grito* (revolutionary *viva*) for Fidel Castro and his Marxist Cuban revolution before 200,000 Cuban workers.

But in the end, a tangled, angry and violent world saw us perhaps as more Pearsonian than Trudeausque – the still-honest mediator and inveterate peace-maker, the generous giver of aid with no ideological strings attached.

We may have worried a good deal in the '70s about our national identity at home. But abroad it was never in doubt.

It's an identity the world expects we will take with us into the next and very uncertain decade of the 1980s.

John D. Harbron, foreign affairs analyst, Thomson Newspapers.

The Campaigns

The federal election campaigns of the '70s were about Pierre Elliot Trudeau. In the first, Canadians warned him; then, humbled, we adored him; and, finally, gods that we are, we were angered at his hubris and destroyed him.

For this cold, proud, private man the defeat in the 1979 campaign was a humiliation hard to bear: Pierre Trudeau, a somebody, was driven from power by Progressive Conservative leader Joe Clark, a nobody.

Curiously, the 1979 campaign was, for the Conservatives, the 1972 campaign stretched that vital few points more. The pattern was the same: Give Quebec to the Liberals, hold on to the west and kill the Grits in Ontario.

Somehow, between 1972 and 1979, Trudeau managed to pull himself together, capture some of the magic of his coronation march of the '60s and walk away with the 1974 campaign, his lovely, faithful wife Maggie, in a flowered dress, at his side.

The first campaign of the '70s was a humbling experience for the high-flying Liberals. Wandering about in buckskins, confident that – as his campaign slogan put it, The Land Is Strong – Trudeau took the high road, rarely descending to specific issues, certain that Canadians would love to be lectured by a philosopher-king. He was, of course, quite wrong.

The Conservatives, led by Nova Scotian Robert Stanfield, who had replaced John Diefenbaker after an epic power struggle within the party, ran a meticulously planned campaign on economic issues: the high cost of living, unemployment, taxes and welfare.

The New Democratic Party, under David Lewis, had the good luck to stumble upon an appealing theme – "the corporate welfare bums" – and pounded in the message that working Canadians were paying too much to help run the country while rich corporations were paying too little.

The score at the end of the campaign: Liberals, 109; Progressive Conservatives, 107, NDP, 31; Social Credit, 15; Independents, 2.

Trudeau was humbled. There were a lot of broken dreams, he said, but, quoting a bit of pop philosophy from the *Desiderata,* allowed that "whether or not it is clear to you, no doubt the universe is unfolding as it should."

Two years later, deserted by the NDP, who had been in bed with the Liberals until they decided to return to their own chambers and a little respect after a tiff over an antiprofiteering bill, the Trudeau government was defeated in the House of Commons and the 1974 campaign was on.

This time, Trudeau put himself back in the hands of the old Lester Pearson campaign professionals – particularly, the man who came to be called The Rainmaker, Senator Keith Davey.

In this campaign, Davey said, "When I tell the Prime Minister to shine his shoes, he shines his shoes."

Shoes gleaming, his lovely young bride at his side– smiling demurely and remarking that Pierre had "taught me all I know about love" – Trudeau waltzed through a happy campaign. He was a politician now, transformed, as Larry Zolf remarked, from a philosopher-king to Mackenzie King.

Stanfield, hemming and hawing, drawling on about wage and price controls to the dismay not only of a great many middle-class Canadians but his own party moguls as well, seemed to lurch from misery to misery. A famous

Above: New Democratic Party leader David Lewis and his wife Sophie after Mr. Lewis's personal victory in 1972. CP

Right: Famous photograph of Conservative leader Robert Stanfield dropping a tossed football came to symbolize his loss of the 1974 campaign. CP

"Would you mind giving this to Joe?"

photograph of the Conservative leader dropping a tossed football came to symbolize his bumbling.

David Lewis and the NDP, faintly tainted by their time in the Liberal bed-chamber, couldn't seem to interest Canadians. In the end, Lewis was defeated in his own riding, by a red-headed mother of four children in her first Liberal campaign.

The 1974 score: Liberals, 141; Progressive Conservatives, 95; NDP, 16, Social Credit, 11; Independent, 1.

By 1979, when, after numerous false starts, Trudeau finally called an election for May 22, the election scene had altered radically. Lewis had been replaced as head of the NDP by a doctor of philosophy, Ed Broadbent. Stanfield was gone, his place taken, after a stormy leadership convention, by a 39-year-old part-time journalist from High River, Alberta: Joe Clark.

Trudeau's wife had fled his house, weaving a trail of marijuana and extra-marital sex – all recorded in her book, *Beyond Reason*. Trudeau, still the most intellectual leader in the western world, had turned cold and arrogant. The Canadian dollar had slipped to humiliating lows. The media was bitter, Ontario rebellious, the West, lost. Trudeau went into campaign miles ahead of his party in the polls; Clark, well behind Trudeau, but behind his party as well. Broadbent was neutral with a kind of pop-eyed charm and more good sense than either of his rivals by most accounts.

A main feature of the campaign was the national television debate in which Trudeau humbled Clark but Broadbent seemed to outdistance them both.

At the end, only Quebec, some parts of Toronto and a few constituencies in the Maritimes remained faithful to Trudeau. Clark, overcoming his early perceptions by the media as a giggling wimp, coasted nicely home with a comfortable majority.

The 1979 score: Progressive Conservatives, 135; Liberals, 115; NDP, 26; Social Credit, 6.

Pierre Elliot Trudeau had nothing to say about the proper unfolding of the universe.

Val Sears, journalist.

Maureen McTeer and Joe Clark on their way to victory, 1979. CP

The Most Newsworthy People

As chosen by newspaper editors and broadcasters in year-end polls . . .

Canadian

Pierre Elliott Trudeau, prime minister of Canada for nine years of the decade.

Bobby Orr, hockey star.

Anne Murray, singer.

Dr. Gerald Herzberg, winner of the 1971 Nobel Prize for Chemistry.

David Barrett, who ended W.A.C. Bennett's political rule in B.C.

David Lewis, federal NDP leader who coined the phrase "corporate welfare bum" in 1972.

Phil Esposito, hockey star.

Paul Henderson, hockey star.

Alan Eagleson, Toronto lawyer; hockey players' representative; organizer of the Canada Cup series.

Harry Sinden, coach of Team Canada.

Margaret Laurence, author.

Bobby Hull, hockey star.

Martin Hartwell, who survived a plane crash on November 8, 1972, in the western Arctic and who lived to tell the tale of 32 terrifying days of survival.

John Turner, former finance minister.

Robert Stanfield, former PC leader.

Clarence Campbell, former National Hockey League president.

Bryce Mackasey, who quit as immigration and labour minister in 1972 and who was postmaster-general in 1975 for the 43-day strike by 22,000 inside postal workers.

Dr. Morton Shulman, former crusading NDP member of the Ontario legislature.

Gerald LeDain, head of the commission that recommended in May, 1972, that penalties be abolished for possessing marijuana for personal use.

Charles Marion, Sherbrooke, Quebec, credit union employee who was held by kidnappers for 82 days in 1977.

Jack Horner, who switched to the Liberals after 18 years as a Tory.

Ed Schreyer, whose NDP government was defeated in Manitoba's 1977 election and who became Canada's governor-general in 1978.

Justice Thomas Berger, whose 1977 report on a proposed northern pipeline recommended a ten-year delay.

René Simard, entertainer.

W. O. Mitchell, author.

Cindy Nicholas, the 16-year-old who swam across Lake Ontario on August 16, 1974.

Farley Mowat, author.

Irving Layton, poet, prophet.

Ferguson Jenkins, pitcher for the Texas Rangers.

Celia Franca, ballet director.

Eugene Whelan, former agriculture minister who received the brunt of criticism for the 1974 rotten-egg scandal.

Jean Drapeau, mayor of Montreal.

Joe Clark, elected prime minister of Canada, 1979.

Brian Erb, captain of the runaway ship *Answer* boarded by RCMP in the St. Lawrence River.

Joe Davidson, president of the Canadian Union of Postal Workers.

René Lévesque, leader of the Parti Québecois, premier of Quebec.

Beryl Plumptre, former head of the Food Prices Review Board.

Dr. Henry Morgentaler, first acquitted by a Montreal jury, November 13, 1973, then sent to jail by the courts in 1975 on charges of performing illegal abortions.

Margaret Trudeau, who married Pierre Elliott Trudeau in 1971; had three children, two on Christmas Day, and left her husband in 1977.

Donald MacDonald, former energy minister.

Greenpeace III, seized by the French in August, 1973, while they were protesting French nuclear tests in the Pacific.

Sandy Hawley, jockey.

Anne Murray. CP.

Bernie Parent. CP.

Former Finance Minister John Turner
cleaning out his Ottawa office after his
resignation in 1975. CP

Rene Simard became Canada's answer to
Donny Osmond. Here he is performing at
the CNE Grandstand. CP

Richard Nixon saying farewell to the White House staff in August 1974. AP

Patty Hearst in front of the Symbionese Liberation Army insignia. AP

Egyptian President Anwar Sadat, U.S. President Jimmy Carter and Israeli Prime Minister Menachem Begin, shake hands at the White House on September 18, 1978, after a peace agreement between Egypt and Israel was announced. Sadat and Begin were awarded the 1978 Nobel Peace Prize for their efforts towards a settlement of the Arab-Israeli conflict. AP

Ken Dryden, hockey star.

Gordie Howe, hockey star.

Peter Lougheed, Alberta premier, central figure in the west, and in the power struggle between the federal government and the provinces over resource revenues.

Mordecai Richler, novelist.

Bernie Parent, hockey star.

International

Richard Nixon: remember Watergate?

Henry Kissinger, former U.S. secretary of state.

Bobby Fischer, for his world championship chess win over Russia's Boris Spassky in 1972.

Willy Brandt, former German chancellor.

George Wallace, former governor of Alabama.

The *Apollo 16* and *17* astronauts.

Mick Jagger, rock singer.

Clifford Irving, for his fake biography of billionaire Howard Hughes.

King Faisal of Saudi Arabia, who instigated the Arab world's cutbacks in oil exports to pro-Israeli nations.

Patricia Hearst, newspaper heiress, kidnapped in 1974 by the Symbionese Liberation Army, who then announced that she had joined them; her capture, trial, conviction, and release in 1979; her marriage to her bodyguard.

Gerald Ford, former United States president.

Harold Wilson, former United Kingdom prime minister.

Yasser Arafat, leader of the Palestinian Liberation Organisation.

Archibishop Makarios of Cyprus.

Jimmy Carter, United States president.

Idi Amin, Ex-Ugandan president.

Ian Smith, ex-prime minister of Rhodesia.

Indira Ghandi, former Indian Prime Minister.

Elvis Presley, entertainer, died 1977.

Bing Crosby, entertainer, died 1977.

Menachem Begin, Israeli premier.

Karak Cardinal Wojtyla of Poland, the first non-Italian Pope in 456 years.

Ayatollah Khomeini, who wrested power from the Shah of Iran.

Generalissimo Francisco Franco, of Spain, who died in 1975.

Jim Jones, People's Church leader.

Anwar Sadat, prime minister of Egypt.

In the '60s, Only Our Lifestyles Changed – In the '70s, Our New History Began

What forms the perception of any decade, what gives urgency to the expectations of its survivors and allows its participants a rationale for their actions, is some deeply shared, common experience. It was the excitement and agony of World War II that formed the '40s; the somnambulism of prosperity that symbolized the '50s; the nerve-wrenching detonations of social, sexual and political change that shook us up during the '60s. Now, we suddenly find ourselves in the final year of the '70s, looking back on a tumble of events that add up to no discernible pattern or structure.

Yet the legacy of the confusing '70s could be even more dramatic than the afterbirth of the pulsating '60s. A decade ago, we merely altered our lifestyles; ten years later we are on the verge of transforming the way we are governed.

The real victim of the '70s was less Pierre Trudeau than his approach to government as a royal court conducted by a self-selected hierarchy dedicated mainly to its own perpetuation. Imperceptibly, a new style of populism emerged during the decade, personified, however reluctantly, by Joe Clark and his faceless crew. Based on no recognizable ideology, its roots are the simple but universal impulse that governmental authority at all levels is overstepping its proper boundaries.

This new brand of politics remained a mood in search of a movement, representing more a decline of faith in middle-of-the-road solutions and the arithmetics of compromise than any drastic shift to the Right. But its objectives are clear: that politicians must stop treating voters as objects that can be bought with their own money at quadrennial auctions called election campaigns; that some way must be found to alleviate the desperation of the young burdened by the shallowness of the education system and the frustrations of a narrowing job market; that the murderous effects of inflation on consumer prices and fixed incomes must be arrested – and soon.

So far, the most obvious outcropping of this new political temper has been the wave of protest against a scale of spending by the federal government that has seen Ottawa's avalanche of expenditures rise to its current level of nearly $1 billion a week. But the issue runs very much deeper.

Political power is about to be assembled and harnessed in new and unpredictable ways. By the end of the '80s, most of our legislatures, federal and provincial, will have undergone one of those rare, historic convulsions that every so often redistributes the coalition of political forces that keep democracies alive and functioning.

Peter C. Newman, editor of *Maclean's* magazine, author of *The Canadian Establishment* and *Bronfman Dynasty.*

The attack on Soviet Premier Alexei Kosygin in Ottawa, October 18, 1971. Toronto *Star.*

A co-ed screams as a classmate lies dead, on the campus of Kent State University. National Guardsmen fired into a crowd of demonstrators. May 1970. AP

Astronaut Thomas B. Stafford and cosmonaut Aleksey A. Leonov, during the Apollo-Soyuz Test Project. They are in the hatchway between the Apollo docking module and the Soyuz orbital module. NASA

Idi Amin, the Big Daddy of Uganda during his palmy days. By the end of the decade he was hiding out in fear of his life. *Wide World*

"Harold's taking a crash course in Iroquois . . . he thinks it may be more valuable than French and sooner than we think . . ." Sid Barron, The Toronto *Star*

About Canadians in the '70s – Some Statistics

In a majority of urban Canadian homes, the head of the household is no longer the father.

Nearly half of us claim to have read a book in the past seven days.

Eighty-five percent of us believe this is the best country in the world.

Most Canadians can name no more than three countries in the Commonwealth.

Seventy-five percent of us have purchased a lottery ticket in the past year.

Our most common phobias are rats, snakes and fire.

A third of us have never seen a Canadian movie.

Most of us believe the police are doing a good job.

Most of us believe labour unions are necessary.

Almost half of us watch less TV than we used to.

Forty-eight percent of us are too fat.

Three-quarters of urban Canadians believe in psychiatrists.

One out of five of us is a victim of crime.

Seventy-three percent of us believe there will be another world war.

Two out of three Canadians say they are not afraid of death.

More than half of Canada's men read skin magazines.

The majority of us prefer classical music to rock.

Sixty-eight percent of Canadians believe the unemployed don't want work.

Forty-two percent of us favour legal betting shops.

Forty-two percent of women consider themselves feminists.

Nine out of ten young Canadians hope to own a home.

Ninety percent of Newfoundlanders are glad the province joined Canada.

Fifty-seven percent of Canadians believe doctors are overpaid.

Canadians are putting less value on university degrees than they used to.

We are losing respect for federal politicians.

Most of us would put strings on foreign aid.

Canada's favourite TV star is Johnny Carson.

Most Canadians want to raise the drinking age.

Sixty-eight percent of Canadians object to four-letter words on TV.

Most Canadians feel American influence is increasing.

We think the ideal age for retiring is 57.7 years.

Most Canadians think "upper class" means rich.

More than half of us want to ban the hunt for baby seals.

Half of us think the postal service is unsatisfactory.

Forty-one percent of Canadians believe television.

Twenty-four percent of Canadians believe newspapers.

Eighteen percent of Canadians believe radio.

Sixty-nine percent of us believe that those earning more than we do should pay most taxes.

Most French Canadians have never flown.

Seventy-six percent of Canadians didn't feel that the Trudeaus' marriage break-up affected Pierre Elliott Trudeau's job.

Eighty-three percent of Canadians said they didn't think Maureen McTeer's keeping her name affected Clark's job.

Most Canadians feel the Queen is just fine.

Ninety-three percent of people in Quebec feel it's important to speak both English and French.

Most Canadians believe in capital punishment in some circumstances.

From the **Weekend Poll,** *Weekend Magazine.*

Seventies-speak

People did not speak in the 1970s as they had spoken before. Our language, even if we tried to resist the current tendencies, inevitably reflected the jargon of the period. This emerged from business, politics and, above all, psychotherapy; regionally, the major source of seventies-speak was California, which now dominates the verbal language of the western world in the same way that it has, for half a century or so, dominated our visual imagination. Some notes, for a future historian, on how we spoke as the 1970s drew to a close:

Turkey: A dolt, a loser, a nebbish, a nothing. First heard among adolescents, later among all age groups. Applied, in 1979, by roughly seven million Canadians to describe their new prime minister.

Different strokes for different folks: Possibly the most odious of all 1970s expressions, implying, as it does, both an imitation down-home corniness and a phony urban sophistication. It means that some people like one thing, some another. Once used by the mayor of Toronto to suggest that body-rub parlours are okay.

Impact: Its use as a verb was characteristic of the 1970s, as in "This will impact negatively on our sales picture."

Hopefully: The most misused word of the 1970s, as in "Hopefully, we'll have a good turnout for the rally." This is wrong, but the people who know it's wrong are almost extinct. The correct use is in a sentence such as "He spoke hopefully," meaning he spoke with hope. No one says this anymore.

I could care less: In the past, there was an expression, "I could not care less," meaning "I don't care at all." Somehow, the 1970s transmuted this into "I could care less," which doesn't mean anything at all. No one can explain how this happened and there is no way to stop it.

Up front: This term neatly straddles the business and psychotherapy worlds, but more of us use it in the latter than in the former. In the business world it fits into a sentence like: "I need a million dollars up front before I sign," which few of us get to say. All of us, however, find a way to say, before uttering something hopelessly banal, "I'm gonna be very up front about this." That means honest.

Head: In the 1950s a nice fellow was described as "a good head." The 1960s brought us a "head shop," which is where you bought hash pipes. In the 1970s "head" came into wider use: "This is where my head is at" came to mean, roughly, that this is the way one was thinking. "Head space" meant a mood, or a perspective on things, but as the 1970s closed it was fading fast. Don't try to use it in the 1980s.

Have a nice day: In the past, no one ever said this. Then, on January 1, 1970, *everyone* began saying it, especially taxi drivers and waiters of ambiguous sexual intentions. The plan is to kill it on January 1, 1980, and everyone hopes that will happen.

Lifestyle: The word was first used by a disciple of Sigmund Freud in Vienna, but it did not achieve widespread currency until this decade. Now it can be used in literally any sentence describing one's existence. "I have a basically yoga lifestyle." "My lifestyle is that of an IBM executive." It became the most-used word of the 1970s because it was the most democratic. Not everyone can afford a Jacuzzi or even a pair of cross-country skis, but the poorest of us can claim to have a lifestyle.

Getting it on: This came to mean the sex act. A related term was *getting your rocks off.* The latter was once bleeped out of a program on Ontario's educational TV network and thus qualified as a 1970s obscenity.

Input: A word from the computer business that came into nearly universal use. Like most such words, it served the purpose of making what was said seem slightly more important than otherwise. People who had once said, "Can I give my opinion on that question?" now said, "Can I have some input on that question?" It was also possible to say, "Let me have your input."

Handling it very well: As the 1970s ground on, "cope" and "coping" began to seem archaic. It was no longer enough, if your wife suddenly left you with three kids under five, to tell your friends that you were coping. So you learned to say, "I'm handling it very well." If a true 1970s person were to find himself the victim of a hydrogen bomb attack, he would explain that he was handling it very well.

Blow away: This began in the underworld: "I'll blow you away" meant "I'll kill you." It soon came to mean the same as "impressed." As in: "I showed him the work print of my film and it blew him away."

I know where you're coming from: A leading California import. It means the same as "I understand you," but it implies profound depths of empathy.

The bottom line: This began in business, where it means the last, crucial number on a profit-and-loss statement. It moved swiftly into the outer world and came to mean the ultimate *raison d'être* of anything or anybody. As in: "My wife and I have our troubles, but the bottom line is the future of our relationship." Uttered, always, with total earnestness.

Into: It was strong in the 1960s, but it was a gigantic force in the 1970s. To be "into" something can mean obsessed by it, or involved with it, or simply interested in it. As in "I'm into Mozart" or "I'm really into mustard."

Bor-ing: The only genuine 1970s innovation in pronunciation. In previous ages it was pronounced "boring," but in the 1970s it turned into "bor-*ing*," with the accent firmly on the second syllable. It seemed sort of more sophisticated that way.

At this point in time: Possibly the most flagrant word-waster of the 1970s – "in time" is totally redundant. In the Watergate hearings many witnesses found they were unable to recall something "at this point in time." Half the people listening thought this sounded silly, but the other half thought it sounded impressive and began using it whenever they could fit it in.

Getting it together: A 1960s phrase that showed amazing staying power in the 1970s. It came to mean anything from getting one's work done to enduring seven years of psychoanalysis.

Dynamite: Few of us got through the 1970s without saying something was "dynamite." It meant impressive, or wonderful, or just good. "That's a dynamite trout stream" did not mean it was a place where you were allowed to plant explosives in the water. It meant there were a lot of trout there.

Gross out: "It grossed me out" meant that you didn't like it. A "*gross-out*" was something one despised. "*Pig-out*", a related term, meant to eat too much.

Relate: In the 1970s, everyone became conscious of relationships, and of relating to one another. During the 1970s, in fact, many people did little else. Many variations on the word came into use, such as "I can't relate to yoga," which meant that you didn't (as the 1960s would say) *dig* it. In the end "relating" was what the 1970s were about.

Robert Fulford, Editor, *Saturday Night.*

Anniversaries & Celebrations

Centennial of the Northwest Territories: 1970
Manitoba Centennial: 1970
B.C. Centennial: 1971
Saskatchewan Homecoming: 1971
Calgary Stampede, Diamond Jubilee: July 6-15, 1972
Fredericton's 125th Birthday: June 30-July 7, 1973
Hector Bicentennial Celebration: 1973
PEI Centennial: 1973
RCMP Centennial: 1973

Riviere-du-Loup Tercentennary: July 7-22, 1974
Yukon's 75th Anniversary: 1973
Newfoundland's 25th Anniversary: 1974
Superfrancofête: August, 1974
B.C. Captain Cook Bicentennial Celebration: 1978
Belleville, Ont., Centennial: 1978
The 100th Canadian National Exhibition, Toronto: August, 1978
The 2nd International Gathering of the Clans: Halifax, Nova Scotia, June 28, 1979

The Canadian Government Office of Tourism

Atlantic Canada – Cables, Pipelines, Waterfalls, Sun, Wind & Tidal Power

Sorry, Gabby, time's up, and your prediction about Fundy Tidal Power looks ludicrous. Gabby is an old nickname for Gerald A. Regan and back in '71, in the early days of his eight years as premier of Nova Scotia, he was noticeably gabby about Fundy Tidal Power. To hear him you'd have sworn that, by the time the '70s gave way to the '80s, the tides of Fundy would be driving the electric toothbrushes of Connecticut, the air conditioners of Manhattan, the unborn industries of New Brunswick and Nova Scotia. He went to New York to announce that Nova Scotia "hopes to harness the bay so Con Ed won't have brownouts here anymore . . . I am extremely optimistic that the necessary engineering and experimentation will go forward rapidly. I would hope to place a target date of 1980 for major development of tide energy to come on stream."

But despite the subsequent rises in oil prices – a punishing fact that should actually have made tidal power appear all the more attractive – no dam-builder yet has so much as sunk a shovel into the gleaming red mud of the Fundy shore. And despite the millions that governments have spent on technical reports, it's still not certain tidal energy will be on stream by 1990, or 2000, much less 1980. Like the broken promise of Sable Island oil, Fundy Tidal Power was a lesson in the gap between high energy hopes and bitter energy realities and, throughout the whole Atlantic region, it was this lesson that set the mood of the '70s. Energy, above all else, was the issue of the decade.

In Nova Scotia, the government's takeover in 1971-'72 of a private utility, Nova Scotia Light and Power Co. Ltd., haunted Regan for the rest of his years in power. Later, high electricity costs drove people out of the province, crippled industry and, miraculously erasing an environmentally sooty reputation, restored the respectability of coal. They also helped defeat a government. About the downfall of Regan's Liberals on September 19, 1978, Ralph Surette wrote in *Atlantic Insight,* "Despite his protestations that the real culprits were OPEC sheiks, the voters turfed him out as premier."

In Newfoundland and Labrador, too, energy decisions, energy controversies, and dreams of energy-based prosperity coloured the times. In the early '70s, the new Conservative government of Frank Moores lashed the old Liberal government of Joseph R. Smallwood for what Moores saw as Smallwood's scandalous sell-out to Quebec of power from the Upper Churchill hydro-electric project. Newfoundland later went to court to break the Quebec contract. Meanwhile, the Gull Island site (potential: 1,600 megawatts) on the Lower Churchill awaited development. But the court battle and Quebec's territorial designs on Labrador scarcely improved chances of an amicable arrangement to transmit Gull Island electricity through Quebec to the Maritimes. Hopes for an underwater cable to Cape Breton (the "Anglo-

Joseph R. Smallwood. CP

Saxon route") faded in '79 when Moores announced a massive industrial development plan for Labrador. Cheap energy in Newfoundland and Labrador would stay home to benefit Newfoundlanders and Labradorians – and to heck with the Maritimes. By mid-'79, eight oil-drilling rigs were at work in Labrador's "Iceberg Alley" and this fact, along with the potential of Gull Island, partly accounted for Newfoundland's new cockiness. She didn't need the Maritimes, she'd outface and outfight Quebec and, at appropriate moments, she'd tell off Ottawa. Her energy potential was now part of her character.

But in Prince Edward Island it wasn't the promise of cheap energy or energy prosperity that helped set the tone of the '70s. It was the threat of endlessly rising oil prices and, since the Island totally depends on oil to generate its power, the threat of endlessly rising electricity bills. (The Canadian provinces with the highest power rates are P.E.I., Nova Scotia, Newfoundland and Labrador, and New Brunswick, in that order.) The Island, under Liberal Premier Alex Campbell, transformed itself into Atlantic Canada's Mecca for devotees of alternate energy. Campbell invented the Institute of Man and Resources to promote conservation and to experiment with the tapping of sun, wind, wood and manure for energy. News from the Island sometimes suggested windmills were busting out all over but, in the late '70s, it turned out Islanders would rely on a new underwater cable to New Brunswick to get power from so environmentally suspect a source as the nuclear reactor at Lepreau. After the defeat of the provincial Liberals in '79 however – and after the historic accident in the nuclear plant near Harrisburg, Pa. – Tory Premier Angus MacLean said the Island could get along without piped-in electricity from a nuclear generator.

Perhaps more than any of the other Atlantic provinces, it was New Brunswick that made the fateful energy decision of the '70s. It decided to "go nuclear," to build a nuclear plant at Point Lepreau, near Saint John. Originally estimated at $350 million, the cost of Lepreau soon approached a billion. The Maritime Energy Corporation, a supposedly cooperative venture to build big energy projects, was conceived in '77, stumbled into existence in '79, gave first priority to Point Lepreau. A few weeks later – Harrisburg. "Is Lepreau a lemon?" Surette asked in *Atlantic Insight.* "If so, write off New Brunswick as a going concern."

Energy, as an issue, was not only central to each of the Atlantic provinces in the 1970s, it was also the clearest proof of their ancient intractability. Newfoundland was determined to go it alone. Nova Scotia, for a while, sounded as though it would build a tidal-power plant without bothering to consult New Brunswick; and, later, one reason why founding the Maritime Energy Corporation took years was inter-provincial distrust, jealousy, prickliness. Some east-coast factions wanted a gas pipeline from Montreal right away; others feared it would hurt their oil refineries. Though the belated MEC may have been the start of something good, the common problem, oil prices, did not result in a huddle that found a common solution.

Unemployment, inflation, the enfeebled dollar, Quebec separatism, the constitution, postal strikes, freight rates . . . all of these mattered down east in the '70s, just as they did elsewhere in Canada. But they didn't seem to matter all the time. What did was energy. We had a decade of talk about kilowatts, British Thermal Units, wood stoves, oil contracts with Venezuela, cables, pipelines, waterfalls, insulation and, as always, weather, winds and tides. Speaking of tides, others have long since begun to carry the ball for Regan. Federal Energy Minister Alastair Gillespie in '78: "Only a disaster can stop Fundy now." Sure, Alastair, sure.

Harry Bruce, journalist.

Natural Gaffes of the '70s

Pierre Trudeau: "Separatism is dead"
Turtlenecks in restaurants
The DC-10
John Dean introducing "at this moment in time" to the language
Joe Clark's world trip
Jimmy Carter: "I've committed adultery in my heart many times"
Otto Lang's nanny flying over the ocean on a government plane
Richard Nixon not burning the tapes
The girlfriend who invited Margaret Trudeau to the Rolling Stones concert
Billy Carter
Alex Haley's research
Francis Fox's penmanship

Bert Lance's arithmetic
Rene Richards
Pierre Trudeau telling Mark Phillips of CBC and Mary Janigan of the Toronto *Star* that he might hang on to power if defeated by a few votes
Hamilton Jordon's dining manners
Anita Bryant
John Munro's phone call to a judge
The press release on Nelson Rockefeller's death
Wilbur Mills and Fanne Foxe
The Big Mac
Pierre Trudeau: "Joe Clark doesn't know his razzamatazz from a hole in the ground."
Joe Clark: "How old are the chickens?"
Jeremy Thorpe's friend shooting the dog

Allan Fotheringham, journalist.

They Like It the Way It Is

You might have known Herman Kahn wouldn't understand Vancouver – not the Vancouver of today, anyway. That all-purpose futurist and adviser-to-everybody came bustling into town one day in November and announced joyfully to an audience of corporate bigwigs that Vancouver, God bless it, could grow in the years ahead from 1.2-million population to ten million. Then (he was speaking to 250 people) he asked everyone who favoured this awesome vision to stand up. Four people did so.

Kahn was aghast – he thinks it's unfair for the present inhabitants of Vancouver to keep it for themselves, just because they got there first. But Vancouverites, getting in some late tennis before dusting off their skis, yawned. They don't need that sort of thing. They have what they want, roughly. Vancouver is now, to an extent never quite achieved before, pleased with itself.

It has passed through urban adolescence and grown up happy. It doesn't any longer feel inferior in the face of Toronto's vastly superior economic clout. It isn't even much worried by the prospect of Calgary becoming the West's most powerful city. Vancouver, which was once described as a setting in search of a city, has blossomed into one of the most attractive places in North America and will become more beautiful still with the completion of the Robson Square project. And, like Toronto a few years back, Vancouver is admiring its own image as reflected in the pages of American magazines – *Esquire,* the *Atlantic, National Geographic,* and the rest.

Vancouver knows what it wants to be, and it doesn't want to be Toronto, Chicago, or Los Angeles. Historians may eventually pinpoint 1968 as the year it solved its own identity crisis: in the Chinatown Freeway debate, the city specifically rejected the idea of a new cross-harbour bridge linked to a freeway through Chinatown. It went on record against unchecked growth and in favour of a city people could enjoy.

Vancouver has had a boom, of course – population has doubled since 1956 – but now it's in a period of consolidation and gradual change. Physically, the city is making itself steadily more handsome – False Creek, the second harbour, once an industrial slum, is on the way to being cleaned up; the waterfront is increasingly edged with parks, marinas, and townhouses. Economically, the city is changing from a port and distribution centre into a financial management centre; and at the same time it's evolving, California-like, a sophisticated science-based industry which produces everything from computers to deep-sea submersibles. Emotionally, it's in the middle of a high: Vancouver these days, to borrow from Mark Twain, displays "the calm confidence of a Christian with four aces."

The Inside Track, *Saturday Night.*

The City

Ten years ago, we discovered the City. There it was, the seething beast, the breeding ground for a radical politics that would transform the Canadian political scene.

The enemy was easy to define. On one corner was the expressway lobby, pumping suburban cars into the downtown. Across the street was the developer group, ready to plop apartment towers into unsuspecting neighbourhoods. Just down the street was the politician, jostling with his developer friends as they worked out the next best scheme to make themselves happy and content. Urban renewal was the key: it would get rid of all those embarrassing neighbourhoods.

And there, perplexed, was the citizen group. Groups of working people tried to fend off highrise towers, or land clearance schemes. The young professionals worried about expressways and road-widenings. The newspaper editorials complained about how city government wasn't an open process, and that City Hall was living in the dark ages.

In Toronto, the turnaround came in 1972, with the election of a reform-minded council worried about downtown development, neighbourhood preservation and the rising cost of housing. Toronto City Council imposed a 45-foot holding bylaw to control downtown development while it looked for other solutions; it formed a nonprofit housing company that later in the decade was to become the largest builder of residential units in the city; and it got planners out of City Hall into neighbourhoods, to devise plans that would protect the traditional Toronto streetscape. Government became more open, more exposed to community pressure, where anyone had a right to depute about anything.

In short, Toronto City Hall welcomed the hordes to share in the process of government. At least that's how the story went.

Other cities weren't so successful. In Montreal, the citizen group lobby produced a sizable opposition, but not a government. In Vancouver, the new politics was represented at City Hall, but its voice was not loud. In Halifax and St. John's, there were fresh faces that quickly blended into the scenery.

By 1975, the world had stabilized. Whatever gains had been made – and save for Toronto those gains were small – were secured. The citizen lobby dissolved in either despair or limited satisfaction. The young professionals found old and secure neighbourhoods close to the downtown, and the working class found themselves dispersed to the suburbs. The hope of controlling the city had dissipated in most urban areas. The spate of publications analyzing the city and its power structure dwindled, and only a few hardy souls discoursed across the country on the state of the city.

Perhaps because of its greater wealth, Toronto was fortunate in maintaining its reform push, sort of.

A new downtown plan reduced office densities, attempted to reintroduce housing to the downtown, and tried to respect the pedestrian. The council pushed its housing program and encouraged community-based nonprofit groups – all this even though the citizen-group base had retired to the smugness of the neighbourhood.

New pressures began to emerge. While across the country public transit was seen as an ultimate good to be encouraged, transit deficits began to skyrocket. The expressway addicts reemerged, although this time they were willing to settle on road-widenings and transportation corridors rather than explicit expressways.

The economy slowed down, and stopped. No longer was it a crime to support a new office complex which would provide construction jobs and new assessment. The apartment tower was laid on its side and called infill housing. Luxury condominiums were sprinkled through the city in the place of rental housing as rent controls were accepted by everyone as one of the few ways to control housing costs.

And provincial governments began to shut off the tap. Grants to municipalities were curtailed, and restraint – or cutbacks – was the slogan of the day. All of us had to do better, to make money magically go further. What was left of the citizen movement began to complain about government

David Crombie (the tiny perfect mayor) and John Sewell, who succeeded him as mayor of Toronto. Toronto *Star.*

expenditures and the annual increase in the mill rate. The focus came on smaller, less consequential issues, as the Big Decisions seemed foreordained or too massive for cogent criticism.

Government became a matter for the politicians, who again had a free hand. Transit fares were raised, as they said, "out of necessity." Those cities that could attracted new development. Citizens kept out of the way.

And so the decade closes. We've learned a few lessons. Some of us are questioning the form of growth rather than growth itself. Some of us are trying to define with more intelligence the real workings of the housing industry. We're looking at how governments spend money, how bureaucracies work, the pressures that politicians face, and what options seem to be at hand.

But few of us are ready for the new start that seemed just around the corner in 1970. We've become too wise, too world-weary. Somewhere out there is the new constituency that will save us from the perils of the suburban form, the commuter society, the shopping centre, and the developers' capital cost allowance deduction. Somewhere out there is a group of people who will help save the city from the ravages of the last decade or two.

John Sewell, mayor of Toronto.

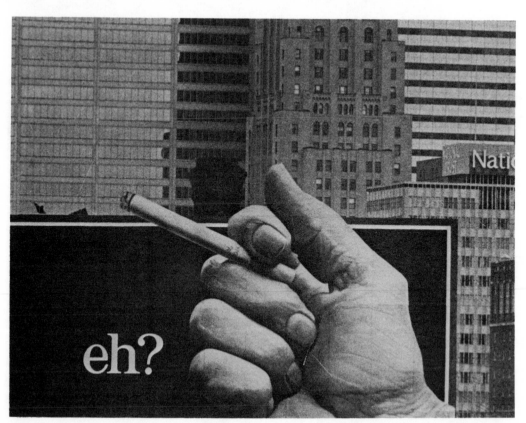

The city of Toronto's anti-smoking bylaw was ignored by most stores and restaurant owners. CP

The Eyes of Toronto – 1969-79

It was a tale of two different cities, returning to Toronto in 1969, then again in 1979. It could all be seen in the eyes. In 1969, the eyes you saw on the street saw you! Eyes that were open, eager, questing . . . full of a spiritual lust. A lust that was at once desire for a more open life, life incarnate, yet also a prayer for something more than the flesh. Nineteen sixty-nine –it was virtually the apogee, in Toronto, of what we think of as the '60s, the decade of the "flower children," the resonances of Yorkville. Rochdale College was still burgeoning (not yet bedlam), with experimental writers like Judy Merrill, John Palmer and Victor Coleman in residence. The House of Anansi, under the editorship of Dennis Lee, was launching a whole new era of young writers. Stan Bevington's Coach House Press mounted the avant-garde of the black humouresque, and had not yet succumbed to trendy respectability and place. McClelland and Stewart could dare to publish my own second novel, on Toronto, as a manuscript in a Birks Blue Box (though it did not dare entitle it *The Smugly Fucklings*).

The subway ads blathered in superlatives. Among the young, words like "beautiful" were in full sway. And they often talked about "holiness" – which did not mean some monastic continence, but a given life, shared and expressed in the body. It was pagan, but with more than a hint of God, or of the gods. And if the revolution of the decade was termed "sexual," there were fine moments when it fringed the erotic, that point at which the finite intersects with the eternal, the body with the spiritual. Leonard Cohen's song, *Suzanne,* said it all.

Eyes that danced, cavorted, sought the adventure they most feared. *That* was Toronto, at its bravest, when I returned here in the autumn of 1969. A city desperately trying to alchemize a rancid inherited Calvinism into a water-bed of roses.

The political correlative of this sexotic hope was, of course, Trudeaumania – a prime minister who was the world's presiding high hip lecher-monk, a kind of Jansenist's Rabelais, for those who followed him behind the scenes. But 1969 was also the high-water mark of the national media. Glossy names like Pierre Berton, Peter Gzowski, Larry Zolf, Richard Needham, Sandy Ross, Bob Fulford . . . at their prime, or entering it, as Pied Pipers to a nation. And Trudeau . . . why he was merely their Parliamentary surrogate, president of the pan-Canadian media!

Oh, we were all drugged on hope. We were all carrying, lodged somewhere in our spines, the impacted orgasms of five centuries of repressive Protestantism. And we were blasting it all out, at longed for last – the Big "O"!

Ten years later, when I returned to Toronto, all that looked absurd! Quixotic, bathetic – the '60s, a world that had dribbled to an end in the '70s, with a whimper and not a bang! Again, the eyes tell the story. Toronto eyes, in 1979, are furtive, withdrawn, working only point to point, or by ricochet, instead of embracing some Brave New World. And when such eyes do peer out, it is a flat flesh-quest. That, and a diffuse chagrin, diffuse fear, everywhere. As if something central has been torn out of everybody – or has it merely been subtly eroded. And the additional fear lurking that whatever is left will be lost as well. Yes, after the mass break-out of the '60s, everyone is in retreat, in a state of psychic seige, and lost in a factitious busyness. The subway ads are no longer superlatives, but couched as an endless conditional: words like "perhaps," "maybe," "possibly" –these tell the new story. And Yorkville, once the drumbeat of a new era, is now the centre of Toronto's chichi carriage trade. The decade of emotional opportunities has been displaced by the decade of furtive opportunisms.

The national election of '79 was fought over all of this, of course. As the unstated major issue. And a nation bloated with chagrin ejected the Liberal Party and Mr. Trudeau, quite simply because they had come to represent a huckster cynicism, an emotionally illogical positivism, a joyless materialism . . . as a form of creeping impotence. Under Trudeau, the Liberals tacitly thought that power would bring potence. It didn't – it brought Maggie Trudeau's pathetic autobiography, and national psychic stagflation.

But Election '79 was not just the defeat of Trudeau Inc. It was also the defeat of the media panjandrums. They had proven themselves dishonest brokers of the public soul, purveyors, at best, of a negative immanence. Their very language and prose, the medium of the national schizophrenia they covertly propagated.

The election of "Joe Who" (despite the bullying by the media) marks the end of the '70s. The spurious "toughness" of the Gliblibs will be replaced by commonplace decency. And a de facto media president of Canada, by a parliamentary prime minister and his cabinet. For Canada, certainly for English-speaking Canada, the '80s will be both the decade of the last chance, and also of some first new chance. And Toronto, which has decisively displaced Montreal as the unofficial capital of Canada, is at once bellwether and centre of all of this.

What will a pair of Toronto eyes be like in 1989? I suspect that one eye will be bright open, and the other torqued in suspicious squint!

Scott Symons, author.

In the '70s, I became 50 years old. I moved to Vancouver. Oddly enough I discovered that there were other joyful matters besides constitutional reform, the Quebec Referendum, and the latest Canadian political polls – ME!

Laurier Lapierre, broadcaster.

The New Narcissism of the West

In the darkness, from 30,000 feet up, Edmonton is so many glittering emeralds strewn across a jeweller's icy tray. On the ground, one discovers a trench slashed through the tray: the valley of the North Saskatchewan River, a writhing dragon upon whose high embankments rise the concrete totems of the West's blustering new affluence. These bleak temples, fashioned of prestressed, precast concrete, make modern Edmonton look like an underground parking garage and effectively mask a history that drifts all the way back to the fur trade and the Hudson's Bay Company. The oil-induced prosperity here is without style or nuance. The new riders of the purple sage have discarded cowboy boots and ten-gallon hats in favour of grey business suits and funny little haircuts featuring nubbly skin at the neck and pipestem sideburns trimmed to the ear lobes. Somehow the new riders all affect open, monotonous faces; young faces, to be sure, but – like the city that makes them beam so proudly – without character. The new riders stand in clusters awaiting elevators at the Château Lacombe, spiking their conversation with names like Syncrude and Diane Jones Konihowski, discussing which steakhouse they will visit tonight – steak and pizza being the gastronomic staples of the city; a gourmet in search of even half a Michelin star might well starve to death.

Women appear to have abandoned the city. Those who remain steadfastly cling to fashion that has not been seen east of Thunder Bay for years, then hide that under layers of parka. Prostitution thrives out here on the Frontier, conducted discreetly, of course, as befits a people shocked by a picture of a girl in their morning paper. Here, the ladies of the night cheerfully knock on your hotel-room door: home delivery, so to speak.

Western chic is embodied in Peter Pocklington, who defies good taste and hangs a $50,000 Emily Carr original in his tiny panelled office just off the showroom of his Ford dealership. There must be $500,000 worth of original Canadian art in the office, lost to an auto dealership. But westerners shrug off the waste, and adore Pocklington. "He is the epitome of everything that is happening in Alberta," notes one observer. "He is the fantasy prince of the province." Pocklington is a transplanted easterner, a wheeler-dealer only 37 years of age who, when he isn't tooling about in his Rolls, leaping aboard his eight-seater private jet or risking his neck jet-boat racing, oversees the Edmonton Oilers of the World Hockey Association. He also operates the largest Ford dealership in the country ($44-million volume in sales last year), consummates vast real-estate and development deals, and campaigns hard so that one day he can become prime minister. It's a far-fetched yet understandable ambition for a man who owns just about everything else. "We need 50 million new immigrants," he pronounces from behind an acre of desk, "and I'm talking about Europeans, not Viet Congs. Undoubtedly they are good people, but for the long view we need people who are used to the climate and are willing to get out and work."

The booming oil town of Edmonton lights up the night sky with all its newly found affluence. *John Reeves*

Pocklington embodies the new narcissism of the West, a shoulders-back, chest-out arrogance that is awesome to behold. The world, to western eyes, has narrowed considerably; it's epicentre has shifted so that now it is located "Out Here." "What we're trying to do *out here* is build a whole goddamned new country," snaps John Lindblad, a former eastern newspaperman who now works (in Ottawa) for the Alberta department of federal and intergovernmental affairs. "There is a spirit of entrepreneurship *out here* that is unlike anywhere else," announces broadcaster turned movie-producer Fil Fraser. "People *out here* are willing to risk everything on a hole in the ground. People *out here* say, 'What's the risk? Let's go for broke.' "

Out here, statistics are the sharply pointed weapons employed to puncture holes in misconceptions about the West, and further show off its superiority. Al Bleiken, the ever-diligent general manager of Edmonton's business development department, is like a machine gun, spraying the room with statistics: Edmonton is not the blue-collar town it is perceived to be – only 20 percent of the population is blue-collar. In fact the city has the fourth-largest disposable income, and more legitimate theatres – seven – than just about any other city in the country. "I would say that, culturally, Edmonton is among the top three cities in the country." Bleiken does not even blink when he says this.

The enemy, of course, is to the east. Snooty Toronto with its gimlet-eyed bankers, upset that the financial world is shifting westward. Hatred of the East is what knits xenophobic westerners together, and that hatred is ill-concealed. It is like a surprising slap in the face to any visitor. "It's something

I'm reminded of all the time," says an uncomfortably transplanted Torontonian. "I'm constantly getting hell from people here because I'm from the East."

Hatred of the East is easily exploited. Alberta's Premier Peter Lougheed is a master of the art of East-bashing, and he has spawned apt pupils. One of the most avid of these pupils is J. Patrick O'Callaghan, the "Green Hornet" to his staff – because he constantly wears a green suit, and usually a matching green shirt as well as a green parka – who is, as his name amply implies, an Irishman – from County Cork. He learned the newspaper business in Yorkshire and Liverpool, then worked for a time at the Red Deer *Advocate,* before joining the Edmonton *Journal* as assistant to then publisher Ross Munro. Southam, the Toronto-based newspaper chain that owns the *Journal,* brought him to the dread East for six years before dispatching him back west to publish the *Journal* in 1976. O'Callaghan, in short, is not a native. Still, there is no more fanatical a westerner than a newly arrived easterner and the Green Hornet is certainly proof of that. He learned quickly that to win the West you must kick hell out of the East. He does so with relish: "After a century of picking the pockets of the West," he will tell any service-club meeting that cares to invite him around, "Upper Canada now finds itself in the difficult position of having to return some of that money, because at least one of the western provinces has something that Ontario lacks – *energy."* He has no hesitation about taking a few swipes at another western bugaboo, the eastern media, neatly overlooking the fact that his bosses at Southam are based in Toronto. "I must confess," he says blithely, "we are a little tired of being analyzed on two-day jaunts from Toronto and then reading or hearing that Calgary is an instant packaged city dropped on the Prairies, or that your typical Edmontonian has oil on his boots, garlic on his breath, and speaks with a Ukrainian accent."

Ron Base, journalist, *Quest* Magazine.

The Most Powerful People in Alberta

Peter Lougheed, premier of Alberta
Robert Blair, president, Alberta Gas Trunk Lines
Peter MacDonell, lawyer, Lougheed confidante
Ron Southern, president, ATCO Industries
F. C. Mannix, chairman, MANCAL Group of Companies (formerly LORAM)
Joe Clark, the man from High River

Merv Leitch, minister of energy
Lou Hyndman, provincial treasurer
Hugh Horner, deputy premier, minister of economic development
Wilbert Hopper, president, Petro-Canada
Max Ward, president, Wardair
Blake Ashforth, regional vice-president, Royal Bank of Canada
Dr. Charles Allard, surgeon, Industrial Conglomerate owner
Jack Gallagher, chairman, Dome Petroleum Ltd.
J. Patrick O'Callaghan, publisher, the Edmonton *Journal*

Our Best Years

The West has always provided the bread and leaven of Canadian life, but the '70s have been our yeastiest years. It was the decade in which we westerners and our institutions came of age and changed the Canadian equation.

Alberta and Saskatchewan, ending the decade three-quarters of a century old, are clearly the fiestiest part of the West and the country. British Columbia continues as Lotus Land, where the lush seduction of the environs makes "goofing off" a way of life. B.C.'s contribution to the rest of us includes the political entertainment of the Bennetts, *The Georgia Straight* (which as the decade ends appears to be going straight), the biggest marijuana burn in our history and Allan Fotheringham. Manitoba, everybody's hinterland, yielded up a governor general and took back James Richardson.

But Alberta and Saskatchewan are the real movers. Their political philosophies – from the ginger groups of the 1930s, through the CCF and Social Credit of the '40s and '50s (such different responses to the same dilemma), to Lougheed and Blakeney, respectively the toughest and brightest politicians in power as the decade ends – have been critical to the Canadian balance. In the '60s, Saskatchewan exported medicare, social conscience, key civil servants and Tommy Douglas to the nation; Alberta sent oil and money, no longer on the receiving end of the equalization payments. In the '70s they sent a new message, a new equation for power that moved the fulcrum of the country westward. By and large, westerners were not surprised when Peter Lougheed chose the premiership of Alberta over the prime ministership of Canada when he quite clearly could have had either. It was a signal that the best action may no longer be at the centre, or where the centre used to be.

The '70s confirmed that we are a nation of urbanites. The back-to-the-land flood of the '60s has become a trickle. This decade belongs to the cities. The city with the excitement is Edmonton.

Winnipeg has always had the ballet; Regina is always full of interesting people; everybody knows about Calgary's Stampede, Americans and building boom; and Vancouver remains the great Canadian escape. But the world is waking to Edmonton – dare I say it? – the new Athens of North America.

Edmonton is a fortuitous combination of wealth, ethnic diversity, entrepreneurial balls (no other word will do) and cultural awareness. It's the place where they ran the XI Commonwealth Games and brought them in on time and on budget. The foundation that organized the games closed its books by giving money back to the governments that had provided grants (some $60,000). The games themselves were among the most successful ever and began a tradition to be carried into future games by pairing a cultural festival with the athletic events.

Edmonton, by population, is served by more theatrical stages and companies than any city in North America, and in absolute terms is probably Canada's most theatrical city. Some 110 productions were mounted on city stages during the '78-'79 season. The Citadel Theatre, with the finest theatrical complex in the land, has set a standard of production equal to anything on the continent. Howard Pechet's *Stage West* (with a second stage in Regina) is the country's, and one of the continent's, most successful dinner theatres, playing to capacity audiences six days a week, 12 months a year, and paying its way without benefit of grants from the Canada Council or anybody else.

Against the background of a fine symphony orchestra, the ITV Concert Series, which brings such musical luminaires as Henry Mancini, Cleo Laine

Alberta Premier Peter Lougheed waves to spectators as he trots along in the Calgary Day Parade at the Canadian National Exhibition, 1975. CP

and Englebert Humperdink into concert with the Edmonton Symphony, has been shown on television stations in more than 50 countries around the world.

The '70s, and Edmonton, produced Horst Schmid, the peripatetic Alberta culture minister for most of the decade. Though he hated flying, he logged thousands of air miles travelling to cultural events the length and breadth of the province and across the country. His incredible personal commitment gave Alberta culture the most dramatic boost given by any government in modern times.

The West provided the spirit and the locale for two films that captured something very important about the Canadian experience. *Why Shoot The Teacher,* based on Saskatchewan-born author Max Braithwaite's personal story and filmed in Alberta, has become one of this country's first true film classics, acclaimed around the world. *Who Has Seen The Wind,* based on W. O. Mitchell's story of prairie boyhood will, with *Why Shoot The Teacher,* become a permanent part of Canada's important film literature.

The '70s have been our best years. We outgrew the "Bible Belt" and came of age culturally, economically, politically. While the "creationists" are still around, our approaches to education have leapfrogged other parts of the nation in scope and enlightenment. W. O. Mitchell and Margaret Laurence are not banned in western schools.

Nothing more needs to be said about the economic boom except that the house we bought near the beginning of the decade will have quadrupled in value at its end.

Did someone mention narcissism? Well, we like what we see in the mirror – but the West is looking out, not in. Look out for us in the '80s.

Fil Fraser, filmmaker.

Royal Visits

In the '70s, the Queen visited Canada seven times:

July 5-15, 1970, for 100th anniversary of Manitoba's entering Confederation, also travelled to North West Territories and Arctic.

May 3-12, 1971, for 100th anniversary of B.C.'s entering Confederation.

June 25-July 5, 1973, 100th anniversary of the formation of the RCMP.

July 31-August 4, 1973, to open the Commonwealth Heads of Government Conference in Ottawa.

July 13-25, 1976, visit to Nova Scotia and New Brunswick and to Montreal to open the 21st Olympiad.

October 14-19, 1977, Silver Jubilee ceremonies, and Queen read speech from the throne on October 18.

July 26-August 6, 1978, to open the Commonwealth Games in Edmonton, August 3. She also visited Newfoundland and Saskatchewan during this time.

Authors (left to right) Pierre Berton, Farley Mowat, Margaret Laurence, and Leslie McFarlane, participate in Canada Day ceremonies by the newly formed Canadian Academy of Authors, April 1977, Hamilton. CP

The Rise & Fall of Serious CanLit

In the past ten years the writing and publishing of Canadian fiction has become a true industry: plentiful, unpredictable – and now depressed.

Although there had been previous periods, most notably the 1930s, when Canadian fiction enjoyed wide public support, the most recent splurge came at an unexpected time. In the mid-1960s Canadian publishing, like publishing the world over, was beginning to suffer from the popularity of television and the movies. It was a time when people were asking why Canadian novelists were cursed with the one-book syndrome. To add to their woes, Canadian publishers were beginning to lose, to the American branch plants, the educational markets that had once supported them.

But during the same period, buoyed by the first major wave of nationalism since the Second World War, there were new small presses starting up to publish political books and novels that weren't sufficiently conventional or international to attract the attention of the more established houses.

In the spring of 1969 one of these new houses put out a novel called *Five Legs,* by Graeme Gibson. It was, even in the quirky canon of Canadian literature, a strange book. Dense and complicated, with large debts to James Joyce and Malcolm Lowry, it did to syntax what winter does to flowers.

Some called it genius, other labelled it pretence. But as the sales began to mount up it became clear that *Five Legs* had achieved the impossible – carried by a new interest in things specifically Canadian, a difficult novel from an unknown press had achieved both critical and commercial success.

Immediately Anansi and other small presses began to publish in quantity. Novels, mostly first novels, suddenly began to appear on bookstore shelves. Where the crop had been a few novels a year, it now became dozens. And they proved, by their very multiple and flawed existence, that novels – highbrow, literary, and even unreadable novels – had a market in English Canada. It was not, to be sure, a very large market, but it was large enough to meet the costs of production, given a little help from the Canada Council.

In the fall of 1970, the rising nationalist sentiments were crystallized in publishing by two events: W.J. Gage sold its educational division to an American firm, and Ryerson Press, Canada's oldest and most respectable publisher, let itself be bought out by the American-owned McGraw-Hill.

The arts community protested loudly and demanded support from the Canada Council before the whole publishing industry met a similar fate. Fortunately, the Liberal Party was in a spending mood. Writers' tours, writers-in-residencies, block grants for publishing programs, new national organizations for publishers and writers sprang up like little voters across the land.

But despite the marvellous growth of infrastructure, and a whole new battalion of cultural bureaucrats, the explosion of new fiction writing continued. And its acceptance widened. Books by such writers as Alice Munro and Margaret Laurence became popular successes. In 1970 a best-selling novel was considered one that sold 5,000 copies. In the spring of 1974 *The Diviners* was published, and a few months later more than 20,000 copies were in print.

The very successful books also increased the audience for the more ordinary sellers, and along with the expanded market for hardcover books came increased paperback sales. For these the prime target was university courses, where a burgeoning interest in cultural nationalism was bringing students to Canadian literature almost faster than the often reluctant (and American-staffed) English departments could handle.

The combination of the college market and the wider public enthusiasm for things Canadian brought this new phase of the Canadian fiction industry to its prime: during this period the normal successful book was a serious literary work which would receive good reviews and achieve sufficient sales in hardback to get into paper and finally onto college courses.

Canadian writers found themselves in a surprising situation. They were writing the kind of books that would have once guaranteed perpetual oblivion, but they were gaining an interested and often demanding audience.

The older publishing houses, especially McClelland and Stewart, with its ubiquitous New Canadian Library series, were quick to take advantage of this trend. And some of the newer ones, like Anansi, Oberon, and Talonbooks, were equally astute – often printing even their first editions in paperback to asure instant access to the educational market.

Writers had stumbled into a fortunate time. They were encouraged by an expanded Canada Council, their royalties were often augmented (in Ontario) by Arts Council grants, and their rejected manuscripts and embarrassing love letters were snatched up by eager libraries and archives. Thanks again to the Canada Council, even their personal appearances became a valued commodity.

While younger writers happily multiplied, major writers long silent – Irene Baird, Adele Wiseman, Robertson Davies, Morley Callaghan – surfaced with new books, books so good that the silences seemed all the more regrettable. Even some expatriate writers began to return to Canada, includng Margaret Laurence and Mordecai Richler.

Between the older writers and the new, a remarkable outpouring of fiction commenced, a cornucopia of work in which anything was possible, books both excellent and terrible in absolutely unpredictable ways. While the rest of the world was breeding novelists who wrote about disasters, Canada was enjoying a flowering of Victorian sensibilities. Beautiful and baroque novels like *Fifth Business, Lives of Girls and Women, Lord Nelson Tavern, Bartleby, Arkwright, Farthing's Fortunes, Scann* were published. And while they were being read with interest, classics that had never really found their audience – books like *As For Me and My House, The Mountain and the Valley, The Stone Angel, The Double Hook* – were becoming popular in quality paperback editions.

Why, people were starting to ask, were there not more Canadian books in the really cheap and available mass-market lines? Like many industries in Canada, book publishing was dominated by foreign firms, but while government-funded organizations were still lobbying the government about foreign control of distribution, General Publishing made a surprise move.

From its low-profile, mass-market subsidiary, PaperJacks, it sent out a blizzard of contracts to an amazingly wide variety of writers. And then went one step further and bought the Canadian franchise for Pocket Books – distribution system and all. Within a couple of years, both McClelland and Stewart and Macmillan were also to announce joint ventures with American-owned paperback lines, Seal Books and Macmillan-NAL.

It is this development – the existence of several mass-market publishing lines – that will revolutionize the writing of Canadian fiction. For the first time it is economically feasible for large quantities of novels to be widely distributed. But this is happening when the ten-year boom in literary publishing is starting to slacken. The major houses, beset by rising production costs and a static market, have been cutting back. The small presses, while they introduced new writers and new styles of writing, never succeeded in increasing their cash base; and they are having, in face of the disappearing gap between costs and potential market, to publish in a more conservative way. Good books and new writers are still being published, but they are no longer centre stage.

Because, as the literary boom falters, it is clear that a new phenomenon is beginning to appear. With the support of mass-market paperback lines, international connections, a budding market-place for Canadian agents, lawyers specializing in contracts, even the occasional film and television adaptation, it has become clear that there is a place for the *intentional* Canadian best-seller.

By the fall of 1978 the fiction lists of most major houses were heavy with these "commercial" novels. There are books being originated for Seal and PaperJacks. There are book packagers in Toronto specializing in putting books together with assured subsidiary and international sales. There are the Alberta fiction and non-fiction awards, and now there is the all-time leader in glitz, the Seal Books $50,000 first-novel award.

The kind of money involved in these commercial novels dwarfs the potential returns from a literary novel, and once again that kind of novel is becoming an economic dinosaur. The 5,000-copy printing that could be such a happy success just a few years ago now seems uneconomical.

Meanwhile, the campus boom has moderated. And the wave of nationalism that carried Canadian culture to such prominence is beginning to recede. It seems that Canada, with its incredible political and economic problems, can't bear to look itself in the face.

Even bookstores are in difficulty. The old-fashioned store, with its huge stock and excellent service, is becoming the well-loved but archaic exception. Chain bookstores have taken over almost half the market, and their share continues to increase. Most are leery of short stories, first novels, experimental novels – anything that might not sell. And for the small presses, chains are a total disaster, often refusing even to speak to small-press salesmen.

After ten years of excitement, the publishing industry is in many ways back where it started, and back in tune with the international publishing world. There are a few large companies – all of them in terrible financial condition – and a lot of equally beleaguered small presses. What can be expected for the future? Will the big companies overcome their fiscal problems? Will the small publishers find new markets for their books?

According to most observers, the answer to both questions is a qualified yes. The big publishers may survive – but they will be rescued by suicidal investors and government loans only on the condition that they trim their costs. And the literary publishers, with their lists shrunken and made conservative by aiming for wider sales, will struggle through hard times by cutting costs and salaries.

But the new wave in publishing, the place where the money and the energy is located, will be book packagers and small publishers doing solely commercial books: coffee-table books for the carriage trade and commercial fiction and non-fiction for the international market.

We had ten anomalous years of bizarre and wonderful books. Much of what was done was silly, vain, pompous, forgettable, but nevertheless that decade was the time when the publishing of Canadian fiction came of age. Now, when a new group of writers and editors must be expected to make their mark, the industry is in trouble and its possibilities are narrowing.

Will the new-style commercial publishers be able to afford the virtues that crippled the old? In shaping books for the best-seller and international market, the publishers may have to de-emphasize books about Canada, about ourselves, in favour of books that blur cultural and national differences. Will they support writers through bad times, publish fiction that might not sell, publish poetry at all?

As the makeshift arrangements of the last decade collapse under the pressure of more conservative and stringent times, everyone agrees that large-scale changes are coming. The next year or two in the publishing industry will be interesting, and dangerous.

Matt Cohen, author.

Canadian Children's Literature

At the Pacific Rim Conference at the University of British Columbia in May of 1976 an earnest interviewer from Access Alberta asked me: "What is Canadian children's literature?" Two British authors waiting their turn at being interviewed suppressed giggles and guffaws without realizing that what they considered a silly question was really a political issue. The extensive and fine output in English by both the Americans and the British had so overwhelmed Canadian publishers and authors that the only books being read with truly Canadian settings were *Anne of Green Gables* and *Wild Animals I Have Known.* Most publishers felt that Canadian children's books didn't sell. In 1974 even the dogged children's librarians' section of the Canadian Library Association had abandoned the Young Canada's Book Week, which was the only event that ever even attempted to draw attention to Canadian children's literature.

Fortunately, there were people in this country who cared that Canadian children should have an opportunity to read about themselves and their country. A move was already afoot to establish the Children's Book Centre for the promotion of Canadian children's literature and to assist authors, illustrators and publishers. The dream, through the funding of the Canada Council, became reality in 1976.

The real change in Canadian publishing for children came in 1974 when Macmillan published Dennis Lee's fanciful collection of rhymes, *Alligator Pie.* To date 75,000 copies have been sold in Canada alone, proving that books rooted in the Canadian setting can sell. "In Napanee I'll eat your knee" is now a part of the language of most Canadian children under the age of 12.

Not until 1976 did other promising

developments occur in the field, the most impressive of which is the growth of magazines for children, beginning with *OWL*, which is published by the Young Naturalist Foundation. A nature study magazine for children from eight to 12, it uses the production expertise of Key Publishers to produce a stunning-looking magazine filled with useful and interesting information. Young Naturalist Foundation and Key combined their efforts successfully again in 1979 to produce *Chickadee* for the four to eight age range.

The *Canadian Children's Magazine* was established in 1976 by Evelyn Samuel of Victoria, who was concerned about our children's knowledge of their country. Here is a general social studies magazine which manages to get children from different parts of the country talking to each other.

Magook (the name indicates a cross between a magazine and a book) appeared in the fall of 1977. Although its creators found they had a reasonable initial success, their sales did not measure up to their expectations so they rethought and revamped their format and concept and reappeared in January, 1979, as a monthly magazine, available on subscription, with a storybook included.

The astonishing commercial but not literary success story is *The Canadian Children's Annual*, which has appeared annually since 1975. The 1979 edition sold around 50,000 in bookstores, supermarkets and department stores in spite of generally bad reviews. The covers have been beautifully designed by Canadian artists, and the content has improved over the years.

The publicity generated by the Children's Book Centre and its Children's Book Festival every November has brought a keener awareness to the public and the children's librarians about the necessity to buy for their children books which help give them a sense of themselves and of the country in which they live. Now fine books such as *Hold Fast, Listen for the Singing, Rebecca's Nancy, A Salmon for Simon, Hey Dad, The Wooden People, Underground to Canada* and others are being read by our children as works of literature and books that will help them to develop a sense of national identity.

Judy Sarick, owner, Children's Book Store, Toronto

Book Publishing

It was a decade of spectacular growth. The issue of Canadian ownership and the burgeoning interest in Canadian cultural identity brought political attention to the book publishing industry for the first time.

The sale of Gage, Ryerson and the threatened sale of McClelland and Stewart to U.S. interests, plus the report of an Ontario royal commission confirming the overwhelming extent of foreign control, spurred instant government action. The Ontario government introduced a subsidized loan program that supports publishers and writers through the Ontario Arts Council. The federal government, through the Canada Council, expanded its block grant program, translation assistance and a variety of technical trade support devices. The Foreign Investment Review Act was passed which effectively prohibits the sale of a publishing house to foreign interests unless it can be proven to be in the public interest.

Small publishing houses developed everywhere in the country. Regional publishing became a force. Applications for block grants grew from fewer than 50 to over 500 overnight. The Canadian books present in the retail trade grew from fewer than ten percent to an estimated 25 percent during the decade. Canadian houses became competitive in mass-market publishing. Foreign-owned subsidiaries expanded their interest in Canadian books. For the first time in history it became a seller's market for the Canadian author.

At the end of the decade, the outward aspect was that of a flourishing industry. Behind the scenes, bankers, accountants and government officials looked with dismay at balance sheets and operating statements and wondered how long it would last.

Jack McClelland, publisher, president, McClelland and Stewart Ltd.

Alligator Pie

The kids' poem that swept the country –
from the book *Alligator Pie* by Dennis
Lee, illustrated by Frank Newfeld.

> Alligator pie, alligator pie,
> If I don't get some I think I'm gonna die.
> Give away the green grass, give away the sky,
> But don't give away my alligator pie.
>
> Alligator stew, alligator stew,
> If I don't get some I don't know what I'll do.
> Give away my furry hat, give away my shoe,
> But don't give away my alligator stew.
>
> Alligator soup, alligator soup,
> If I don't get some I think I'm gonna droop.
> Give away my hockey-stick, give away my hoop,
> But don't give away my alligator soup.

Dennis Lee, poet.

The Governor General Literary Awards

1970

La femme de Loth
Monique Bosco (Roman)
Quand nous serons heureux
Jacques Brault (Théâtre)
The New Ancestors
Dave Godfrey (Fiction)
Still Water
bp Nichol (Poetry)
The Collected Works of Billy the Kid
Michael Ondaatje (Prose & Poetry)
Les actes retrouvés*
Fernand Ouellette (Autres genres littéraires)

1971

The Last Spike
Pierre Berton (Non-fiction)
Le cycle
Gérard Bessette (Roman)
La fin d'un règne
Gérald Fortin (Autres genres littéraires)
Selected Poems
John Glassco (Poetry)
Le réel absolu
Paul-Marie Lapointe (Poésie)
St. Urbain's Horseman
Mordecai Richler (Fiction)

1972

The Manticore
Robertson Davies (Fiction)
Histoire économique du Québec 1851-1896
Jean Hamelin et Yves Roby (Autres genres littéraires)
Signaux pour les voyants
Gilles Hénault (Poésie)
Civil Elegies and Other Poems
Dennis Lee (Poetry)
Don l'Original
Antonine Maillet (Roman)
Lies
John Newlove (Poetry)

*Prix refusé par le titulaire.

1973

Painters in a New Land
Michael Bell (Non-fiction)
L'hiver de force
Réjean Ducharme (Roman)
Québec en Amérique au XIXe siècle
Albert Faucher (Autres genres littéraires)
La main au feu*
Roland Giguère (Poésie)
Lions at Her Face
Miriam Mandel (Poetry)
The Temptations of Big Bear
Rudy Wiebe (Fiction)

1974

Don Quichotte de la démanche
Victor-Lévy Beaulieu (Roman)
Mécanique jongleuse suivi de Masculin grammaticale
Nicole Brossard (Poésie)
Habitants et marchands de Montréal au XVIIe siècle
Louise Dechene (Autres genres litteraires)
Fire on Stone
Ralph Gustafson (Poetry)
The Diviners
Margaret Laurence (Novel)
The Siren Years
Charles Ritchie (Non-fiction)

1975

Chouennes
Pierre Perrault (Poetry)
Hallowed Walls
Marion MacRae and Anthony Adamson (Non-fiction)
Les enfants du sabbat
Anne Hébert (Fiction)
Nordicité canadienne
Louis-Emond Hamelin (Non-fiction)
The Great Victorian Collection
Brian Moore (Fiction)
The Island Means Minago
Milton Acorn (Poetry)

1976

The Writing of Canadian History
Carl Berger (Non-fiction)

Bear
Marian Engel (Fiction)
Les rescapés
André Major (Fiction)
Le Bas Canada 1791-1840 changements structuraux et crise
Fernand Ouellet (Non-fiction)
Poèmes 1946-1968
Alphonse Piché (Poetry)
Top Soil
Joe Rosenblatt (Poetry)

1977
The Wars
Timothy Findley (Fiction)
Ces enfants de ma vie
Gabrielle Roy (Fiction)
Essays on the Constitution
Frank Scott (Non-fiction)
Le développement des idéologies au Québec des origines à nos jours

Denis Monière (Non-fiction)
Under the Thunder the Flowers Light up the Earth
D. G. Jones (Poetry and drama)
Les Célébrations suiviede Adidou Adidouce*
Michel Garneau (Poésie et théâtre)

1978
Go Boy
Roger Caron (Non-fiction)
Poems New & Selected
Patrick Lane (Poetry)
Who Do You Think You Are
Alice Munro (Fiction)
Mon refuge est mon volcan
Gilbert Languin (Poésie)
Paul-Emile Borduas
François Marc Gagnon (Essaie)
Les grandes Marées
Jacques Poulin (Roman)

Edward Schreyer takes the oath of office as Canada's 22nd Governor General, 1979. CP

Great Children's Books

In choosing a list of books to represent the '70s, consideration has been given to wide-ranging interests and different age levels, literary quality and the physical properties of each book.

There is little that is not discussed in today's children's books. Unlike children's books of the '30s, which kept children apart in a world of their own, the '70s placed the child in the mainstream of things.

Although many of the interests and issues of the '70s are reflected in these books, it is their vitality and originality that makes them among the best of the decade.

Abel's Island, William Steig
Aio the Rainmaker, Fiona French
Anno's Journey, Mitsumasa Anno

Bridge to Terabithia, Katherine Paterson
Frog and Toad Are Friends, Arnold Lobel
John Brown, Rose and the Midnight Cat, by Jenny Wagner, illustrated by Ron Brooks
Mickey in the Night Kitchen, Maurice Sendak
Mr. Gumpy's Outing, John Burningham
Nobody's Family Is Going to Change, Louise Fitzhugh
Season Songs, Ted Hughes, illustrated by Leonard Baskin
The God Beneath the Sea, Edward Blischen and Leon Garfield, illustrated by Charles Keeping
The Magic Orange Tree, Diane Wolkstein
The Machine Gunners, Robert Westall
The Stone Book, Alan Garner
The Stronghold, Molly Hunter

Bob Barton, teacher of Children's literature.

Best of the Bestselling Mass-market Paperbacks

1970
The Godfather, Mario Puzo
Love Story, Erich Segal

1971
The Sensuous Woman, J
Everything You Always Wanted to Know About Sex and Were Afraid to Ask, Dr. David Reuben

1972
The Exorcist, William P. Blatty
The Happy Hooker, Xaviera Hollander

1973
Jonathan Livingston Seagull, Richard Bach
Chariot of the Gods, Erich Von Daniken

1974
The Exorcist, William P. Blatty
The Sybil, Flora R. Schreiber

1975
Jaws, Peter Benchley
Fear of Flying, Erica Jong

1976
Rich Man, Poor Man, Irwin Shaw
Love's Tender Fury, Jennifer Wilde

1977
Passages, Gail Sheehy
Your Erroneous Zones, Dr. Wayne W. Dyer

1978
Thorn Birds, Colleen McCullough

Jack Jensen, Metro News.

Bestsellers

1974

Charlie Farquharson's Jogfree of Canada, Don Harron

Charlie Farquharson's Histry of Canada, Don Harron

Monty Python's Brand New Paperbok, Monty Python's Flying Circus

Peter Gzowski's Book About This Country in the Morning, Peter Gzowski

Colombo's Canadian Quotations, John Robert Colombo

Drifting Home, Pierre Berton

Canajan Eh?, Mark M. Orkin

Howie Meeker's Hockey Basics, Howie Meeker

Mike: The Memoirs of the Right Honourable Lester B. Pearson, Volume 2: 1948-1957, Lester B. Pearson

Six War Years 1939-1945: Memories of Canadians at Home and Abroad, Barry Broadfoot

1975

The Canadian Establishment, Peter C. Newman

The Snow Walker, Farley Mowat

One Canada, Volume 1, John George Diefenbaker

The Canadian Limerick Book, Hugh Oliver and Keith MacMillan

Bring on the Empty Horses, David Niven

More Joy of Sex, Alex Comfort

Moneychangers, Arthur Hailey

Curtain, Agatha Christie

Will Gordon Sinclair Please Sit Down, Gordon Sinclair

Exodus U.K., Richard Rohmer

1976

Charlie Farquharson's K.O.R.N. Allmynack, Don Harron

My Country: The Remarkable Past, Pierre Berton

The Pioneer Years: 1895-1914: Memories of Settlers Who Opened the West, Barry Broadfoot

The Golden Age of B.S., Fred C. Dobbs

Between Friends/Entre Amis, National Film Board of Canada

A Man Called Intrepid: The Secret War, William Stevenson

Blood, Sweat and Bears, Stanley Burke, illustrated by Roy Peterson

René: A Canadian in Search of a Country, Peter Desbarats

Your Erroneous Zones, Wayne W. Dyer

Separation, Richard Rohmer

1977

The Silmarillion, J.R.R. Tolkien

Act of God, Charles Templeton

Tom Thomson: The Silence and the Storm, Harold Town and David P. Silcox

All Things Wise and Wonderful, James Herriot

Garbage Delight, Dennis Lee, illustrated by Frank Newfeld

The Dionne Years: A Thirties Melodrama, Pierre Berton

One Canada, Volume 3, John George Diefenbaker

Roots, Alex Haley

Canada: Cancelled Because of Lack of Interest, Eric Nicol & Peter Whalley

Dear Me, Peter Ustinov

1978

Bronfman Dynasty: The Rothschilds of the New World, Peter C. Newman

The Wild Frontier: More Tales From the Remarkable Past, Pierre Berton

Olde Charlie Farquharson's Testament, Don Harron

War and Remembrance, Herman Wouk

Swamp Song, Stanley Burke, illustrated by Roy Peterson

The Joy of Hockey, Eric Nicol, illustrated by Dave More

Chesapeake, James Michener

The Canadian Book of Lists, Jeremy Brown and David Ondaatje

Illustrated Hobbit, J.R.R. Tolkien

Gnomes, Wil Huygen, illustrated by Rien Poortvliet

D. W. Quick, vice-president of marketing, W.H. Smith.

Ten Best of Crime Fiction

God Save the Child, Robert Parker: Spenser is to the '70s what Archer, Marlow and Spade were to earlier decades. Perhaps more so.

True Confessions, John Gregory Dunne: Distinguished mainstream crime fiction.

The Friends of Eddie Coyle, George V. Higgins: The symbiotic relationship between minor villains and cynical prosecutors; violent and sardonic.

A Pinch of Snuff, Reginald Hill: The human comedy includes murder and kinky sex, even in provincial England.

The Blackheath Poisonings, Julian Symons: Murder mysteries in a prosperous late-Victorian household; touching, funny and realistic.

Death of an Expert Witness, P.D. James: Classic modern detective story with feeling and intelligence.

The Laughing Policeman, Maj Sjowall and Per Wahloo: The Swedish homicide squad brought new dimensions to the police-procedural genre.

The Fan, Bob Randall: Thriller with terrifying suspense. Showbiz flavour.

The Theban Mysteries, Amanda Cross: Multilevel detective novel with style, wit and perception. Academe flavour.

Murder To Go, Emma Lathen: Clever, funny detective story. Wall Street flavour.

Five Best of Spy Novels

The Human Factor, Graham Greene: Civil servants cannot necessarily remain neutral.

The Honourable Schoolboy, John Le Carré: Nor can they necessarily remain committed.

Twinkle, Twinkle, Little Spy, Len Deighton: The other side of defection.

The Levanter, Eric Ambler: The other side of neutrality with Middle East terrorism.

Other Paths to Glory, Anthony Price: Contemporary significance of truth behind a First World War legend.

Derrick Murdoch, book reviewer and author of *The Agatha Christie Mystery.*

Canadian Radio Highlights

1970
CRTC imposes the 30 percent Canadian music content regulation; the rest is history.

1971-'72
Inauguration of new CBC-AM schedules, including:

- local information programming in prime time: morning, noon and afternoon replacing (in morning and afternoon) local disc shows that features primarily American music with minimal local news;

- *This Country In the Morning* (now *Morningside),* the first daily magazined program to attempt to capture the spirit and happenings of the country in talk, music and documentary from all locations;

- *As It Happens,* the nightly Canadian institution.

1973-'74
Public hearings and subsequent establishment of CRTC-FM policy: that the FM band should not be used (as in the U.S.) for AM formats; foreground programming with limited commercialization should make it a separate medium from AM radio (this policy applied to the private sector; the CBC had already met these requirements and was expected to increase its programming innovation).

1975
Inauguration of the CBC stereo FM network, the longest such system in the world, with intent to reach 95 percent of the country before the mid-'80s.

1976
Inauguration of CBC music, arts and drama policies leading to:

- *Mostly Music* – nightly program of serious music on AM mono (repeated from FM stereo at noon) featuring all major Canadian orchestras as well as other festival and choral achievements;

- *Arts National* – weekday afternoon stereo network program featuring analysis and in-depth commentary of the arts with major festival and other musical achievements, both national and international;

- *Festival Theatre* – FM stereo drama with major productions that have included the Stratford Festival production of *Judgement* starring Richard Monette; the Shaw Festival production of *Man and Superman;* Albee's *A Delicate Balance* with Kate

Reid from Vancouver; Hume Cronyn and Jessica Tandy's *The Many Faces of Love;* Halifax production of *Cardinal Tosca* starring John Neville as Sherlock Holmes;

- popular drama – *Johnny Chase,* the first radio science fantasy series since *Star Wars,* and *Sussex Drive,* the very popular series written by Marian Waldman of the lives of a mythical prime minister, his family and staff.

1977-'78
Achievements:
- live stereo feed of the Beyreuth Festival in Germany;

- first live-to-Europe stereo production of *International Music Day* from the National Arts Center in Ottawa featuring Maureen Forrester, the NAC Orchestra and a work by Murray Schaefer (carried in a dozen countries);

- recording of the Tchaikovsky Competition in Moscow (the only medium; in North America to do so) in which Canadian Andre Laplante won second prize.

Above all, in 1970, CBC Radio, excluding national news and special events (including hockey broadcasts), had fewer than 350,000 regular listeners to its English service; today, CBC Radio has close to five million weekly listeners. Radio has made an impressive comeback in the public sector.

Robert Blackwood, manager,
Program Development Project, CBC.

After many years, there is no doubt that FM radio broadcasting in Canada has come of age. It will increase its audience in the years to come. But it's my opinion that it is just another part of radio broadcasting. While FM will get more people listening to radio, I don't believe it will substantially affect AM's audience. I believe they will both do extremely well in the future.

Allan Waters, president, CHUM, Toronto.

A steamy performance by Mick Jagger and guitarist Keith Richards of The Rolling Stones at Maple Leaf Gardens in 1972. CP

Brutal Chic

Rock began the '70s dazed and lazed. Janis Joplin, Jimi Hendrix and Jim Morrison were all dead, the Beatles gone, and the culture had lost its counters. Show business had replaced social activism and if you traced the Rolling Stones' financial holdings you ended up in Liechtenstein. Money replaced reality-altering herbs as *the* stimulant. A period of pragmatic fragmentation followed in which every minority had its musical ghetto: soul, reggae, disco, rock-a-billy, middle-of-the-road, heavy metal, progressive rock, teeny-bopper rock, '50s revivalism, album-rock, glitter-rock, jazz-rock, fusion-rock, folk-rock, and you-name-it-we've-got-it rock. Rock had come to learn corporate-think – or was it vice versa? – and to appreciate megabucks.

This is where punk came in, which, taking into account its later development as "new wave," became the *real* history of pop music in the '70s. Admittedly, punk – excuse me, new wave – didn't begin until the '70s were well on their way, but that has more to do with the idiosyncrasies of the times than with the music. You see, no one realized that the '70s had begun until about 1977, when they were nearly over. In fact, for a time there, many believed that the '60s had been a decade in which time had actually rolled backward and 1971 was 1959 in disguise. Once we'd got the truth sorted out, it was almost too late and we had to play catch-up ball. So when a brand-and-nasty new music appeared, a music with such figure heads as Sid Vicious of London's Sex Pistols and Nazi Dog, of Toronto's Viletones, a lot of history had to be compressed into a relatively short time.

That is how punk barely began when it was replaced by new wave; a new street-style was barely out of the basement when it became a couturier item; the media had barely figured out what was happening when something else started to happen. Briefly, then, the history of the new wave can be outlined as follows:

1. The formative stage: Lots of general nastiness here. Bands had names like Dead Boys, the Ugly, Curse, the Clash, the Damned and Teenage Head, while their lead singers were given to self-mutilation with shards of glass from broken beer bottles, safety pins or just about anything that would draw the maximum amount of blood and do the minimum amount of permanent damage. (As I mentioned, '70s rock was pragmatic to a fault – a nice, neat slash along an arm yielded just as much media coverage as something far less visible, and much more painful: a groin injury, for example.)

2. The derivative stage: In which much of the same happened as in the formative stage, but usually it happened in the suburbs where the kids were merely following inner-city trends. Still more bands arrived on the scene, though, and some of these – particularly one led by Elvis Costello and a group of would-be androids out of Ohio called Devo – came close to being household words.

3. The post-derivative stage: In which the record industry discovered there was actually money to be made from all of the above and bands like Blondie and Talking Heads attained hit-record status. Of course, as soon as this happened, those who wished to preserve the integrity of the new music realized they were being coopted by big money, and there followed:

4. The aesthetic stage: In which the more commercial aspects of the new wave – the sheer loudness of any particular band's presentation, the simple chordal patterns and lyrics laden with cliché and irony – were separated from the more experimental aspects, such as new wave activism (the Tom Robinson Band, by which both gay liberation and left-wing politics were hustled into a first-rate collection of songs), and sheer avant-gardism (by the likes of Brian Eno, Robert Fripp or Devo). This is pretty much where the matter stood as the '70s ended, leaving everyone happy with the situation. Those who wanted to make money could, those who were in it all for the art could be called artists.

Running through this sped-up evolution was a certain consistent tone that could be seen in everything from the new fashion to the choice of publicity photos. The favourite colours were black and white, the favoured expression a sort of bored blankness that implied a certain amount of pent-up anger bristling just beneath the surface. Anything that took you up – pot, say – was out, while anything that brought you down – for example, booze, a depressant – was definitely in. And four-letter words took on a new zinginess, as they were used often and usually in great hell-bent-for-leather flourishes. The new wave was rather egalitarian in terms of sexual politics, except that it pretended to play the old sexual stereotypes to the hilt. Thus male singers were not above talking, singing or bragging about their chicks, while female singers exaggerated their sexuality.

To add one further complication, all of this style of confrontation took on a certain trendiness, which, in turn, took the edge off the confrontation. Call it brutal chic, or SM for the masses.

To some, this was the final stage in the decline and fall of western culture: fascist decadence. And indeed it was decadent, in its way, but the fascism was just a ploy – a ploy to break through all the smug liberalism that had glossed over pop culture. If anything, the new wave was far less fascist than '60s pop-think that had come to dominate the music industry in the '70s. Brutal chic had its shock value and to that extent it served its purpose. And just in time. The '70s were darn near over and we were still living in the '60s.

Peter Goddard, journalist.

Great Canadian Art Events

1970-72

Works of art from the Douglas M. Duncan collection were distributed nationally to all the major art galleries in the country, contributing immeasurably (in a qualitative sense) to their Canadian (and other) collections.

At approximately the same time, the Charles S. Band and J.S. McLean collections come to the Art Gallery of Ontario (the latter on loan from the Ontario Heritage Foundation), which, along with the Duncan bequest, almost doubled the collection in terms of its significant Canadian works.

May 1, 1970

The Group of Seven's original exhibition, mounted in 1920 at the Art Museum of Toronto, was reconstructed at the Art Gallery of Ontario. The exhibition seemed to herald a new dawn of interest in Canadian art on the part of both the general public and young Canadian artists.

June 18, 1970

The Group of Seven exhibition at the National Gallery of Canada was the first exhibition of its kind to study the group with scholarly detachment, and to indicate a new attention toward documentation.

July, 1971

Duncan Cameron, an ex-Royal Ontario Museum staffer, became director of the Brooklyn Museum and tried to initiate "established museology procedures."

October 29, 1971

The Art of Tom Thomson, a retrospective of the legendary artist and woodsman, opened at the Art Gallery of Ontario. The exhibition was the first to focus on the art, not the legend, as well as being the first retrospective of the artist's work (46,957 in attendance over 45 days).

July 3, 1972

Richard J. Wattenmaker, an American art historian from Philadelphia, came to the Art Gallery of Ontario as chief curator. The reaction of both artists and the public was indicative of the rise of nationalism in cultural affairs.

November 10, 1972

Toronto Painting opened at the Art Gallery of Ontario. In one of its many "first" times, Toronto realized it had an indigenous cultural life. The careers designated by this exhibition were later to be examined individually, in retrospectives at the Robert McLaughlin Gallery, Oshawa: Nakamura (1974-75), Ronald (1975-76), Coughtry (1976-77), Burton (1977-78) and Rayner (1979-80). In a striking coincidence, both the Ronald and Coughtry shows had a total attendance figure (which includes the national tour) of 33,919. By the time of Burton's show, attendance had built up to 60,070.

May 10, 1973

Dr. O.J. Firestone gave his significant collection of Canadian art to the Ontario Heritage Foundation.

February 4, 1974

A summons was issued to Av Isaacs, the dealer for the Canadian artist Mark Prent, charging him with exhibiting disgusting objects "contrary to the Criminal Code."

October 26, 1974

The Henry Moore Centre opened at the Art Gallery of Ontario (followed by the opening of the Canadian wing and library, September 24, 1977) in a long-awaited "new" building.

December 10, 1974

J.H. Moore donated to the London Regional Art Gallery his collection of Canadian drawings and paintings (277 works). This generous gift, which specialized in artists of the London area, was followed by gifts of international paintings, graphics, sculpture and multiples on

The Henry Moore Sculpture Centre opened October 26, 1974 at the Art Gallery of Ontario.
Jim Chambers/AGO

November 26, 1976 (61 works), and Canadian and international drawings, prints and sculptures on December 31, 1976 (114 works).

January 17, 1975
The *Chairs* show, an extreme and happy example of populism in the arts, opened at the Art Gallery of Ontario (79,681 in attendance over 45 days).

September, 1975
David Mirvish Gallery opened its photography section. This move on the part of this prominent, important, commercial gallery heralded a change in taste on the part of the Canadian public. (Later Jane Corkin, the curator, opened her own space.)

November 8, 1975
David Craven's first show opened at Sable-Castelli Gallery, Toronto. This marked the beginning of the rise in interest on the part of the public in the younger generation of artists in Toronto.

November 20, 1975
Some Canadian Women Artists opened at the National Gallery of Canada, one of the first signs of the awakening of a national feminist consciousness in the arts.

February 18, 1976
Projects: Michael Snow – Photographs was held at New York's Museum of Modern Art along with a retrospective of Snow's films at the Centre Nationale d'Art et de Culture Georges Pompidou, Paris.

October, 1976
The Willem de Kooning exhibition at the Pollock Gallery, Toronto, was the first and only exhibition of the painting and sculpture of this renowned contemporary American painter in a Canadian gallery *ever*.

June 30, 1976
Jean Boggs, the director of the National Gallery of Canada, left to teach at Harvard University.

August 5, 1976
Joyce Wieland's movie *The Far Shore* was shown at the National Arts Centre in Ottawa to mixed but often pleasantly surprised reviews.

October 8, 1977
The Silence and the Storm by Harold Town and David P. Silcox sold 50,000 copies at a relatively high price for the time ($29.95 till December 31, 1977, and $42.50 thereafter).

November 3, 1977
A Terrible Beauty: The Art of Canada at War opened at Rodman Hall Arts Centre, St. Catharines. The exhibition involved an important reexamination of one of the nation's most fascinating but forgotten historical episodes. This was the nation-wide exhibition with the greatest number of bookings and highest attendance in the country in this decade.

January 9, 1978
The Allan Fleming memorial service was held at Massey College, University of Toronto. (There wasn't enough room for those who wanted to honour Canada's finest designer.)

January 13, 1978
Lawren S. Harris: Urban Scenes and Wilderness Landscapes 1906-1930 opened at the Art Gallery of Ontario. A monumental tribute to one of the original members of the Group of Seven, the exhibition examined only the representational period of this important artist's work. Attendance during this exhibition was the highest in the gallery's year (68,183 over 45 days).

May 3, 1978
The *Louis de Niverville Retrospective* opened at the Robert McLaughlin Gallery, the first extensive public recognition accorded an important Canadian artist whose career was parallel to, but apart from, the Toronto "gang."

July, 1978
David Mirvish Gallery closed. This commercial gallery entertained notions of quality, backed a certain moment in art (American colour field painting) and gave credibility to its artists through the purchase of their work.

July 20, 1978
The *A.J. Casson Retrospective* opened at the Art Gallery of Ontario, 58 years after the founding of the Group of Seven of which Casson is the only remaining living member. The show was a surprisingly fresh example of what it means to explore the "regional neighbourhood" (here, Ontario's small towns).

March 8, 1979
Gallery Moos opened in Calgary (to be followed by the Mira Godard Gallery, September, 1979). This is one of the first times eastern commercial dealers opened a facility in the west.

May 1, 1979
"Twas ever thus! The Price Collection of Eastern Canadian Folk Art opened at the Robert McLaughlin Gallery. This exhibition of the most important private collection of folk art in the country was the first of its kind to travel nationally.

Joan Murray, director, the Robert McLaughlin Gallery, Oshawa.

Mark Prent's Aquarium. Life-size figures in plexiglass aquarium—more than one ton of water. Bubbles rise from lower figure. *J. Littkemann* The Isaacs Gallery

Non-Art Events

The single most important non-art event in Canada in the 1970s was the disgraceful whithering away of any semblance of national influence on the national art scene by the National Gallery of Canada. In the first part of the decade, under the feckless direction of a charming scholar, Jean Boggs, and now during the invisible stewardship of Dr. Hsio-Yen Shih, the National Gallery wallows in the murk of past curatorial policies. Even deckhands such as Pierre Théberge and Dennis Reid, who contributed so remarkably to the voyage of no discovery, are abandoning ship, eager to direct other craft to the shoals. The general excuse given for this flaccidity is that they need a new building in Ottawa. Taking into account the level of sensibility at the National Gallery over the last ten years, a phone booth would have done as an exhibition hall.

The second significant event was the collapse of American art career director Clement Greenberg's power to manipulate Canadian art, which had reached its zenith with a retrospective exhibition of his protégé Jack Bush at the Art Gallery of Ontario. Greenberg's influence began to decompose with the closing of that temple for the cardinals, priests and choir-boys of his ministry, the David Mirvish cultural hobby gallery. There remain, however, pustular pockets of Greenbergian cant, mainly in Edmonton, where Terry Fenton presently scrambles to make himself over into a champion of home-grown art, and in that collection centre for wet finger critical writing, Toronto, where Andrew Hudson, Karen Wilkin and Ken Carpenter stagger around in the wilderness of perceptual orthodoxy, blind to the map markings of history, vainly searching for another prophet and a burning bush.

The brightest aspect of the last decade is the strength of galleries that provide creative alternatives to the beefed-up, fund-sapping bureaucracies of the larger cultural machines, such as the Art Gallery of Ontario and the National Gallery of Canada. Smaller, intimate, understaffed galleries – the Windsor Art Gallery directed by Ken Saltmarche, the Robert McLaughlin in Oshawa under Joan Murray and the lively if uneven Harbourfront Art Gallery complex in Toronto – deal with the heart matter of Canadian art: Canadian art.

Harold Town, artist.

The '70s were the time when the impact of the '60s was felt on lives set in the '50s. Everything was up for challenge: marriage, career, moral values, self-image. The result was a sublime confusion from which some emerged with a joyous sense of freedom based on self-reliance. Others began a limp and bleeding return to the warmth and security of conventional wisdom.

Sylvia Fraser, novelist.

Great Musical Events

Mariposa Folk Festival: The unscheduled appearances of legendary folk/rock musicians Bob Dylan, Joni Mitchell, Neil Young and Gordon Lightfoot at the 1972 festival on Toronto Island almost caused mob scenes, but Mariposa had survived far worse problems in its earlier years. During the decade the festival continued to provide a platform for young and unknown performers and composers as well as showcasing some of the biggest names in the music industry.

Anne of Green Gables, written by Don Harron with music by Norman Campbell, is a perennial favourite that, despite the critics, enjoys continuous popularity and ever-increasing audiences. It has been performed annually at the Charlottetown Festival since 1965.

Indigo, a celebration of the birth and evolution of the blues starring Salome Bey, played to capacity audiences for 11 months at Toronto's Basin Street during 1978-'79.

Lois Marshall, accompanied by Anton Kuerti, sang Shubert's *Die Winterreise,* a role usually performed by a male singer, in a magnificent performance at Toronto's Sheridan College on November 11, 1976.

The Canadian Opera Company's Canadian premiere of Alban Berg's *Wozzeck,* conducted by Raffi Armenian, directed by Lotfi Mansouri and starring Allan Monk, Lyn Vernon and Phil Stark, was staged at Toronto's O'Keefe Centre October 21-29, 1977.

The National Arts Centre Festival's presentation of Tchaikovsky's *The Queen of Spades* in July, 1976, marked the first time the opera had been performed in English. Conductor was Mario Bernardi, director Vaclav Kaslik; the cast included Jon Vickers, Maureen Forrester, Cornilis Opthof and Janice Taylor.

Gordon Lightfoot. CP

Gordon Lightfoot, making his 12th annual appearance at Toronto's Massey Hall, filled the room for nine consecutive concerts March 17-25, 1979.

The Orpheum Theatre, Vancouver, celebrated its opening on April 2, 1977, with Maureen Forrester accompanied by the Vancouver Symphony Orchestra, performing Pierre Mercure's *Triptyque,* Ravel's *Scheherazade* and Mahler's *Symphony No. 1 in D.*

The Edmonton Heritage Festival, held as a one-day event in 1977 and 1978 and a two-day event in 1979, included participants from more than 30 ethnic communities.

Maureen Forrester, accompanied by Benjamin Luxen and pianist John Newmark, presented Hugo Wolf's *Itallenisches Liederbuch* at Toronto's St. Lawrence Centre on December 13, 1974.

Krzysztof Penderecki's *The Magnificat* was performed by the Mendelssohn Choir under the direction of Elmer Isler at Toronto's Massey Hall on April 6, 1977.

Anton Kuerti, in a four-year period, twice performed the Beethoven sonata cycle and the *Diabelli Variations* in live concert as well as recording these works for Aquitaine Records – a feat very few musicians have achieved. Only six recordings have ever been made of the complete Beethoven sonatas.

Eleanor Sniderman, president, Aquitaine Records.

The Top Songs

1970
Let It Be, The Beatles

1971
Joy To The World, Three Dog Night

1972
American Pie, Don McLean

1973
Tie A Yellow Ribbon, Tony Orlando & Dawn

1974
Seasons In The Sun, Terry Jacks

1975
Love Will Keep Us Together, The Captain and Tennille

1976
Silly Love Songs, Paul McCartney & Wings

1977
Tonights The Night, Rod Stewart

1978
Stayin' Alive, The Bee Gees

Compiled from the top 100 of the year courtesy of 1050 CHUM Toronto

The Bee Gees—still going strong. AP/*Wide World.*

Censorship

If civilization has anything to do with the achievement of freedom, censorship belongs with the forces opposed to the cultural evolution of man, and the struggle against it charts our intellectual history.

Canada had to become a centenarian before it began to outgrow the constipating effects of WASP traditions. The revolt of the '60s struck a blow for freedom on all fronts, including the area of censorship. Sexuality – that bogeyman obsession of the puritan – suddenly became a subject that could be treated publicly (within limits) in films, books, plays and magazines. It began with the legalization of *Lady Chatterley's Lover* in 1959 and reached a climax when a national CBC broadcast of the launching of the Oxford anthology *Modern Canadian Verse* in 1968 included the word "fuck" and there was not a single protest call from anywhere in the country. The permissive society had arrived.

But those who thought that censorship was on its way out were confusing moral weathers with the social climate. The '70s began with a brutal reaffirmation of the principle of censorship: the War Measures Act. It was unjustified political repression, and in its public condonation the essentially unchanged conservative nature of Canada surfaced again. Since then we have witnessed, alongside a gradual drift to the political right, a resurgence of various forms of censorship.

In 1971, after 18 months of legal equivocation, two actors of the Gallimaufry company in Vancouver, along with their technical director and the proprietors of the Riverqueen where they staged Michael McClure's *The Beard*, were found guilty of "unlawfully giving an obscene performance." It took two years and the B.C. Court of Appeal to reverse those verdicts. In Toronto, in 1972, the police attempted to close down an exhibition of the sculptured environments of Mark Prent, charging Av Isaacs with "publicly exhibiting a disgusting object" in his art gallery. Although the case fizzled, two years later the police laid the same charges against Av Isaacs for another exhibition of the same artist. This time costly legal battles were required to get the charges dismissed. In the following year, the actors, stage manager and director involved in the Theatre Passe Muraille production of *I Love You, Baby Blue* were arrested and charged with "performing an immoral stage performance." The prosecution had to withdraw the charges, but the writing was on the wall.

The second half of the '70s was marked by increasingly virulent censorship activity in all parts of Canada. Ontario banned films like *Pretty Baby* and *In Praise of Older Women* on the grounds that they were "obscene." The fact that *Pretty Baby* was a powerful indictment of the commercialization of human relationships escaped the censors. In the Maritimes, W.O. Mitchell's *Who Has Seen the Wind* came under attack for blasphemy. On the same grounds, a Quebec Superior Court granted a temporary injunction banning the sale of Denise Boucher's play *Les Fées Ont Soif,* a protest piece against the exploitation of women. On the Pacific coast, Bill Bisset was castigated for the generous use of "obscene language" in his poetry, a matter that reached Parliament in Ottawa and was used to censure the Canada Council for subsidizing pornography by giving grants to such poets and to magazines publishing their work. Meanwhile, the police in Toronto confiscated and burnt 80,000 copies of an issue of *Penthouse* and the courts fined the distributor $100,000 for possession of "obscene magazines." In 1979, to top it all, the City of Hamilton tried to pass a bylaw that would have made an "adult entertainment parlour" of any newsstand, drugstore or bookstore selling literature that "appeals to or is designed to appeal to erotic or sexual appetites or inclinations," making it illegal for anyone under 18 to enter such an establishment, and requiring, among other things, every salesclerk to be "properly dressed, neat and clean in his person, satisfactory to the medical officer or chief inspector . . . " It took the efforts of several groups and individuals concerned with civil liberties to forestal this Orwellian extravaganza.

More serious and more effective were – and still are – the activities of Renaissance, an organization founded in 1974 by the fundamentalist preacher Ken Campbell to lead an assault upon our educational system, which he described as "the key stronghold of Satan in our society." The protest and pressure tactics of this small but nationwide and militant group has resulted in the removal of such books as *The Diviners* by Margaret Laurence, *Lives of Girls and Women* by Alice Munro and *Surfacing* by Margaret Atwood from high school reading lists and their banishment from many classrooms across the nation. This often involved acrimonious public controversies. There is evidence to suggest that to avoid these, school boards have become reluctant to put forward books that might be considered controversial, thereby engaging in an invidious form of censorship.

More ominous still were the proposals the Liberal government brought before the House to amend paragraph 159 of the Criminal Code, which defines obscenity essentially as the "undue exploitation of sex." The proposed amendment would expand the definition to include "the undue exploitation of sex, crime, horror, cruelty or the undue degradation of the human person." The proposal died twice with the dissolution of Parliament under the Liberals, but with the PCs now in power we shall no doubt see renewed efforts to pass this bill into law. If that happens, we will have taken a giant step toward a repressive society.

The reactionary trend in the '70s was particularly disturbing in view of the mounting evidence that censorship is counterproductive. In the area of sexuality, for instance, the cathartic function of pornographic material was repeatedly argued and demonstrated by psychologists. From the Institute of Criminology in Copenhagen came several studies establishing a direct link between the abolition of censorship in Denmark in 1968 and the decline in the number of sexual offences since then – by as much as 60 percent in the case of sexual crimes against children. As for the suppression of works of contemporary literature in our schools, its perversity was self-evident. By attempting to suppress central aspects of experience and reality, such book banning prevents the schools from developing precisely the appropriate levels of understanding and judgment which the youngster needs to deal responsibly with the world into which he is growing. But censors are generally motivated by fear and fanaticism and are not readily accessible to reason.

In 1978, the Book and Periodical Development Council, an association of eight organizations of writers, publishers, distributors, booksellers and librarians, set up a Freedom of Expression Committee to stem the rising tide of censorship. In its statement of principles the committee affirmed the absolute freedom to write and read as "essential to the preservation of a free society and a creative culture." Without this freedom "democracy will become extinct and people will fall prey to the dictatorship of the few." If the conservative momentum continues into the '80s – and with the continuing instabilities and insecurities of the times it certainly will – the committee will have its hands full. Perhaps in the heat of battle between enlightenment and dogmatism, it will occur to someone that what Canada needs most of all are constitutional guarantees for the rights and freedoms of the individual which are threatened on all sides today. In the absence of such guarantees both censorship and liberty are mere caprice.

Henry Beissel, playwright, chairman of the Book and Periodical Development Council's Freedom of Expression Committee

---

Dance

The '70s was the decade when dance finally came of age in North America. No longer confined to the stage with its select following, dance became a fitting subject for popular art forms such as movies, TV, radio, even glossy coffee-table books. In Canada, dance finally cracked the academic barrier.

1970
York University opened Canada's first undergraduate program in dance. Not only did it provide scholarly credibility to the art form, it also turned out the first generation of writers, choreographic notators and teachers who were academically trained.

1971
The premiere of *Eight Jelly Rolls* by Twyla Tharp, the U.S. choreographer who set the dance world spinning. She broke away from the cerebral avant-garde by marrying virtuoso classical dance with popular music forms. Tharp choreographed for ballet star Mikhail Baryshnikov, Olympic gold medallist ice-skater John Curry and the film of the rock musical *Hair.*

1972
Rudolph Nureyev's production of *The Sleeping Beauty* for the National Ballet of Canada opened. At $375,000, the most lavish Canadian ballet in history, it almost bankrupted the company. But a year later it propelled the National into the upper reaches of international ballet

ranks when it played at the Metropolitan Opera in New York.

The New York City Ballet held the month-long Stravinsky Festival, an orgy of old and new works to 23 Stravinsky compositions. The festival was the culmination of the George Balanchine/Igor Stravinsky collaboration, the greatest choreographer/composer partnership of the century.

1973

Dance in Canada, the first Canadian national service organization for dance, was incorporated. It acted as a catalyst for dance through its sometimes fractious, sometimes stimulating annual conferences and its quarterly magazine. More important, it put the far-flung Canadian dance community into regular communication for the first time.

Canadian dancers Karen Kain and Frank Augustyn won the gold medal for best pas de deux at the Moscow International Ballet Competition. For Kain, it was the stepping stone to becoming a national celebrity, a household word.

1974

The first national Jean A. Chalmers Award in Choreography was introduced, a breakthrough in recognizing that you can't have Canadian dance without home-grown choreography. Among its winners are ballet's Lawrence Gradus and modern dance's Judith Marcuse and Danny Grossman.

Mikhail Baryshnikov defected to the

Karen Kain and Frank Augustyn, principal dancers with the National Ballet, became the most captivating dance team Canada had ever seen. CP

West while appearing in Toronto with the Bolshoi ballet. Perhaps the greatest male dancer of this generation, his brilliance and daring in his subsequent North American career set new standards for dance.

15 Dance Laboratorium opened in Toronto. This tiny 41-seat dance theatre spurred the emergence of an indigenous Canadian avant-garde dance, a phenomenon unique to the '70s.

1976

The Dance, the first serious weekly critical program on the art form, appeared on CBC radio. Its broad-ranging format makes it unique in the world.

1977

Rudolph Nureyev, the most popular dancer of the generation, starred in the film *Valentino.* The first time a major dance personality has played a leading role in an essentially non-dance film, it is evidence of the mass box-office appeal of the dancer-celebrities of the '70s.

Mikhail Baryshnikov took a leading role in the movie *The Turning Point.* The film proved to be the biggest missionary influence for classical ballet on the public since *The Red Shoes.*

1978

The first national seminar on choreography was held at York University. Of major importance to the dance profession, the seminar took dance composition out of the realm of mystique and into the realm of craft.

In addition, with a series of landmark anniversaries, the 1970s proved that classical ballet was firmly entrenched in Canadian culture and that modern dance had taken solid root. The Royal Winnipeg Ballet, plagued by financial and personnel problems, nonetheless survived its 40th birthday; the National Ballet Company turned 25; and Les Grands Ballets Canadiens and the National Ballet School reached 20. Modern dance's Le Groupe de la Place Royale, Toronto Dance Theatre and the Judy Jarvis Dance Company each celebrated their tenth anniversaries.

Susan Hilary Cohen, founding editor of *Dance in Canada* magazine.

The Canadian Film Industry

The end of the '60s marked the beginning of change in the Canadian film industry, brought about by the rise of one government agency and the fall of another. What rose was the Canadian Film Development Corporation, what fell was the National Film Board of Canada. As the desire on the part of Canadian filmmakers to make feature films rose, they began to depart from the NFB, and with the help of the CFDC, to begin the long road to a Canadian feature film industry.

In Quebec they had already started several years earlier and during the early years of the 1970s, the Quebecois cinema enjoyed critical and financial success. In English Canada the beginning was slower, more sporadic and less culturally and financially organized. There was a Quebec cinema, just as there was a Czech cinema, but there was no Canadian (English) cinema. There were English Canadians making films but there was no cohesive effort, and hence to the world at large no Canadian cinema other than Quebec cinema. But all that was to change. The Quebec cinema was really a house of cards. A few artistically valid efforts were shored up by a raft of "pepsi" comedies, with the standard blend of sex and anticlerical and anti-English jokes. But the public in Quebec soon tired of these and the financial base of the industry collapsed.

In English Canada the writing was on the wall. Sooner or later the trend would be to duplicate Hollywood. Whereas initially the French language gave the Quebec cinema a uniqueness, in the end it would be its undoing. By the mid '70s the pressure to make Canadian films with phony American locales was starting to build and by the end of the '70s almost every film shot in Toronto or Montreal was passed off as some American city. In Montreal the centre of filmmaking switched from the French language to the English and the Quebec cinema, which had been welcomed warmly (if somewhat over-praised) was now persona non grata.

1978 and 1979 brought an even more definite switch in the direction of Canadian cinema. Firstly, producers now were able to go to public auction to raise their funds and the budgets shot up dramatically as investors rushed to gain tax advantages. Secondly, one could almost strike the word "Canadian" from the producers' vocabulary. A turning point appeared to be the 1977 Canadian Film Awards, when the NFB seemed to win most of the awards for two not very good features. Suddenly the idea seemed to take hold that there were two kinds of films to be made in Canada: the "international" movie and the "Canadian" movie.

Producers, along with the money brokers newly arrived to the industry, seemed to view the two as mutually exclusive. The real directors and producers were to make the international films while the NFB and a host of navel-contemplating filmmakers in Quebec were to make the "Canadian" movies, of course at a considerable budget difference. Their argument was that Canadian movies did not make money, which was not true, and they put forth examples that were not examples of Canadian films so much as they were examples of "bad" films.

Now at the end of the '70s there is a film industry in Canada, but is it a Canadian film industry? Surely not every film made in this country needs to have the maple leaf stamped on it, and if we chose to make films about other countries and other people's histories that is all quite valid and should be welcomed. But surely no one would ever claim that *Madame Butterfly* is Japanese and not Italian to its core. To totally negate the idea of a "Canadian" film is tantamount to self-genocide. To say that the rest of the world will not go to see a movie set in Canada is pure nonsense. If it is a good movie they will come to see it regardless of its locale. What we have to sell to the world is our own uniqueness. Only those who have no sense of themselves and their country will argue against that.

Donald Shebib, filmmaker.

Canadian Feature Films

The 1970s brought feature-film production to Canada in a serious way. For decades our features had been few and isolated and mostly ignored by Canada and the rest of the world. Creation of the Canadian Film Development Corporation by the Pearson government in 1968 laid the foundation for an industry that by now often makes money on its product and sometimes even produces good movies. The 1980s beckon, shimmering with promise.

These seem to me the best of the scores of films we turned out in the 1970s (in order of appearance):

Goin' Down the Road, Don Shebib, 1970
Mon Oncle Antione, Claude Jutra, 1971
Between Friends, Don Shebib, 1973
Les Ordres, Michel Brault, 1974
The Apprenticeship of Duddy Kravitz, Ted Kotcheff, 1974
Outrageous! Richard Benner, 1977
J.A. Martin Photographe, Jean Beaudin, 1977
Why Shoot the Teacher, Silvio Narrizano, 1977
Who Has Seen the Wind, Allan King, 1977
Skip Tracer, Zale R. Dalen, 1978

Marshall Delaney, *Saturday Night* magazine film cricket.

A young Richard Dreyfuss in *The Apprenticeship of Duddy Kravitz,* listens to advice from Zvee Scooler who played his grandfather. It premiered in Montreal in 1974. CP

The Best Films

1969
Midnight Cowboy
They Shoot Horses, Don't They?

1970
Women in Love
I Never Sang for my Father

1971
Sunday, Bloody Sunday
Klute
A Clockwork Orange
The Go-Between

1972
Cabaret
The Heartbreak Kid

1973
Last Tango in Paris
Summer Wishes, Winter Dreams

1974
Amarcord

Alice Doesn't Live Here Anymore

1975
One Flew Over the Cuckoo's Nest
Dog Day Afternoon
Shampoo

1976
Bound For Glory
Seven Beauties
Cousin Cousine
Network

1977
Julia
The Turning Point
Annie Hall

1978
International Velvet
Autumn Sonata

1979
Agatha
Manhattan

Brian Linehan, TV host.

Liza Minelli in her most famous and riveting role as Sally Bowles in *Cabaret. Wide World*

English Canadian Theatre

"Until we develop competent playwrights of our own, Canadian theatre must remain a minor and rather snobbish form of entertainment. I'm not prepared to say that such playwrights are appearing . . . that would be too bold a prediction . . . but I do think the upsurge of belated nationalism is begging to assume an identity of its own . . . and to me, nothing would be more satisfying. To witness the birth of creative drama is a sensation few are privileged to experience . . . and I honestly believe I shall be among the lucky ones."

That was Nathan Cohen speaking in a 1948 CBC radio broadcast. His comments were a bit premature and, in fact, Cohen died just before the great period of Canadian playwrights began. In the 1970s, we had a revolution in the creation of our own drama that is still astonishing, even in retrospect.

As Urjo Kareda once summed it up, all hell broke loose in the early 1970s. Suddenly a whole group of small Toronto theatres, operating on tiny budgets and dependent on arts councils, began to flourish. Original Canadian plays, which had been an embarrassment only a few years earlier, were not only getting produced at these places; they made a stunning impact. David Freeman's *Creeps*, on the unlikely subject of cerebral palsy victims, scored a hit at the Factory Theatre Lab and went on to New York. Bill Glassco's Tarragon Theatre, dedicated to original Canadian plays, adopted a couple of regulars: David French, whose naturalistic plays about a Newfoundland family living in Toronto resurrected naturalism in our theatre; and Michel Tremblay, the prolific Quebec radical who rejected respectable notions of classical French theatre and filled the stage with outlandish freaks of the Montreal Main who not only spoke in *joual* but even threw drag parties. Meanwhile, at the Toronto Free Theatre several important new talents emerged, including Carol Bolt with *Red Emma* (about the anarchist feminist Emma Goldman) and Martin Kinch, who put the world of Toronto underground media chic on stage in *Me?*

But the emergence of a new Canadian theatre was by no means happening only in Toronto. In Montreal, even with its minority anglophone population, the Centaur Theatre became a thriving regional institution with its own resident playwright: David Fennario, who wrote plays about his own working-class neighbourhood. In Vancouver, a whole group of new playwrights emerged in a hothouse atmosphere nurtured by such local phenomena as the New Play Society and the Vancouver East Cultural Centre. Vancouver talent kept bursting out and surprising the rest of the country with shows such as *18 Wheels, British Properties* and *Billy Bishop Goes to War* – this last a tour de force written by John Gray and acted by Eric Peterson, due to hit Broadway in the spring of 1980.

The regional theatre that John Hirsch pioneered in the 1960s at the Manitoba Theatre Centre became the model for others all over the country,

Jean Richard (left) and James Rankin battle it out in a scene from Theatre Passe Muraille's *Les Canadiens*. CP including the Citadel in Edmonton, which has one of the most architecturally dazzling spaces anywhere in the world, and the Neptune in Halifax. The most controversial regional theatre remains the National Arts Centre in Ottawa – controversial because it has delusions of being our national theatre, and gets special treatment from the government for that reason.

Cultural nationalism has now become such a hot issue that foreigners are under attack. There was a huge controversy when Robin Phillips came from England to take over the Stratford Festival, though no one can argue with his record: He has turned Stratford into one of the world's most dazzling classical repertory companies in just a few short years. But the mood in this country is fighting: Peter Coe, who came from England to take over the Citadel, has been told by the immigration department that he will have to leave next year.

We have plenty of problems: Toronto's alternate theatres seem to be going through a middle-age crisis, and the CBC seems to have stopped doing original stage plays on television altogether. But to look back on this era is to be struck by the richness of it.

If I were compiling an anthology, it would have to include Rick Salutin's *Les Canadiens,* Carol Bolt's *One Night Stand,* John Gray's *Billy Bishop Goes to War,* David French's *Jitters,* Theatre Passe Muraille's *Farm Show*, George Luscombe's production of *Ten Lost Years* at the Toronto Workshop Productions, and possibly several others. That's a fat list.

Martin Knelman, critic, author of *This Is Where We Came In.*

The Little Paper That Grew . . .

The journalistic story of the 1970s is probably the Toronto *Sun.* At least it is for those who were involved with it.

The bare bones of the story are fairly well known – the Toronto *Telegram* surrendering to competition and closing its doors forever and selling its subscription lists to the rival Toronto *Star* in the fall of 1971 for some $12 million – thus throwing some 1,200 employees onto the job market. Then, the first publishing day after the *Tely* shut down, 68 ex-*Tely* employees set up shop on the fourth floor of the Eclipse Whitewear building in downtown Toronto and began publishing a daily tabloid which would depend on street sales only, no home delivery, and would aim at the commuters riding the public transit system.

All the experts predicted failure.

As one of the "originals" with the *Sun* I will say without qualifications that my partners, Doug Creighton and Don Hunt, and I didn't have the suggestion of a doubt that it would succeed. Personally, I thought the Jeremiahs were nuts to be so pessimistic.

As it turned out, the *Sun* was a success story beyond even our expectations – going from a circulation that first month of 60,000 a day to around 220,000 a day in 1979, and 360,000 on Sundays; from 68 employees to 500; from a profit that first year of $50,000 to nearly $7 million in '78-'79; from owning nothing except the typewriters and renting space in a bankrupt office, to owning land, erecting a building, owning presses. And starting another *Sun* newspaper in Edmonton and assuming controlling interest in a wire service – United Press Canada.

While the *Sun* has the reputation of being right-wing and hard-line, in a classical sense it is really the most "liberal" paper in the country. That is, columnists and writers can – and do – argue, disagree and feud with one another and with the paper's editorial stance.

What other newspaper has been "raided" twice in two years by the RCMP under terms of the Official Secrets Act – once to recover a letter from the security boss that had been leaked, and the other to lay charges against the publisher and the editor for running a story about Soviet espionage in Canada?

What other newspaper continues to get cakes and greetings from its readers on the anniversary of its birth? What other newspaper has been labelled in parliament by the prime minister as "scurrilous, vicious, vindictive, inaccurate"?

There are all kinds of flaws in the *Sun* journalistically. And here I speak as the editor (and a reader) and must share corporate responsibility. We are best at covering fires, crime stories and running provocative pictures of pretty girls. We have one or two reporters capable of exploring complex stories, and until recently ran no business news except the stock market reports which we used to steal from the Toronto *Star.*

But the *Sun* is relatively tough. It grew up on the streets of Toronto, asked no favours and expected none, and fought the *Globe and Mail* and *Star* relentlessly, irrepressibly, cheerfully, mischievously. We are always ready to give the *Star* and *Globe* advice, and one of the proudest moments was when the *Star* moved into its new highrise offices at 1 Yonge St. and a dictum was issued that coffee and sandwiches were not to be consumed in the newsroom in order to protect the new broadloom. A night editor was suspended for drinking coffee at two a.m.

The *Sun* wrote an editorial applauding *Star* management's decision because it is well known that reporters are messy fellows inclined to drool and dribble. The *Sun* reminded *Star* management that the Third Reich began to crumble when discipline failed, and that reporters need to be kept in line.

The no-coffee order was rescinded next day with the admonition that while it was now okay to drink coffee in the newsroom, "Don't let it get around!"

The *Sun* can and should be a lot better. But it has grown from a runt without a chance to survive into the fifth largest paper in the country – and the second largest weekend paper. It long ago passed the *Globe and Mail* in Toronto. The *Sun* sometimes says of the *Globe* that if it had to invent competition it would invent the *Globe.*

For all its fun and games, it can still be a solid newspaper. In seven years it has won six National Newspaper Awards, 20 Police Association awards and eight Firefighter Awards.

Sun ads refer to itself as "the little paper that grew" and its editorial motto is "Toronto's Other Voice." Both are true. Editorially the *Sun* sees the world differently from its competitors, and this fact alone gives the people of Toronto a varied journalistic viewpoint. No other Canadian city has three English-language newspapers. The *Sun* basically sees its role as kicking the shins of the various levels of government and, like it or loathe it, it is very difficult to ignore it.

A creation of the '70s, the *Sun* is self-proclaimed saviour of democracy and will likely continue this role into the '80s, unless, of course, it is struck with a severe case of maturity and pomposity. Neither of which is likely.

Peter Worthington, editor, the Toronto *Sun.*

The Decade for Magazines:
A Personal Recollection

On January 2, 1970, I saw *Hair* for the first time. Montrealer Galt McDermott had written this brilliant groupie rock musical as an expression of our entrance into the Age of Aquarius complete with communal love, flower power, marijuana and precious little work. Little did he dream that within a short decade this blissful society would revert back to a time of isolated "me-ism." Suits and ties are again the order of the day, the hair is short and it's back to business.

One thing was clear during that January – things were going to be different and McLuhan was probably right: the medium was to become the message (in Canada, anyway), be it television, motion pictures, magazines or newspapers. At that time I had no idea how personally involved I would become in most of those mediums.

January, 1970, was to be prophetic in terms of the meetings I went to and people I talked to during that month.

Michael Spencer was just finding his feet at the Canadian Film Development Corporation and a suspect film crowd didn't know what to make of him.

Jim Crang, a Toronto architect, was mesmerizing the people around him with the idea of a floating concrete airport in the middle of Lake Ontario (it was to serve Toronto, Rochester, Niagara, Hamilton and Kingston). Everybody loved it, except the banks and the fishes.

The money market was once again tense, as it perceived that the Trudeau government was antigrowth; a campaign was required and meetings were attended at the Toronto Stock Exchange to counter this development.

Allan Fleming, Canada's foremost graphic designer, was to introduce me to his artist friend, Alex Wise, whom he was championing at the time. Alex's career blossomed shortly thereafter and my friend, Allan Fleming, was to die of a heart attack a few short years later.

Cable operators across the country were jockeying for territories and the City of Toronto became the biggest pie. New Toronto personalities emerged: Ted Rogers, Jeff Conway, Sylvain Walters, Ed Jardine, Sruki Switzer, David Graham and Jerry Grafstein.

Author Bob Kroetsch had recently published his terrific *Studhorse Man* and during January we talked film.

Ron Thom, the west coast architect, who had recently moved east, finally let me see his "Cathedral of the Arctic", a pet project of Bishop Marsh.

Financier Ben Webster had just put together Helix Investments, one of the first of the venture capital organizations to spring up in the early '70s. Two of his original hit-men were to turn up later in the decade in important media positions: Mike McCabe became head of the CFDC in 1979 and Moses Znaimer was to lead a group (including myself) to capture a new television license – CITY-TV in Toronto. Interestingly, also during that month the first meetings regarding this proposed station took place.

Unbeknownst to me at the time, Bill C-58 was being hatched in Ottawa by Keith Davey and *Saturday Night* magazine was once again heading into troubled waters.

There were many surprises during the '70s. The biggest for me happened in 1974. That year I was seconded into the *Saturday Night* problem by editor and friend Bob Fulford and the then major investors, Eph Diamond of Cadillac Fairview, Ray Wolfe of Oshawa Wholesale, and Arthur Gelber, financial and cultural leader. By January of 1975 I found myself as the publisher, fund raiser and national spokesman for the downtrodden Canadian periodical industry. Who could forget the Senate Commons Committee hearing on the now infamous Bill C-58.

That event, together with *Maclean's* announcement about publishing weekly, was to mark the beginning of the greatest period of magazine growth and diversification the country has ever known. Since the mid-'70s many significant events occurred:

Controlled circulation (free) magazines (*Homemaker's, Quest, City Woman, Calgary Magazine, Vancouver Magazine,* etc.) flourished.

The big city service magazines, such as *Toronto Life,* the *Calendar* magazines, *Vancouver Life,* telling people where to eat, shop, entertain and do whatever is in at the moment, came into their own.

Maclean's became a newsmagazine and went biweekly, then, miraculously, weekly, just like they promised Ottawa.

The Atlantic provinces tried twice to produce a new regional magazine; first with *Axiom* (it went down the tube after fewer than a dozen issues) and currently the bright *Atlantic Insight*, published by ad man Bill Belliveau and edited by Harry Bruce.

One of the big winners was *Harrowsmith*, published and edited by Jim Lawrence; it took the publishing industry by storm by first clearly identifying and then publishing directly at the new urban farmer and the growing environmentalist groups. Another was *Decormag*, a snappy Quebec publication, edited and published by Ginette Gadoury. The magazine sold 60,000 copies on the newsstand and averaged more than 11 readers per copy. By 1978, in a rare reversal, this same group began publishing an English version.

The troops also finally got busy and writers' organizations sprung up everywhere: the Writers' Union of Canada, the Periodical Writers' Association and the Writers' Development Trust. On the other side of the desk, the publishers got organized – for the smaller magazines it was the Canadian Periodical Publishers Association. In 1978, the Magazine Association of Canada changed its name to Magazines Canada and opened up its membership to all types of magazines and rotos.

Two national magazine awards programs were launched and became instant successes and magazine distributors began to integrate themselves and play a more visible role in this flourishing industry.

On the business side, the larger established magazines closed ranks and produced the finest media research study ever done anywhere on magazines. The Print Measurement Bureau provided a new and solid underpinning in the industry's fight for professional and accurate advertising information.

The '70s proved to be the decade when the magazine industry matured. With that maturity came the middleman: agents for writers and lawyers who specialized in libel and slander.

Most important was the realization that magazines, books, recordings, movies and theatre were all part a new world – the emerging cultural industries – a world of Half-back programs, lotteries, development funds and special low-interest loans. Magazine publishing was at the heart of a vigourous cultural upsurge. What was once considered a series of cottage industries now commanded as much consideration as tourism, shipbuilding and fishing.

For me, personally, it was a decade for magazines and I wouldn't have missed it.

Edgar Cowan, publisher, *Saturday Night.*

Stars	
Frank Augustyn	Glenn Gould
Bachman-Turner Overdrive	Karen Kain
Carroll Baker	Anton Kuerti
Genevieve Bujold	Gordon Lightfoot
Diane Dufresne	Monique Mercure
Denise Filliatrault	Anne Murray
Maureen Forrester	Ginette Reno
Doug Henning	Royal Canadian Air Farce
Harmonium	Rush
Peter Gzowski	Craig Russell
	Veronica Tennant
	Sid Adilman, columnist, the Toronto *Star.*

Significant Canadian TV

House of Commons broadcasting: allowed the Canadian public to see the high and low points of parliamentary proceedings – and boosted sales for tailors and haberdashers in the Ottawa area.

Canada-Russia hockey series: proved it took only a spark to reignite the feelings of nationalism Canadians had during Expo and Centennial year.

Connections: proved we have homegrown, as well as branch-plant, crime syndicates.

Rainbow Country: proved we can produce unique television; and when it was dropped, that we want to stay on imitating foreign programming.

Homage to Chagall: a masterpiece of artistry and creative skill, proving that in this program as well as in the entire series Harry Rasky will not compromise art.

Encounter 79: finally established that when politicians (federal leaders in this case) accept constricted and artificial media event surroundings, they become prisoners of televison.

The National Dream: proved that Canadians are starved for recreations of their own history.

Harry J. Boyle, broadcaster and author.

The 1970s was the era when TV news took over.

It was the decade when Canadians became more dependent on television for their knowledge of what's happening and placed greater reliability on TV news than on any other form of mass communication.

As a TV journalist you might think that pleases me. It doesn't really.

In the first place, it underlines the critical importance of television journalism doing more than it now is. It must offer not just headline news, but documentaries and analysis to provide substance, texture and nuance to what's happening and why. TV must have more information and much more explanation.

In the second place, nobody can really be considered well-informed by only watching TV journalism. To be a fully aware citizen, you clearly have to read newspapers, magazines and books as well as listen and watch.

So while the 1970s have seen TV become the dominant news force in our lives, it's a mixed blessing and a warning that TV had better measure up to its increasing public responsibilities.

Knowlton Nash, CBC newscaster.

The Cable TV Explosion

Canadians had a love affair with cable television during the 1970s. First invented in Ontario and British Columbia (and Pennsylvania) in the early '50s as a way to bring in distant signals, cable TV acquired some popularity during the '60s. But it wasn't until the '70s that the regulatory impediments were cleared away. Then, in one decade, Canada became the most heavily cabled nation in the world, with nearly 60 percent of all households taking the service.

The reason for the popularity was that cable provided more viewer choice, more distant stations (often U.S.) and better picture quality. Television viewers demonstrated that they had an insatiable appetite for programming. In Toronto, for example, there are now 16 broadcast television stations delivered to households (80 percent of which take cable).

Cable television developed in other ways. Encouraged by the CRTC, and particularly Harry Boyle, cable began to undertake local community programming, which turned into an important neighbourhood communication service. Then cable began to expand into organizing other minority audience services: multilingual programming, children's programming, financial and consumers' information programming. Indeed, some cable TV systems produce an additional 12 channels to supplement the broadcasting stations. But not pay television. The regulator denied repeated requests to begin this service.

This phenomenal growth was not accomplished without some impact on existing communications media. Some television stations sagged under the increased competition from distant stations. TV stations in smaller markets were hurt, yet urban stations prospered in spite of (and in some cases, because of) cable TV. Cable was widely blamed for being the vehicle that fostered the mass importation of American television culture. Yet, to many people's surprise, viewing of U.S. stations by Canadians remained almost static during the decade. This was because the cable systems were able to use

Gordon Pinsent in *The Rowdyman.*

electronic switching to transfer audiences to Canadian TV stations, which restored the principle of the local license.

But Canadians became strongly attracted to U.S. television programming. In fact, more than 75 percent of all viewing by Canadians is of U.S. programming – programs that appear for the most part on Canadian television stations. This lack of popularity of Canadian programming is a serious problem and it is imperative that ways be found to repatriate viewers to Canadian productions. For, as Pierre Juneau noted, if we don't have a national communications system, we don't have a nation. And cable can be an important ingredient in the solution by providing greater opportunities and more money to create better programs.

The future for the cable industry looks promising indeed. Cable systems will become a vital programming force. In the United States, which until recently held second place to Canada in cable development, there are 25 programming services available on its satellite. Canada, which pioneered both cable and satellite, has yet to allow the two to develop a relationship. But that will come, as will the interface with the computer. This will allow interactive, two-way television, particularly important in an energy crisis, for home shopping, information-retrieval services and alarm systems. Pay television, allowing further audience specialization, will revolutionize the concept programming choice as cable systems deliver more than 100 channels.

The '70s saw radical changes to the Canadian communication structure, changes that will continue into the '80s.

Phil Lind, senior vice-president and director of Canadian Cablesystems Limited and Rogers Telecommunications Limited, former chairman of the Canadian Cable Television Association.

TV Personalities

Adrienne Clarkson, *the fifth estate*
Robert Cooper, *Ombudsman*
Robert Homme, *The Friendly Giant*
Bruno Gerussi, *The Beachcombers, Celebrity Cooks*
Helen Hutchinson, *Canada AM, W5*
Harvey Kirck, *CTV National*
Knowlton Nash, *The National*
Ernie Coombs, *Mr. Dressup*

Lise Payette, talk show hostess of *Appelle-mois Lise*
Gordon Pinsent, *A Gift to Last*
Lloyd Robertson, *The National, CTV National News*
Second City
Rene Simard, *The Rene Simard Show*
Joan Watson, *Marketplace*
Wayne and Shuster
Al Waxman, *King of Kensington*

Sid Adilman, columnist, the Toronto *Star*.

The '70s were a time of great personal growth for me. My whole professional career has blossomed during this time as I joined the National Ballet of Canada in the 1969/1970 season.

Karen Kain, principal dancer, National Ballet of Canada.

The Mounties Under the Microscope

For a century, as the Mounties became a world-wide symbol of Canada, they remained the least known of all our great institutions. The government and the press usually left them alone, and the Mounties liked it that way. But now the pendulum has swung in the opposite direction. Soon the RCMP may join the CBC among the most-studied Canadian agencies.

It started in 1966 when Ottawa appointed a royal commission under Maxwell Mackenzie to look into national security. The full text of the report is still secret, but an abridged version, released in 1969, contains a passage that will chill the blood of every civil libertarian in 1979: "A security service will inevitably be involved in actions that may contravene the spirit if not the letter of the law, and with clandestine and other activities which may sometimes seem to infringe on individuals' rights."

In 1974 Ottawa established a royal commission under Judge René Marin to study internal discipline, grievance procedures, and methods of handling public complaints. It released a 220-page report in March, 1976, detailing a list of internal problems and recommending many improvements – most of which have not yet been made.

The ink on the Marin report was hardly dry when the Nova Scotia government set up a judicial inquiry into the RCMP's treatment of Dr. Ross MacInnis, a medical doctor from the town of Shubenacadie and the victim of some bizarre and spiteful treatment from the local RCMP detachment. The inquiry provided a look at operations at the detachment level.

In 1977 the official investigations came in a flurry. In the spring, Alberta Attorney-General Jim Foster ordered a judicial inquiry into the police investigation of a Florida-based carnival company, Royal American Shows. The charge that the company had provided kickbacks was thrown out of court because evidence had become "tainted" as a result of police indiscretion in handling it. The inquiry, headed by Supreme Court Justice James Laycraft, found evidence that the force had signed a secret swapping agreement with the Department of National Revenue, giving Mounties access to income-tax information. The RCMP in return would give DNR information gathered from wiretaps and general investigation work.

The commission of inquiry that worried the federal government most was conducted in Montreal by a former Parti Québécois candidate, Jean Keable, a young labour lawyer from Quebec City. The Keable Commission started as an inquiry into the illegal 1972 police raid on the radical Montreal news agency, Agence de Presse Libre du Québec, but mushroomed into a general probe of RCMP tactics. The Keable inquiry uncovered the celebrated barn-burning and the theft of dynamite, and it revealed the existence of the special G-4 unit. It was an impending revelation from the Keable commission that prompted the federal government to disclose the RCMP's break-in of the Parti Québecois's Montreal office in January, 1973. In November, 1977,

Solicitor-General Francis Fox went to court to try to limit Keable's powers of investigation.

And of course the federal government established its own royal commission, which immediately created jurisdictional battles between Quebec and Ottawa. The federal commission, headed by Alberta Supreme Court Justice David McDonald, has the widest mandate and is the only inquiry with sanction to rummage through the RCMP's own filing cabinets. It could last three years.

The old days are definitely over. The organization that was once the most secretive in Canada may soon have few secrets left.

The Inside Track, *Saturday Night.*

"...judging by the ruckus in Ottawa, this country is teetering on the brink of democracy..."
Bierman, *Victoria Times*

Important Criminal Cases

Wray

At John Wray's first trial for the murder of a Peterborough service station attendant, the jury was not told of his admission to the police that he had thrown a rifle, the murder weapon, into a swamp, nor were they shown the rifle, because Wray's statement had been obtained by trickery and duress. However, in 1970, the Supreme Court of Canada ruled that a trial judge has virtually no discretion to exclude that part of an admission which leads to a discovery of material evidence. At his retrial, John Wray was convicted of murder.

Scallen
Tom Scallen, entrepreneur and former assistant attorney-general of Minnesota, brought the NHL to Vancouver in 1969. But before the Canucks reached the top of their division, he had been convicted in Vancouver of issuing a false prospectus and stealing $3 million of the cash raised from investors in the new club. In confirming his conviction, the B.C. Court of Appeal ruled, in 1974, that the object of a "theft" was wide enough to include intangibles such as bank credits and wasn't restricted to tangibles.

Brownridge
Clarence Brownridge was stopped by the Toronto police and taken for a breathalyzer test. He was charged with refusing to provide a breath sample because he said that he wanted to speak with his lawyer before taking the test. However, in June of 1972, the Supreme Court of Canada decided that he had had a reasonable excuse to refuse the test because the police had deprived him of his right to retain and instruct counsel without delay, as guaranteed by the Canadian Bill of Rights.

The Breathalyzer. Toronto *Star*

Hogan
Twenty-six days before the Brownridge decision was released, Mr. Richard Hogan was stopped by police while driving in Dartmouth, Nova Scotia, and taken for a breath test. Before he blew into the machine he wanted to speak with his lawyer who was at that moment pounding on the door of the breathalyzer room. But, because the police told him that if he did not immediately provide a breath sample he would be charged with refusing to do so, Hogan took the test without speaking to his lawyer. At trial he was convicted on the basis of his blood-alcohol reading. The Supreme Court of Canada upheld his conviction, ruling in 1974 that evidence, such as breathalyzer results, was admissible notwithstanding that in the course of its being obtained a citizen's rights under the Canadian Bill of Rights are violated.

Dr. Henry Morgentaler in front of the Supreme Court of Canada. CP

Morgentaler
Dr. Henry Morgentaler was charged with performing an illegal abortion in his Montreal clinic in 1973, and as a result became the central figure in the public debate over the morality of abortions in the mid-'70s. Although a jury acquitted him at his trial, the Quebec Court of Appeal reversed that decision and sent

him to jail. The matter went on to the Supreme Court of Canada, which upheld the conviction in 1975. Public outrage resulted in parliament amending the Criminal Code to provide that appeal courts could no longer substitute a conviction for a jury's acquittal.

Doyle

Multimillionaire John C. Doyle of Montreal, Quebec and Panama, friend of Joey Smallwood and the force behind Canadian Javelin, was charged in Newfoundland on December 7, 1973, with fraud and breach of trust. Free on $25,000 cash bail, he came to court for the commencement of his trial to find that the Crown wanted a four-month adjournment. Despite Doyle's objections, the magistrate granted the delay. Rather than wait, Doyle departed for Panama, and has never returned. Furthermore, his cash bail was returned to him. The Newfoundland courts had ruled that a magistrate has a discretionary power to adjourn cases for as long as he wants but, in 1976, the Supreme Court of Canada held that a magistrate's powers are limited to those given to him by the Criminal Code, which only allows a delay of eight days without consent. In granting the adjournment, the magistrate had exceeded his powers and lost jurisdiction over Doyle. Of course, the proceedings could start all over again if he returns.

Cooper

Norton Cooper, in the course of applying for DREE grants in 1972 for his private mint and mining companies in Ontario, became close friends with a senior DREE employee. In the month before his companies received over $700,000 in federal grants, Cooper treated his friend to two trips to Florida. Two more followed the awarding of the grant. Cooper was convicted of conferring benefits on a government employee. In the appeals that followed, the Supreme Court of Canada, in 1977, upheld his conviction, but more importantly, swept away a Canadian rule

of law, based on an 1838 English case, that required a judge to give a jury special instructions in cases involving circumstantial evidence.

Demeter

Wealthy builder Peter Demeter was convicted of having had, in 1973, "a person or persons unknown" bludgeon his wife to death in the garage of their Mississauga home. His trial lasted 51 days; his appeal to the Ontario Court of Appeal suggested 26 errs in law but was dismissed, as was, in 1977, his further appeal to the Supreme Court of Canada. Now he is suing as the beneficiary of his wife's $1 million life insurance policy, continuing his courtroom battles from a prison cell while serving a life sentence.

Leary

From 1962 until this decision in 1977, drunkenness was a defence to a charge of rape in Ontario, but not in British Columbia. The disagreement ended when six of the nine members of the Supreme Court of Canada, in upholding the conviction of Allan Leary for a 1974 rape at Nelson, British Columbia, ruled that rape is a crime to which the defence of drunkenness has no application.

Celebrity Enterprises Ltd. et al

Brothers Joseph Philliponi and Ross Filiponne, operators of Vancouver's 100,000-patron-per-year New Penthouse Cabaret and others, had a 61-day trial on two charges. Their conviction of conspiracy to live on the avails of prostitution was quashed and an acquittal was entered in 1977 by the British Columbia Court of Appeal, which held that indirect benefits accruing from the offering of services to prostitutes were not "avails of prostitution." The court also dismissed the Crown's appeal from the accused's acquittal on the charge of conspiracy to produce a public mischief with intent to corrupt public morals, holding that neither this conspiracy, nor committing public mischief with intent to corrupt public morals, nor the English common law offence of conspiracy to corrupt public morals is a criminal offence in Canada.

Moore
The right to remain silent was dealt a heavy blow in October, 1978. Mr. Thomas Arthur Moore, who ran a red light on his 10-speed bicycle, ended up charged with obstructing police because he refused to identify himself. The majority of the Supreme Court of Canada decided that because the officer who had witnessed the offence had a duty to ask Moore to identify himself, Moore had a duty to answer, and his failure to do so amounted to criminal obstruction, which was punishable by up to two years imprisonment.

Clay M. Powell, Q.C.

Art Theft: The Runner-up Crime of the Decade

Drug trafficking, to no one's surprise, is the '70s number-one internationally committed crime. But who would name art theft as the runner-up?

Ten years ago, art thefts seemed a foreign problem. Newspapers occasionally reported heists from a poorly guarded Italian church, a French chateau, an archaeological site in Turkey. Toward the end of the decade, the date-lines were closer to home and more frequent: a chalice pilfered from a church in Nova Scotia; two Calgarians, an assistant professor and a high-school teacher, convicted of filching about $5 million worth of collectibles from friends' homes and public displays; armed robbers made off with a Picasso crayon drawing from a Toronto apartment; in a midnight smash-and-grab, burglers removed a $500,000 painting from a Toronto gallery.

With organized criminals directing the main action, art theft today is a world-wide, multibillion-dollar business. The estimated recovery rate of stolen works is five percent. That disheartening statistic relates to another. In 1970, not one police officer in Canada or the United States specialized in art theft full time; today, there is one. He is Robert Volpe of the New York City police department who says that he has "brought back more than $3 million worth of art over the last few years. My recoveries are personally gratifying, but they're only a drop in the bucket." Detective Volpe conjectures that in New York City alone art thefts are averaging an alarming $2 million a month in 1979. Statistics show that since 1970 international art thefts have risen 400 percent.

Tied to the dramatic escalation of thefts is the rapid rise in prices paid for works of art. The lucrative field has attracted organized criminal rings that have altered the mode of thievery. Freelance picturenapping used to be the most prevalent. A thief would nick a painting from a museum, dealer or private collector and hold it for ransom; insurance companies – often on the quiet and outside the law – would make a cash deal to recover the work. In 1974, when political art thefts were in vogue, $20 million worth of art was stolen from Sir Alfred Beit's home outside of Dublin; the unsuccessful ransom demands were $1.2 million and transfer of four members of the Irish Republican Army from English to Irish jails.

Customized theft has now become the trend. A collector makes it known that he wants a particular painting, thus setting in motion a criminal network of thieves and fences, dealers and brokers. Perhaps he wants a Rembrandt or Cézanne or Picasso – they are all available.

On Christmas Day, 1978, cat thieves entered the M. H. de Young Gallery in San Francisco and made off with four paintings, including Rembrandt's *Portrait of a Rabbi,* valued at $1 million. Two days later, the Art Institute of Chicago discovered the disappearance of three Cézannes, valued at $3 million. Within two months, the $10 million touring collection of 28 Picassos at the Mira Godard Gallery in Toronto was minus the half-million-dollar *Woman with a Hat Holding the Head of a Sheep.*

"A thief doesn't steal such things unless he knows where they are going," observes Robert Volpe. And where's that? Perhaps to adorn the walls of a shady collector, or into storage for ten or 20 years (a Rembrandt in the vault is better than money in the bank). Perhaps too they made their way to closed-mouthed dealers and auctioneers in Switzerland who channelled them to Germany, Saudi Arabia, Japan or back to North America. They might also be in the possession of South American drug-lords who seem happy to receive inflation-proof art treasures rather than unsteady dollars as payment for their wares. These are the likely illicit homes of 18 paintings (including a Rembrandt, Rubens, Corot, Courbet, Delacroix, Gainsborough and Millet) looted from the Montreal Museum of Fine Arts by three armed bandits. The Old Masters, which were last seen in September, 1972, have never been heard of since.

Belatedly, law-enforcement officials are beginning to recognize that art thieves have created a cultural crisis. Says RCMP Corporal Albert Rivard, appointed in April as the representative to Interpol's new "works of art" section in Ottawa: "We never identified art theft as a serious problem in Canada, and we were proven wrong." But as officials are slowly becoming more concerned, art thieves are rapidly becoming more sophisticated. No signs indicate that the decade's new crime epidemic is about to abate.

Winston Collins, journalist.

The Major Libel Cases

Diefenbaker v. The Canadian Magazine and Tom Alderman, 1971

Mr. Alderman wrote an unflattering piece about John Diefenbaker. The tone was negative, to say the least, and there was a mistake of fact in the article. The *Canadian* is printed throughout Canada and Mr.Diefenbaker sued in Saskatchewan, his home base. The *Canadian* paid $12,500 to Mr. Diefenbaker's favourite charity. It is the only time Mr. Diefenbaker ever sued for libel.

Murphy v. LaMarsh, 1970

Judy LaMarsh, in her first political book, *Memoirs of a Bird in a Gilded Cage,* said some uncomplimentary things about a radio reporter, Ed Murphy. She said he was "heartily detested" by most of the press gallery and the members. Miss LaMarsh was very wrong. Result: $2,500 damages to Mr. Murphy and the publisher had to pay large legal costs. The trial court said: "Miss LaMarsh's memoirs were, her publisher tells me, expected to be a lively and colourful account of her political career. A good deal of the book fits readily into that definition and if Mr. Murphy's head is left bloody, it is not the only one."

Bennett v. Sun Publishing Co. Ltd., 1973

Newspapers have to watch their headlines. The Vancouver *Sun* suggested in a headline that the then premier's sons, Bill and Russell, who managed hardware, furniture and appliance stores under the names of Bennett Stores, had been engaged in corrupt practises. The story didn't support it, and neither did the facts. The *Sun* apologized, but talk is cheap: $16,000 damages and costs were levied. Bill Bennett is now the premier of B.C.

Holt v. Sun Publishing Co. Ltd., 1978

Simma Holt, a member of parliament, was accused of passing a message from Squeakie Fromme, convicted of trying to assassinate Gerald Ford, to the infamous Charles Manson. She didn't, but the *Sun* suggested she did. Holt was awarded $2,000 for the libel.

Lougheed v. CBC, 1978

A fictional television show, *The Tar Sands,* portrayed Alberta Premier Peter Lougheed in a less than attractive way: as a weak and irresolute figure being out-manoeuvered by major corporations. The trial has not been reached as of yet, but it shows that politicians are more willing to sue.

Chernesky v. Armadale Publishers and Sterling King, 1979

The Saskatoon *Star Phoenix* published a letter from two law students that suggested a local alderman was exhibiting "racist resistance" to the establishment of an alcohol rehabilitation centre; the paper put the heading "Racist Attitude" on the letter. The alderman involved sued for libel. In court, both the editor and publisher of the paper stated that the letter did not express their opinions and Cherneskey was awarded $25,000. The judgement indicated that letters to the editor in newspapers, in some circumstances, must express opinions supported by the editors of the paper.

Netupsky v. Craig, 1972

Netupsky, a professional engineer, had a judgement at trial for $250,000 – the highest award ever made in a Canadian libel suit – against architects who suggested his opinion about the safety of a stadium was absolutely wrong. His success was short-lived: the Supreme Court of Canada overturned the judgement.

Vander Zalm v. Bierman and The Times, 1979

A cartoon of British Columbia Minister of Human Resources William Vander Zalm tearing off wings of insects that appeared in the *Victoria Times* was found to be libellous. One cartoonist's wit is another man's libel.

Most Significant Legal Events

Here, in chronological order, are the ten Canadian legal events of the '70 which I consider the most significant:

Invocation of the War Measures Act, October 16, 1970, 4:00 a.m. The only time the Act has been used outside war-time.

Establishment of the Law Reform Commission of Canada. The Act came into force on July 15, 1971. The Commission's legislative track record has not been great, but the potential is there.

Capital Gains Tax. Valuation Day, December 31, 1971. One of the results of the massive Carter Commission Report of the '60s.

Lavell Case, decided by the Supreme Court of Canada on August 27, 1973. The case showed that the Bill of Rights would in future likely be given only a limited application by the Supreme Court.

The Queen v. Morgentaler, decided by the Supreme Court of Canada on March 26, 1974. An abortion case which may be remembered primarily because the result of the various prosecutions and the subsequent amendment of the Criminal Code, which reaffirmed the sovereign right of the jury to acquit.

Abolition of Capital Punishment came into force on July 26, 1976. The legislation ended capital punishment but substituted very lengthy prison sentences, without eligibility for parole.

The Queen v. Paquette, decided by the Supreme Court of Canada on October 5, 1976. The case will be remembered by lawyers as the first case in which the Supreme Court of Canada openly overruled itself.

Bill 101. Became law in the province of Quebec in 1977 under the title "Charter of the French Language."

Family Law Reform Acts. The Ontario Act came into force March 31, 1978. Among other changes, it provides for the equal division of family assets on the break-up of a marriage.

The Toronto Sun and Treu prosecutions under the Official Secrets Act. Both ended in 1979. Both illustrate the tension between secrecy and freedom of information, which will be a major issue in the '80s.

M.L. Friedland, professor of law, University of Toronto.

LTR – Sex in the '70s

I asked my friend the journalist how he and Elaine were getting along. "Just great," he said. "She likes me to tie her up."

At the beginning of the 1960s, this sort of thing would have remained one of those horrible little secrets, like what you do with the contents of your nose after you've picked it. By the end of the 1970s it is close to cocktail party chatter.

One of the big sexual developments of the 1970s is the legitimizing of B&D (bondage and domination), S&M (sadism and masochism) and all those other grimy sets of initials in which people lash each other to the bed or strut around in motorcycle outfits. If it has become okay it's because the Village People say it's okay because Mick (you know, good old when-the-whip-comes-down-Mick) says it's okay and because Robert Fulford says it's *not* okay.

Here we have all those couples who 20 years ago were just doing it in the missionary position, he rolling off her to get some z's, she lying sleeplessly in bed staring at the ceiling. Then blam blam blam blam, Marilyn French (*The Women's Room*) rides in and machine-guns the 1950s marriage, and suddenly all these liberation groups start rumbling back and forth across the bedroom. The women become liberated and start touching and feeling one another. The homosexuals become liberated and begin holding hands as they walk their poodles. The leather fetishists become liberated and turn up in chains and dog collars at punk-rock concerts.

The really startling development is not that all this wild stuff should have appeared in the first place – it surfaced, for example, in Victorian England. The amazing thing is that it has been so smoothly integrated into mainstream sexuality. Canada's national newspaper, on the front of its lifestyle section, runs a color shot of a group of men dressed like cowboys, construction workers and bikers whose message is you'll be beaten if you have oral sex with people who look like us, but you'll love it. So one feat of the '70s is hammering those gongs way down there in our unconscious where power, domination, fear and Eros all brew like the fog in 1930s movies about Jack the Ripper. Just think what a departure this is from 1,000 years of the missionary position!

A second sexual development of the 1970s is the emergence of the Living Together Relationship, the famous "LTR," where he says, "Listen, what's the point of you paying for a separate apartment when we're spending all our time together anyway," and she says, "Well, okay, but if I sew on any buttons and we later break up, it'll cost you half your savings account." I live on Markham Street in Toronto, one of those gentle, leafy streets with three-storey rooming houses. And if you sit out on a sunny day you'll see the LTRs parading by, arm-in-arm, on their way to the green-plant store or Gonzo Stereo. Marriage? No way, because all that repressive stuff is for people like our parents. Children? Maybe, but only if we can have them in a commune.

You'll scoff and say, how many people actually live like this? Plenty. Just think of how many lives the Sexual Revolution has kissed. The whole point of the LTR is sexual: it has all the advantages of a permanent date – so that you don't have to negotiate about intercourse each time over a restaurant table – with none of the institutional entanglements of marriage. What is actually happening is the eroticizing of our entire society, the LTRs being only the leading wedge. We see the shock waves rippling over supermarket profits: they decline as more and more people, held together mainly by sexual affiliation, skip the family togetherness which meal times once offered and go out for fast food. We see the LTR spin-off in census data: enormous increases in the number of unrelated individuals cohabiting. We see the LTR blow-back as we struggle to introduce the people with whom we're living to others: "Mother, I'd like you to meet my Marvin."

In lots of other areas too the '70s have seen major changes in sexuality – sex for the aged (or at least its legitimation), sex for the handicapped, sex for 14-year-olds, as dating gets going about a year after puberty. This stuff is all over the family sections of the country's newspapers, and because it's now more than three days old, it's old hat in the headlines.

But it's not old hat in real life. In the context of the history of our civilization it's absolutely revolutionary. We're talking about the breakdown of an entire system of family life in which sex (for women, at least) was confined to marriage, because extramarital intercourse could have devastating consequences for the family dynasty, or for the disposition of the inheritance, or for the ability of the village to support large numbers of unwanted bastard children.

Nowadays we don't have family dynasties, and the notion of the family tree produces yawns in most people under 25, and an open-fisted welfare state has even effaced all differences between legitimate and illegitimate children, supporting both when they decide to leave home and have a lifestyle of their own.

As the family's need for stability vanishes, its repressive functions become unnecessary. The gates are opened to the dark urges that slumber within all our breasts.

Dark urges? Well, not necessarily. There's nothing nasty about having sex outside of marriage; nothing about the missionary position is essential to the preservation of civilized life; nothing in anal sex among homosexuals is necessarily more repellent that anal sex among heteros. The point of the '70s revolution in "lifestyles," however, is that formerly all those urges were buried deep in the libidinal vault, and meant social ruin for those so indiscreet as to let them take form as conscious desires, or acts. Now they're highlighted on the vast movie screen that our culture dances across. That heavy, libidinal backbeat which makes you want to screw your brains out after 15 minutes of it? The 12-year-olds are lining up for the "clean" version of *Saturday Night Fever*. Black-booted legs with spurs that one formerly saw only in bookstores next to theatres featuring *Swedish Fly Girls*? Look at the shop windows. Splitting the marriage because you aren't getting off anymore? Unthinkable for 1,000 years, and now it's the justification for the LTR.

Edward Shorter, professor of history.

Parents in the '70s continue to be beset by uncertainties. Relatively less attention than in the previous decade was given to the generation gap and to the optional degree of permissiveness in child rearing, but other questions loomed larger. On the one hand, the interests of parents as individuals were recognized – mothers were freer to take jobs and couples were freer to separate or divorce with their own happiness paramount. On the other hand, a rights-of-children movement led by social agencies and buttressed by the all, they should treat their sons and their daughters and how they, as parental models, should behave.

1979 International Year of the Child was especially concerned with parental abuse of children, the just claims of the handicapped and the rights of children of divorce. Parents were also especially affected by the women's movement and they were uncertain how differently, if at

Dr. Frederick Elkin, professor of sociology.

Love

Love has always been considered to be something of a miracle: the miracle of the '70s was that love survived.

Never has the emotion been so assaulted. There were even attempts to euphemize it out of existence, replacing love with something called a "relationship," sometimes preceded by "one-to-one"; occasionally, "meaningful."

Love came into the '70s on a wave of advice from a spate of love doctors eager to promote the emotion as a set of gymnastic exercises that could be performed only by the very fit, or a culinary concoction to which you could add whipped cream or liver paste, depending on your fancy. Emotion was lost in the feverish attention to the clinical: Joy was advertised but what you got was an earnest preoccupation with the number of orgasms worked out to a mathematical ratio whose ideal was three (for her) to one (for him). People were too busy counting to feel.

That emphasis on the clinical led to a tendency to analyze love to death. Pursuit of the clinical flourished in a pornographic climate that confused lovemaking with having sex. And, everywhere you looked, people were doing that – in magazines, on the stage, in films. Mystery died. Lovers were hard pressed to believe that was what was happening between them was unique. Why, right up there on the screen, Marlon Brando was basting his lady's rump with butter and to Andy Warhol's camera eye, fellatio was ho-hum. What was left for ordinary mortals to discover? It's a wonder that we didn't turn into a generation who perceived love purely as a spectator sport.

We did respond to a world of instant soup and instant tea with a demand for instant intimacy. Courtship was out: the meat-market atmosphere of the singles' bar was in. Where some might have thought that sexual liberation gave women the right to say no, most of its male proponents believed that liberated women should always say yes. More and more people were having more and more innovative sex, at a younger age, with more and more partners. But their complaints to their sexologists about their sexual dysfunctions seemed to indicate that they were doing it with less and less pleasure.

Women's lib affected love. Many already performance-oriented men were rendered impotent by the pitiless and seemingly endless complaints of women about male performance. And women discovered that they had lost traditional respect without gaining a significant replacement.

Venereal disease and teenage pregnancy increased and many sexual partners, waking up to a strange and nameless face in their waterbed, discovered that the aftermath of lovemaking without love was frustration, acute loneliness and alienation.

There were some very important couples in the '70s, two of whom proved to be very loving in that they took responsibility for their actions. Nena and George O'Neill coined the label "open marriage." When they realized that was interpreted as a licence for promiscuity, they publicly regretted the phrase and tried to emphasize the importance that fidelity and exclusivity could play in creating an intense relationship.

William H. Masters and Virginia E. Johnson, who pioneered in the detached measurement of sexual response with calipers, married each other and proceeded to write a book called *The Pleasure Bond*. In this book, there were no charts or statistical data. Instead, they presented the theory that pleasure could be the bond that held a couple together, that infidelity could weaken that bond.

The third couple made headlines around the world with a "palimony" dispute. Lee and Michelle Marvin were like many couples of the '70s who decided to live together without getting married. Etiquette had to be rewritten to accommodate them as panicky mothers wrote letters to society editors asking, "How do I introduce my daughter's male roommate? Do I let them share a bedroom under our roof?" These couples loudly declared that a marriage licence – which was, after all, just a piece of paper – didn't make any difference.

The court decided they were right. Lee Marvin, who gave love a new definition by comparing it to a gas tank that might be anywhere from one-quarter to completely full, was ordered by a judge to assume financial responsibility for the rehabilitation of his former roommate. Palimony suits broke out like the measles and the decade closed with the realization that, with or without a piece of paper, love brings its own responsibilities.

There were moments in the '70s when the statistics seemed to indicate that love, as a fact, had died. By the end of the decade, one marriage out of four – in urban areas, one out of three – was ending in divorce. But the marriage – and remarriage – statistics, clearly indicate that love, as an idea, is as powerful as ever.

Love in the '70s: we measured it, computerized it, renamed it, psychoanalyzed it, stripped it of privacy, and rejected it, all the while longing for it, looking for it, and leaping into it. We proved in the '70s what the poets have known all along: that love conquers all, that it springs eternal and, as Lennon and McCartney said in song, *all you need is love.*

Joan Sutton, columnist, the Toronto *Star.*

Famous Marriages

(Not in order of importance)
Robert Stanfield and Anne Austin; August 10, 1978
René Lévesque and Corinne Cote; April 12, 1979
Conrad Black and Shirley Gail Walters; July 14, 1978
Peter Newman and Camilla Jane Turner; August 5, 1978
Christina Newman and Stephen Clarkson; September 1, 1978
Joe Clark and Maureen McTeer; June 30, 1973
Pierre Elliot Trudeau and Margaret Sinclair; March 4, 1971
Anne Murray and Bill Langstroth; June 20, 1975
Princess Caroline of Monaco and Phillippe Junot; June 28 and 29, 1978
Elizabeth Taylor and Richard Burton; October 10, 1975
Elizabeth Taylor and John William Warner; December 4, 1976
Princess Anne and Captain Mark Phillips; November 14, 1973
Jane Fonda and Tom Hayden; January 20, 1973

Sheila Shotton, broadcaster.

Fashion

Startling changes set in rapid succession identify the '70s. The decade saw rapid and drastic changes in fashion – in styling, in resources and in market focus. It opened with the mini versus midi controversy, offering a choice (at least) for the mature woman, but ultimately proving that Paris could no longer dictate to the masses. The *prêt-à-porter* became much more influential than couture and the fashion innovators in Paris, Milan and New York began looking to the Orient (long known for superb workmanship) for mass production of their designs. Fashion became a complex, multicultural happening.

Meanwhile the youth (flower children of the '60s) matured into the job-oriented career seekers – the "contemporary women" of the '70s – and with them fashion adapted . . . from faded patchwork blue jeans and T-shirts, to today's business suits.

The decade began with a confusion of choice – mini, midi or maxi. Women solved the dilemma by opting for the

The ethnic look. *The Fashion Bureau*

Platform shoes became the big footwear item during the early '70s. CP

pantsuit and wearing it everywhere. Pants of all kinds became the uniform of the time and blue jeans reigned supreme.

The middle of the decade brought a return of the dress – now soft, feminine and below the knee. This drastic contrast, along with the growing universality of fashion, brought an explosion of costume looks of many ethnic origins. The "folklorique" inspired by both peasant and primitive was just the beginning of a whole new way of dressing. From soft, full, peasant blouse and dirndl over petticoats evolved the whole layering style of the sportswear collectibles. The pendulum had started its swing back.

This layering spawned an emphasis on classics, versatility and value. The contemporary woman, now mature and educated, was wooed with the seasonless advantages of the more conservative parts and pieces.

Throughout the decade, the famous designers continued to emphasize and expand their ready-to-wear divisions. Many women's wear designers expanded into men's wear (and vice versa) with great success, as well as branching into all types of accessories. Soon the designer logo was a must on eyeglasses, luggage, cosmetics and ultimately on the "status" jean.

In reaction to the plastic '60s, the '70s

The fitness boom brought out a whole new interest in sports clothes.

focussed on the "natural." In fibres, fabrics, fashions and living, the interest was in ecology. A rage for herbs, health foods and gourmet cooking resulted in a fitness boom that saw active sportswear brought into fashion and a body-conscious, casual approach to everyday dressing.

The city suit grew through a paring down of the silhouette, the acceptance of the versatility and practicality of separates and the trend to conservatism, the tradition of the business world.

Hemlines are now rising, shoulders broadening. Fashion is looking back again, but it never repeats itself. The cycle continues. The focus of the decade as we enter the '80s is refinement.

The Mid-'70s brought mid-calf skirts into vogue. AP

Inge Wood, Toronto-area fashion coordinator, Eaton's.

When the mini-midi controversy set most women in a tizzy, they moved instantly into hot pants, panty hose, boots: an aberration that even women who hadn't taken up mini-skirts tried for about ten minutes.

Jeans and **T-shirts** were so prevalent that even the most middle-class embraced embroidered, studded jean jackets, followed closely by safari suits in faded blue (carefully polyestered) with butterfly collars and shirts unbuttoned at least down to the sternum (both male and female).

The string bikini: marvellous on the lithe, bronzed bodies of jet-setters lollygagging about the beaches of Rio de Janeiro, but didn't quite translate to Kitsilano Beach in Vancouver.

Platform shoes: hallmark of the insecure. A fad that worked only for thousands of orthopedic surgeons, who made a fortune out of people stumbling about. The ultimo plat was three-inch high sneakers.

Jewelry for men: the gold necklace on men, pioneered by disco chaps and eventually adopted even by athletes (and even when they were battling one another).

The string bikini was obviously designed only for the very young and very fit. *Wide World.*

Wretched excess took over in the late '70s, when even straight men were finding their jewelry tangled up with chest hair. By 1979 the real macho look was not to wear any jewelry at all: a pussycat revolution on the part of men who'd been afraid of being tagged as homosexuals. Earrings on gays were fading as the younger generation took it up as just something fun to do.

The Diane Keaton Look: Everybody thought it was the *Annie Hall* look masterminded by Halston, but it became evident with *Manhattan* that most of the people in the lineups wanted to look like Diane Keaton, not Annie Hall.

Battle fatigues just kept going on and on. They may have been offensive to some during the Vietnam War, but kids found out that they were cheap and durable; and what did they know about war, anyway? Good street stuff – as long as one wore a fedora.

Punk chic: ripped, torn and safety-pinned – almost anything worked, but hair was the issue. Super short. Spikey orange, bleached blonde, pink or puce was for a moment almost riveting, especially when it wasn't your hairdresser sporting it.

Diane Keaton and Woody Allen gave us the *Annie Hall* look from the movie of the same name. Any old thing put together became the height of chic. *United Artists.*

112

An Encyclopedia of Cults

Since the new age of faith began in the 1960s, an estimated 3,000 cults have arisen in North America. One Massachusetts sect was started in a tree house. In Montreal a lama lives in a monastery with 11 women. A Toronto commune runs a vegetarian restaurant. A California cult practises soul travel. This is a survey of the unorthodox new creeds of the 1970s:

Alamo Christian Foundation
Jewish record promoter Tony Alamo says he and his wife Susan started the Jesus revolution in 1968 when they began preaching to hippies and handing out leaflets on Sunset Boulevard. About 250 members live in sex-segregated communes in Saugus, California, and Alma, Arkansas, and do not talk to the opposite sex except during meals. A U.S. Senate committee has investigated complaints of mind control, beatings and slave labour. There's an Alamo television program. Annual revenues exceed $1.3 million.

Ananda Marga
The "Path of Bliss" was founded in India in 1955 by guru Shrii Shrii Anandamurtii, 58, a "pure reflection of the deity" who was recently charged with conspiring to kill seven former disciples; the charges were dropped, but to protest Anandamurtii's imprisonment (and other social injustices) several Europeans immolated themselves. Members (called Margiis) practise vegetarianism, yoga and meditation, and give ten percent or more of their wages to Ananda, which sells shampoo, soap and health foods under the label Golden Lotus. Headquarters were recently moved from India to Denver, Colorado. Ananda has 300 hard-core followers in the United States and 80 in Canada.

Anthroposophical Society
Austrian-born Dr. Rudolph Steiner was once a Theosophist but left that cult in 1912 to start Anthroposophy. A mixture of Theosophy and Christianity, it is headquartered in Dornach, Switzerland, and has tens of thousands of adherents who believe in reincarnation, the supernatural and Jesus. Canada's 400 members support the Toronto Waldorf School (where a pupil is taught by the same teacher from grades 1 to 8), numerous spiritual bookstores and the Biodynamic Farming Association, which opposes fertilizers.

Apostles of Infinite Love
Founded in France in 1952 as a breakaway Roman Catholic sect that denounced the Pope because of his imagined connections to freemasonry. Founder Michel Collin, a defrocked priest, called himself Pope Clement XV; he ordained Gaston Tremblay, now known as the Reverend Jean Gregoire de la Trinité, who founded a monastery in St. Jovite, Quebec, and recently was charged with abducting two children of a former disciple. Followers of the Apostles number about 1,000 and are as far afield as Vermont, New Brunswick, Alberta and Europe.

Aquarian Foundation
The Reverend Keith M. Rhinehart of Seattle heads the largest psychic and occult centre in the United States. Rhinehart, who has been photographed with ectoplasm coming out of his mouth, sells cassettes of communications with Jesus, Gandhi and other "ascended masters" at $10 each. Members are in seven U.S. cities, Vancouver and Victoria.

Arica Institute
About 50 Esalen associates went on a pilgrimage to Arica, Chile, to study Oscar Ichazo's "scientific mysticism" in 1970, and ten months later brought it back to New York, San Francisco and other North American cities. Ichazo, now a New Yorker, combined Sufi, Zen, Buddhist and other teachings into a 40-day course that Aricans call "an experience

in higher education." About 100 people have taken the Arica training in Montreal, Toronto, Edmonton and Vancouver.

Assembly of Yahowah the Eternal
Vancouver pastor Gordon Keith Pearce says that God (Yahowah), his son Yaho-Hoshu-Wah and Satan live inside the earth (which is hollow) and emerge periodically from the North Pole in flying saucers to appear before humanity in these "last days." Though 75 people are on the mailing list, only nine attend meetings; financial support comes from a civil servant.

Astara
More than 100 lessons in world religion, philosophy, mysticism, nutrition and yoga comprise Astara's *Book of Life*, which traces a course from prebirth to afterlife. Drs. Robert and Earlyne Chaney, who formed Astara in 1951, maintain a ten-acre retreat in Upland, California. At least 25,000 members have paid $10 membership fees in 90 countries, including Canada.

Bhagwan Shree Rajneesh
From Poona, India, comes Rajneesh, author (*Nothing To Lose But Your Head*) and sex guru who teaches that people should say yes to every bodily impulse. His 35,000 or so disciples (sannyasins) around the world (30 in Vancouver) wear orange (the color of sexual energy), a string of 109 beads (representing the 108 names of God plus one more for Rajneesh) and practise one of the guru's meditations daily (a sample Rajneesh song, for singing meditation: *Thank you, thank you Bhagwan/Thank you for giving me me*).

Bible Speaks
Carl Stevens started Bible Speaks after a few short conversations with his maker in the late 1960s. The World Outreach missionaries have entered Russia on the pretext of being college students (exits may be harder), and since "God opened the doors" earlier this year they may soon enter China as well. Their main source of funds, a daily radio show called *Telephone Time,* is heard by millions across the United States; distraught callers ask the audience to pray for them. Headquarters are in Lennox, Massachusetts, where 1,000 members live and 700 students attend the Stevens Bible School.

Children of God
Arizona minister David "Moses" Berg, 65, began proselytizing hippies in Huntingdon Beach, California, in 1968. He led a flock of 150 out of the state in 1969 after receiving a revelation that it would fall into the sea. Members live together and earn up to $300 a day selling "Mo" letters – comic-style pamphlets glorifying sex. "We have a sexy God, and a sexy religion, and a very sexy leader with an extremely young following," says Berg. "So if you don't like sex you'd better get out while you can." Berg's "Sex Letters" contain exhortations such as "Sex Works!" and "In the Beginning – Sex!" Some of these missives are directed at the public; others are for members only. In 1973 Berg had a vision that the comet Kohoutek would destroy North America and at his urging most of his followers left for Europe. The Children believe the world will end in 1993. There are about 5,000 Children in 800 colonies. Canada has 150 members.

Church of Bible Understanding
Stuart Traill reconditioned and sold old vacuum cleaners until he found Jesus in 1968. Three years later, he was head of a band of fundamentalist Christian zealots in Pennsylvania which he baptized the Forever Family, a name that the 1,700 members changed in 1976 because Traill's messy divorce made it inappropriate. The church now has some 2,000 followers in eastern cities; in Montreal and New York members staff a carpet cleaning company, Christian Brothers Cleaning Service, Inc., the church's main source of revenue.

Church of Hakeem

The Reverend Hakeem Abdul Rasheed's "Dare To Be Rich" success program has enticed about 9,000 southern Californians to chant "richer faster, richer faster" and invest $500 to become "ministers of increase." After some early donors received 400 percent of their money, he coaxed more than $20 million from his audiences. Law officials say the church is a pyramid scheme. Hakeem says, "The goal of this church is to make 10,000 millionaires."

Church of the Redeemer

A Houston, Texas, Episcopal community where 180 of the 800 Born Again Christian members live together in 29 houses and pool all or part of their wages. Other such Born Again communities exist in Ann Arbor, Michigan, Woodland Park, Colorado, Washington, D.C., Augusta, Georgia, Cleveland and Cincinnati, Ohio, and Evanston, Illinois.

Church of Satan

Anton La Vey says the group he founded in Daly City, California, in 1969 is not a religion. "Satanism demands study – not worship." About one million members worldwide have paid $50 for a medallion, an ID card, the name of a local contact and a year's worth of the *Cloven Hoof* newsletter. Additional moneys came from the sale of La Vey's *Satanic Bible,* now in its 13th printing.

Church Universal and Triumphant

This jumble of natural foods, vegetarianism, backpacking, Montessori educational methods and anti-Communism was founded by Mark L. Prophet when he set up the Summit Lighthouse to publish the *Pearls of Wisdom* newsletter in 1958. Three years later he formed the order of the Keepers of the Flame. In 1973 he left the physical plane to join the Great White Brotherhood (an association of "ascended masters"), but his wife, Elizabeth Clare Prophet (Guru Ma), continued to publish the latest news from Pallas Athena, Gautama Buddha and K-17 (Head of the Cosmic Secret Service). This convoluted spiritual bureaucracy emanates from Malibu, California; 10 Keepers of the Flame and 100 subscribers to *Pearls of Wisdom* are Vancouverites.

Cold Mountain Institute

Started in 1968 by the late Richard Weaver and now run by his widow Jean, Cold Mountain offers Vancouverites courses and workshops in dream discovery, self-discovery, sexuality and other self-awareness subjects on a barge moored in False Creek. Month-long and week-long residential programs and weekend courses are conducted on a 23-acre site on Cortes Island in the Strait of Georgia. Fees range from $75 for a two-day Vancouver workshop to $290 for five days on Cortes.

Dharmasara

Baba Hari Dass, an Indian-born guru, teaches Ashtanga yoga, which stresses non-injury, non-lying, non-stealing, sexual moderation and a type of meditation that leads to "samadhi," transcendental awareness. Hari Dass has not spoken since 1952 – he writes on a chalkboard. The Dharmasara centre in Vancouver has 30 members.

Divine Light Mission

The plump and pimply Guru Maharaj Ji imported DLM from northern India in 1971 when he was 15; his 50,000 devotees have made their Lord of the Universe fabulously wealthy with millions of tax-exempt donations. "Goom Rodgie," as they affectionately call him, is partial to diamonds and fast cars. He owns a flashy pad in Denver and an estate in Malibu. Initiates ("premies") may attain oneness with the universe through four meditative techniques: close your eyes to see the light, close your ears to hear the music, roll your tongue back into your mouth to taste the "divine nectar," and concentrate on "primordial vibrations" to receive God's word. There are 200 ashrams in North America. Headquarters are in Denver, Colorado.

Doomsday Cult
Roch (Moses) Theriault, 31, and a group of five men, ten women and a two-year-old child were so certain that the world was going to end last February that they holed up in a log house in Paspebiac, Quebec, to wait for the apocalypse. So far as is known they're still there.

Eckankar
The science of soul travel was established in Las Vegas in 1965 by the late Paul Twitchell, a former journalist. Students ("chelas") pay $65 a year for seven years of introduction, than pay $40 in annual membership fees. Eckankarians say they leave their bodies at home when they escape the physical realm to explore "the upper planes." Three million people practise Eckankar. The group rents administrative offices in Manlo Park, California.

Esalen
The first encounter group originated in New Britain, Connecticut, in 1946. The technique was taken west by Richard Price in 1960. In San Francisco he met Michael Murphy, who had just returned from the Indian ashram of Aurobindo Ghose; together they moved to the 75 acres along the Big Sur coast once owned by the Esalen, a tribe of Indians, and later by Murphy's grandfather. Esalen was formed in 1962 as a live-in centre of eastern and western religions, pop and occult psychologies, encounter group interactions, meditation and martial arts. Mentors have included Arnold Toynbee, Aldous Huxley, Rollo May, Norman O. Brown, Ken Kesey, Paul Tillich, B.F. Skinner and Carlos Castaneda. About 80,000 people have taken Esalen courses.

EST (Erhard Seminars Training)
Jack Rosenberg, a former encyclopedia salesman and graduate of Scientology, Mind Dynamics and Leadership Dynamics, changed his name to Werner Erhard and, after a revelation in 1971, started est as a 60-hour course designed to teach people to really *experience* experience. For $350, trainees receive two weekends crammed with Zen, behaviour modification and positive thinking. The trainees are not allowed to eat, use the toilet (except during several short rest periods), smoke, take drugs, wear watches or sit beside friends; they are told their discomfort is evidence that they are not in control of their bodies.

The Farm
Acid guru Stephen Gaskin conducted a weekly hippie gathering in San Francisco called Monday Night Class, and when he left it in 1970 for a speaking tour around the United States a caravan of 65 vans and school buses followed him and finally settled on 1,750 acres near Summertown, Tennessee. Now 1,200 people live there; a further 900 live on 15 other farms in the United States and Guatemala. In Canada there is a farm of 28 folks (as members are called) near Lanark, Ontario. Gaskin's wife, Ina May, and her crew of 12 self-trained midwives have delivered 1,000 babies for visitors at no charge. All the folks are vegetarian and involved with relief work; they listen to taped sermons from Gaskin each Sunday, then meditate for an hour. Most practise a mix of puritanical Christian, Zen and naturalist ethics (no tobacco, drugs, birth control, divorce or cutting hair).

Father Divine
The Reverend M.J. Divine had 1.5 million followers in the '30s and a multimillion dollar empire that included a 73-acre Philadelphia estate. Since his death in 1965, his second wife, Mother Divine (formerly Edna Rose Ritchings of Vancouver), has been spiritual head of operations of his Peace Mission Movement, but Father Divine is still God. The 7,000 remaining followers pay all bills immedi-

ately, refuse mortgages and never buy anything on credit; they are also celibate.

Fellowship of Christians
Members of this Wyevale, Ontario, congregation live together in a large redwood building called the Mill. They turn over their bank accounts and weekly pay cheques to the fellowship; in return they receive food, shelter and $10 a week. The leader, Hector Haynes, preaches that medicine and drugs are evil. He is said to have performed healing rituals such as laying on of hands. Last year a 29-year-old diabetic member died after he stopped taking insulin.

Foundation Faith of God
The Foundation Faith was founded in 1974 when a number of ministers broke away from the Process Church, a Christain street ministry preoccupied with satanism. The 75 ministers in Toronto, Montreal and Vancouver are tithed ten percent, sell leaflets and crafts on the streets. Their 300 American brethren raise money with radio shows such as *The Kingdom Crusade, The Glory Road Crusade* and *The Jewish Crusade for Jesus.* International headquarters are in Phoenix, Arizona.

Great Heart Buddhist Monastery
Tyndale Martin, the son of an evangelist who got rich in Montreal land deals, proclaimed himself the Panchen Lama of Tibet eight or nine years ago and founded a monastery. A powerfully built, magnetic man in his 30s, he lives in the female wing with 11 disciples with whom he practises Tantric yoga sexual exercises. Six of the young women have borne children by him. The male group, which obtained grants from Ottawa and the Roman Catholic Church, has gone into decline since the existence of the female followers became known. Tyndale has told his harem that if anything happens to him it would be better for their spiritual health if they killed themselves.

Gurdjieff-Ouspensky
The 19th-century Russian magus Charles Gurdjieff combined Christianity, Sufism and Buddhism into a system of thought (elucidated by his associate Peter Ouspensky) that saw man as a stimulus-response machine who could wake from his deep mechanical sleep only through concentrated self-scrutiny. The present Fourth Way movement was started by an "awakened" master in California in 1970 and has since spread to Canada and Europe. Many of the 1,200 students of the Fourth Way Schools around the world (35 in Canada) donate part of their wages and live together; others just pay to attend meetings twice weekly.

Hanuman Foundation
The guru is Baba Ram Dass, formerly Richard Alpert, who with Timothy Leary started the LSD cult at Harvard University in the '60s. In 1969 he returned from a Himalayan holiday and held his first ashram on the lawn of his New Hampshire house. Later he found "the only enlightened being in the West," Joya Santayana (real name: Joyce Green), a Brooklyn housewife who became Divine Mother to his disciples until he denounced her in 1975. These days, Ram Dass has lost his ardent following, though his several books continue to sell. Joya, however, claims to have 200 followers living in "Joya Houses" in New York, Florida and California.

Hare Krishna
His Divine Grace Bhaktivedanta Swami Prabhupada, just off the boat, squatted beneath a tree in New York in 1966 and began chanting a mantra and crashing a cymbal. He was an instant hit. Hare Krishna's 350 full-time devotees in Canada shave their heads, dress in saffron-colored robes, live communally and get up at four a.m. to chant. Rules: no meat, fish, eggs, gambling, drinking, smoking, excessive television, junk reading or sex outside of marriage. Members split their salaries with Krishna, then sell books,

Hare Krishna members on Ottawa's
Sparks Street mall. CP

candles, incense and their magazine,
Back to Godhead, on the street to make
Krishna even richer. The society runs
Spiritual Sky, the second largest incense
factory in the United States, and diverse
real-estate holdings including 108
Krishna centres worldwide. Their assets
total $50 million. Krishna has attracted
about 5,000 casual followers in Canada,
about 50,000 in the United States and
millions in India. U.S. headquarters are in
Los Angeles.

3HO (Healthy Happy Holy Organization)
A secular branch of the Sikh religion,
which has 12 million followers
worldwide. HHH offers courses in such
subjects as prenatal yoga, vegetarian
cooking and massage. There are 100 3HO
centres in the United States and five in
Canada. About 200,000 people have paid
$3 per class or $25 a month to take the
courses.

Holiness Church of God
Scattered in tiny congregations through

the mountains of Tennessee, Kentucky
and Virginia, the Holiness Church's
3,000 members are Christians who test
their faith by handling poisonous snakes
or drinking strychnine. In 1969, one man
was bitten by a rattler and died, and in
1973, a further two members fatally poisoned themselves. After the first death,
laws against snake-handling were passed
in every Appalachian state except Kentucky.

Holy Order of MANS
Jesus appeared in divine revelation to
Father Paul in the Haight-Ashbury dis-
trict of San Francisco in the mid-1960s
and told him to found the order MANS, an
acronym of four Greek letters. Brothers
and sisters of this Catholic sect live communally and take vows of poverty, hum-
ilty and purity. Missionaries wear brown
friars' robes, women a knee-length blue
habit. A publication, the *Golden Nuggets,*
offers advice on how to disappear: " . . .
draw energy from the outer atmosphere
into your shell until it becomes cloudy,
then you disappear. Don't bother to try
this if you are a neophyte." There are 750
members of the order, 13 in Vancouver.

Kabalarian Philosophy
After an $80 introductory course in num-
erology and name analysis, members
take new names (such as Lindoro, Norill
and Valana) and pay $13 a month to
continue their training. No meat, tobacco, alcohol or profanity allowed. Kabala-
rian headquarters (a residence, office and
lecture hall) are in Vancouver; they also
have a resort on Lake Kalamalka, British
Columbia, and six other centres in western Canada, California and Holland.
Current membership is about 1,000,
though many more have taken the course.

Kerista Village
You're celibate until you join a Best
Friend Identity Cluster, but then the fun
starts: sexual intercourse with each member of your cluster. Members also practice what they call Gestalt-O-Rama, a

psychological exercise designed to eliminate their "Inner Uglies" – fears, bad habits, everything but acne. Since its formation in 1971, Kerista has observed four holy days per year when members may smoke marijuana or get drunk. It has 17 members in San Francisco.

Krishnamurti Foundation
J. Krishnamurti, now 83, has been blissing them out since 1922, preaching spiritual freedom from authority, fear and the past. The foundation began in Ojai, California. Now schools in four countries (including the Wolfe Lake School in Victoria) charge $4,000 for full-time tuition per year and market books, tapes and video cassettes. An estimated 10,000 followers.

Lifespring
John P. Hanley gave his first seminar in San Francisco in 1974, offering 50 hours of "personal growth" training similar to that offered by est founder Werner Erhard. The basic course is $350 in Canada; the Interpersonal Experience, $750. More than 30,000 people have taken Lifespring training in 11 centres in the United States and one in Vancouver. Headquarters: San Rafael, California.

Light of Truth
A tea-and-muffins spiritualist society for elderly ladies in Vancouver, the Light of Truth is based loosely on the Church Universal and Triumphant. The "ascended masters" speak through founder Isabel Pearson, who collects $3 a week from her 14 steady members and "the many others who come and go." One of the six spirit guides who are assigned to each soul, she says, is an Indian chief who sits on the car roof while you drive and keeps you out of accidents. At her last big gathering, a spiritualist brought Plato over from the other side.

Local Church of Witness Lee
In 1962, Witness Lee brought his anti-denominational, anti-Christian pulpit from Taiwan to Anaheim, California, where members have burned banners reading "Religion" and worn T-shirts with the motto "God Hates Christianity." Lee, 74, teaches that only through intuition and divine experience can we know God; the Bible and other books only confound us. His 8,000 followers in North America and 70,000 in the Orient are forbidden to read anything except what the church prints through its Living Stream Ministry Publishing Company. Lee sends a taped, weekly sermon to the elders of his churches. They repeat it verbatim to their flocks, who must live no farther than three miles from the nearest church. Members donate about $750,000 a year. There are more than 50 churches in North America, including one in Toronto.

Love Israel Family
A one-time real estate salesman, Paul Erdman, changed his name to Love Israel and founded the church of Armageddon in San Francisco in 1970. A year later he brought his flock to Seattle. Members take new first names (Serious, Reverence, Solidity), and use the last name Israel. They observe a form of kosher, smoke hash and hyperventilate. Two members died from sniffing an industrial solvent in 1972. Women cut and brush the men's hair, bow when entering a room and speak only when spoken to. There are 200 active members (including Logic Israel, the son of Steve Allen) and 1,000 followers in Seattle and Vancouver.

National Research Institute for Self-understanding
His name is Ghanshyam Singh Birla and he reads the lines and bumps on your right hand. They reveal your past, present and future, chapter by chapter. From his Institute in Montreal, and on the road trips he's made across Canada, he's seen more than 3,000 people, who have paid $35 for readings, up to $65 for workshops.

New Age Centres

New Age is a spinoff of Mind Dynamics, Inc., created by the man who headed Canadian operations of that outfit until it folded in 1975. George Raynault of Toronto has made New Age the largest mind school in Canada by offering a smorgasbord of palmistry, numerology, astrology, ESP, biofeedback, dream analysis, biorhythm and transactional analysis. The Mind Awareness course runs weekends at $190; an advance course costs $225. As many as 10,000 people have graduated from 19 centres in Canada and two in the United States.

Nichiren Shoshu Academy

Chant "Nam Myoho Renge Kyo" daily in front of the holy scrolls (gohonzons) and be richer than your wildest dreams: so said Academy representatives to college kids in a campus crusade in the late '60s. Based on the teachings of Nichiren Daishonin Ikeda, a 13th century sage, Nichiren Shoshu was brought to the United States in 1960 and where there are now 35,000 adherents there. Recruitment incentives are less materialistic these days and involve changing "negative" to "positive" destiny. Some 15 million members worldwide pay handling charges to receive their gohonzons.

People Searching Inside (PSI Institute)

This southern Ontario mind school run by Joseph Dippong, 43, offers courses based on eastern mysticism and group encounter techniques. Inward Bound IV, the $225, four-day introductory course, is the most popular: the $1,200 followup, Inward VII, is more intense. Several people who took courses were committed to psychiatric hospitals. Participants drive in convoys to any one of several small-town hotel hideaways, where they surrender their car keys and privacy. In "the arena," a fast-moving group encounter battleground, members tearfully confess to matricide or incest fantasies, a musical theme such as *Climb Every Mountain* is played at top volume, and they are hap-pily reaccepted into the group. At least 5,000 people have taken PSI courses in Toronto, Hamilton and Kitchener.

Rastafarian Brethren

When Marcus Garvey was deported back to Jamaica from the United States in 1927, he began preaching for a return of blacks to Africa. Since then the Rastafarians, who worship the late emperor Haile Selassie of Ethopia, have grown in number in Jamaica, Toronto, New York and other North American cities with significant Jamaican populations. They believe they are descended from one of the tribes of Israel. They smoke the holy weed ganja (marijuana). Reggae singer Bob Marley is a central figure in the movement.

Renaissance Community

In 1968 Michael Rapunzel, then 16, set up shop in a tree house in Leyden, Massachusetts, and managed to convince ten friends that he was the reincarnation of Saint Peter and Robert E. Lee. Later he established the Brotherhood of the Spirit, which by 1973 had gathered 2,000 members who ate two meals of brown rice per day and each contributed $50 a week. Money also rolled in from a lighting and sound company, Rocket's Silver Train Bus Service, whose clients have included Yes, Peter Frampton and Linda Ronstadt. Rapunzel was the lead singer for the rock group Spirit and Flesh, which recorded *Stash the Cash*. About 200 members live in a commune in Turner's Falls, Massachusetts, where they await the end of the world.

Scientology

Since its formation by sci-fi writer L. Ron Hubbard in 1954, Scientology has grown into perhaps the world's largest cult. A religion for tax purposes, it is also a commercially packaged psychological "science" based on the principles expounded in Hubbard's book, *Dianetics*. Members pay $2 for a seminar, then another $30 for a 12-hour course in which encounter group techniques are used. Hubbard's E-meter, a sort of homemade lie-detector, determines psychological weak points; courses designed to strengthen these are then offered at prices of $1,000 to $5,000 or more. Scientologists have been known to harass enemies such as journalist Paulette Cooper, who wrote *The Scandal of Scientology*. Eleven members face charges arising from the Watergate-like break-in of several Washington offices where files on Scientology were stored. Some 2.5 million Americans have tried Scientology, including John Travolta, Karen Black and, during his imprisonment in the early '60s, Charles Manson. There are about 60,000 graduates in Canada and an estimated four million worldwide. Annual revenues are in the hundreds of millions.

Seicho-No-Ie

As soon as we realize that we're already perfect, teaches 86-year-old Masaharu Taniguchi, PhD, then our lives will be perfect, too. This rules out the possibility of disease: cancer, he says, is "the symbol of a stubborn mind." Church members, called Holy Missioners, pay $2 or $5 a month and meditate twice daily. An amalgam of Christian, Buddhist and Shinto teachings, Seicho-Ne-Ie has three million adherents in Japan (where it began), one million in Brazil and a growing mixed following in Canada and the United States.

Self-Realization Fellowship

Paramahansa Yogananda brought SRF to the United States in 1920, and lived a total of 30 years in North America, the first Hindu master to teach in the West for such an extended period of time. He taught Kriya yoga and used the Bhagavad Gita and the Old and New Testaments as scriptures. There are 150 nuns and monks at SRF headquarters in Los Angeles, and thousands have taken the courses ($9 for 15 weeks) through 180 groups around the world, including 11

Death upon death—in Jonestown, Guyana, more than 900 cultists committed suicide, 1978.

groups in Canada from Nanaimo, British Columbia, to Westmount, Quebec.

Silva Mind Control

Need a new brainwave synchronizer? Silva markets the Trainer I, complete with silver-coated electrodes, for $37.95. The Big Daddy of mind control schools, Silva was started in Laredo, Texas, in 1962 by Mexican-born José Silva, a former radio repairman who claims his original intention was merely to upgrade his kids' marks at school. Silva combined Norman Vincent Peale optimism, Emile Coué auto-suggestion, Asian mysticism, brainwave meditation and self-hypnosis into a highly marketable package designed to reduce tension and drastically improve memory, imagination, intuition, health and happiness. Silva offers its 38-hour, $195 course in cities from White Horse to Windsor, and has produced about 15,000 graduates in Canada.

Spice of Life

The 14 members of this Toronto commune share beds, clothing and property and operate the Spice of Life vegetarian restaurants. They'll soon publish a new magazine, *Alternative to Alienation.*

Sri Chinmoy

Sri Chinmoy, 47-year-old spiritual master from Bengal, is credited with 350 books, 2,000 songs and 130,000 mystical paintings, but he found time to win, with 179 followers, the group prize in the Pepsi Cola Memorial Day bicycle marathon in Central Park last year. He also meditates daily on each of his 1,000 disciples around the world, who must shower, wear clean clothes and put out flowers beforehand so their images will be pleasant. Chinmoy centres in Vancouver, Toronto and other Canadian cities teach "path of the heart" yoga, supported by student donations.

Subud

Subud's most interesting feature is the Latihan, a spiritual exercise in which members stand in a room and sing, dance, chant, shout, vibrate, hum or make funny noises for half an hour to get in touch with whatever God each believes in. Men and women do this in separate groups, each meeting two or three nights a week, in cities from British Columbia to the Maritimes as well as in the United States, Europe and Indonesia. The practice originated in Indonesia with Bapak, 77, every Subudian's spiritual guide. Canada has about 400 members; international headquarters, which rotate every four years, are now in Toronto.

Sufi Order of Canada

Sufis believe that all religions represent basic truths about our existence; they light six candles for the major world religions during their Universal Worship ceremony, then a seventh for the remainder. Next they read from various scriptures, chant, and do a little dance for each religion. There are 10,000 members in North America, based in six Canadian cities from Vancouver to Ottawa, and 100 centres in the United States.

Sunburst

On 5,000 acres purchased with a lump settlement for a back injury, Normal Paulson, a Self-Realization Fellowship graduate, built a community near Santa Barbara, California, where he was joined by 350 disciples from across the United States who say they had visions of Paulson and his project. Sunburst operates food markets, a restaurant, a juice factory, a bakery and a publishing company. Members share their money and live in harmony with nature according to the "12 virtues" said to have been transmitted from God to Paulson.

Synanon

Fanatical, frighteningly violent, Synanon was started in Santa Monica, California, by an ex-alcoholic, Charles E. Dederich, 66, whose throne is now worth $20 million. The 900 hard-core members are mainly former junkies, alkies, cons and crazies who have traded all worldly possessions for salvation from their addictions and militaristic combat training. Upon Dederich's suggestions, members have shaved their heads, undergone mass vasectomies, undertaken abortions and divorced old partners to marry new ones. Dederich and two other Synanites have been charged with putting a rattlesnake in the mailbox of a Los Angeles lawyer who had won a $300,000 legal judgment against Synanon. The lawyer was bitten but recovered.

Theosophical Society
Occultist Madame H. P. Blavatsky, Civil War Colonel H. S. Olcott and lawyer William Q. Judge formed the Theosophical Society in New York in 1875 to explore the supernatural and the spiritual powers of man. Blavatsky, though exposed as a fraud in 1884, had more than 100,000 followers at the time of her death in 1891. There are more than 1,000 casual and active members from Vancouver to Montreal, and thousands more around the world. Headquarters are in India.

Therafields
Welsh-born Lea Hindley-Smith, 63, began offering therapy in her Toronto home in the mid-1950s. She has since become the matriarch of a therapeutic community of more than 800 members, of whom 200 or so pay as much as a third of their incomes to receive live-in therapy in one of 18 Therafields-owned houses in mid-town Toronto. A company formed in 1971, Therafields Environmental Centre (York) Ltd., owns an apartment building, four houses, a stretch of buildings from 310 to 320 Dupont, and several large farms north of Toronto. As part of therapy, members refurbish old houses or work on the farm on an unsalaried basis. Poet bp nichol is a vice-president and therapist.

Transcendental Meditation
Though it has been around for 5,000 years, it wasn't until 1959 that TM was exported from India (and made widely popular by the Beatles in the late '60s). Singularly responsible for this revival is Maharishi Mahesh Yogi, who is to meditation what Colonel Sanders is to fried chicken. More than one million North Americans have studied his method of attaining deep relaxation: silently concentrating for 20 minutes twice daily on a personalized mantra, eyes closed, incense optional. (The one-week course costs $150, $80 for students.) Some advanced meditators are told they have the ability to levitate. Maharishi regularly dispatches advanced TM teams to world trouble spots to exert a calming influence. There are 83 World Plan Centres in Canada, and 1,500 in the world.

Turning Society
The local representative of this dervish order, a 45-year-old former antique dealer named Sheik Reshad Feild, lives in North Vancouver. The 30 Vancouver members meet on Thursday nights for prayers and, if the sheik agrees, for sema exercises which include a whirling dance that takes 1,001 days to master. The society is part of the Mevlevi tradition, the only one of 12 dervish brotherhoods that admits women and does not require conversion to Islam.

UFO Cult
In April 1975, 26 people renounced their families, sold their possessions and left Los Angeles with the money to join Herff Applewhite and Bonnie Trusdale Nettles (a middle-aged couple also known as The Two, Bo and Peep, Winnie and Pooh, or Chip and Dale) on a UFO cult journey to "the next evolutionary kingdom." The Two now operate from a postal box in Mississippi; their 1,000 followers, who travel in small groups across the United States, get weekly reminders not to mingle too much with ordinary earthlings and to avoid sex, liquor and drugs.

Unfoldment of Kenneth G. Mills
A New Brunswick-born former concert

pianist, Kenneth G. Mills, has attracted hundreds of disciples and formed a "brotherhood" that extends from Toronto, where he now resides, to such cities as New York, San Francisco, Austin, Texas and Tucson, Arizona, where he has a second residence. Poet, author, musician and philosopher, Mills often lectures to students in rhyming couplets; he also conducts the Star-Scape Singers, who have performed at Carnegie Recital Hall and have recorded several albums, sometimes using his teachings as lyrics. His disciples see the "perfection inherent in every human being." They often live together, and may pay to study with Mills.

Unification Church

A millionaire industrialist, the Reverend Sun Myung Moon founded his Unification Church in Korea in 1954 and brought it to the United States in 1972. His 15,000 North American devotees call him the Messiah: some have stated they would die for him and according to one report have rehearsed their own suicides

The Reverend Sun Myung Moon in New York's Madison Square Garden. AP

in case such action becomes necessary – an ominous reflection of Jonestown. Their bible is Moon's *Divine Principle,* which mixes Christian fundamentalism, patriotism, puritanism and old-fashioned American anti-Communism. Moonies live together, sell flowers, beads, candles, donate their salaries to the church and collect money through more than 50 front organizations. Moon lives in godly splendor in a $750,000 home along the Hudson River, with two limousines in the drive and two yachts in the dock. There are 120 Moonie centres in North America.

Venusian Church

Ron Peterson founded the church in Seattle in 1975, but he says, "We consider Venus worship to be the oldest religion going. Venus was the goddess of love. Worship of the fertility goddess goes back to cavemen days." Activities include watching porn flicks ("hard-core religious erotica") and having orgies. About 50 people came to their New Year's party this year for special midnight services.

Vivaxis Energies International Research Society

According to Frances Nixon, who lives on Thetis Island, British Columbia, your vivaxis is your lifetime individual energy pattern which forms shortly before you are born; X-rays and certain drugs interfere with the energy flow. Nixon's 1,500 followers, concentrated in British Columbia, California and Florida, apply dried kelp powder to their bodies and use lead and cadmium inactivator boxes to restore the normal flow of energy. For these techniques, they pay $15 yearly and spend additional sums on Nixon's books. Her latest work is *Mysteries of Memory Unfold* ($4.50), although no one interested in the subject would want to miss *Born To Be Magnetic* (two volumes, $16).

The Way International

"Doctor" Victor Paul Wierwille, 61,

founded The Way in New Knoxville, Ohio, in 1942 and taught "Power for Abundant Living" courses through the '50s. He says God has talked to him, and he is the one true teacher of his time (he denies the divinity of Jesus). The Way College of Emporia, Kansas, was opened in 1974 to offer self-improvement tips and Bible studies to an enrolment of 500. Way stations in 50 American states, three provinces and more than 50 countries offer courses for donations of $100 or more if you've got it.

Worldwide Church of God
The United States is one of the 12 lost tribes of Israel, say these Christian fundamentalists who celebrate the Sabbath on Saturday. Founded in Pasadena, California, in 1934 by a former advertising executive Herbert W. Armstrong, the church collects about $70 million a year from an estimated 75,000 members. Sued for "pilfering" funds, Armstrong and top aides were recently relieved of their powers by the California attorney general's office. Armstrong's son, Garner Ted, 48, who made the church famous with his weekly radio broadcasts, got out just in time. Ousted from the church last year, he launched his own venture, The Church of God, International, with offices in Tyler, Texas, Membership, culled from a computer mailing list, is 3,000 and rising.

Bill Gladstone, journalist, *Weekend Magazine.*

Preoccupations

Looking back at the '70s, the era of the short attention span, the most outstanding preoccupation seems to have been preoccupation itself. The '60s may have been sloganized as the "do your own thing" decade, but it will go down in history as a time when masses of people marched on behalf of other people: Vietnamese villagers, Birmingham blacks at the back of the bus, not to mention the occasional self-immolation in the cause of world peace. There were also sit-ins in the college chancellor's office on behalf of liberal arts education (Bakunin, Trotsky, and Franz Fanon), but the most famous sit-ins were the Woodstock and Altamont rock festivals on behalf of the dope dealers of the world.

In the '70s we seemed to break up into smaller groups, at first touching and feeling each other, and eventually, under Werner Erhard and est, willingly submitting to tongue-lashings at weekend sessions of Dickensian cruelty that cost upwards of two hundred bucks a shock. All this was in the interest of self-development. It is facile to generalize, but the '70s seem to have been spent by most of us looking in a mirror and checking for the appearance of middle-aged hickies.

Canadians are particular suckers for this sort of hype, since they are told constantly that they have no identity, and are in grave danger of losing the country that might give them some (i.e. Canada, not the U.S.). But Canadians are reluctant faddists. Very few of them are on to the latest thing, and if they are aware of the primal scream group meeting in the church vestry for practice at four p.m., they tend, in droves, to shy away from it. Instead they will furtively attend small discussion groups at their local YM or YWCA on "The Terminal Family" or "Are Children Passé, eh?"

I feel a bit foolish pronouncing upon an entire ten years of human existence. In the first place, social history doesn't divide itself up into neat packages, even though social historians would have it so. It's easy to label the '50s as "Eisenhowerish" and the '60s as "Timothylearyish." If so, what would that make the '70s? "Idi Aminish"?

Some parlour analysts feel the '70s have been the second coming of the age of Eisenhower. They point to the return of narrow lapels and stove-pipe pants as proof. That was the age when college graduates did not burn the dean, even in effigy, but rather sucked around the registrar hoping for a good pension plan with Parke Davis. There are elements of that return to the 20-pay-life philosophy, but with rampant inflation it doesn't make much sense.

One of the non-preoccupations of the '70s was with democracy. Eisenhower's legacy was to warn his nation about the dangerous power presence of a military-industrial complex. The average citizen of the '70s has got far more than that to worry about. The old preoccupation of the '50s – atomic annihilation – is with us again, but this time it's from within rather than from without. How do you build a bomb shelter against Ontario Hydro? Most people feel powerless to deal with any of these national and multinational threats, the 1,000 unnatural shocks that flesh is heir to.

The '60s were the age of the environmentalist. Voters would tend to write their elected representatives to pass an anti-pollution law every time a loon got a migraine from an outboard motor. Now we just write them off. But in that bygone age more than ten years ago poverty was voluntary. Remember the thousands who opted out of the rat race because money just wasn't their thing? Today, for at least a million people in this country, poverty is compulsory, and most of them are quite willing to opt back into the Protestant work ethic. And as far as the environment is concerned, when it comes to the crunch, the gas tank will win every time over clean air and organic food in the hearts and minds of average citizens.

Open marriage was one of the preoccupations of the '60s. Living together became quasi-respectable, and most young couples' conception of "tieing the knot" was planning a vasectomy. In the late '70s the emphasis was on the rights and responsibilities of an illicit relationship (the "screw you, Lee Marvin syndrome"). There is no stronger indication of the Me Generation than this: women's lib in the '60s, women's Progressive Conservative in the '70s.

If the opiates of the '60s were LSD, hashish and marijuana, then the opiates of the '70s are Excedrin, marijuana and horseradish (the poor man's cocaine). But an even stronger drug has existed through both decades: the Media. For 20 years people have searched the weekend papers to find out where to go and how to act. At least, I'm *told* that people do this, but then I'm being told this by the media. Frankly, I don't believe it.

Here's a case in point. I was born in Toronto, one of the few natives, I'm sure, still living and working in the old birthplace. I read in magazines (*Fortune* and *People* and *National Lampoon*) about the cloud-capped towers of the New Ilium, the most sophisticated megalopolis in the world. I don't believe a goddam word.

Oh sure, the Royal Bank building shines in reflected sunlight like the fabled Eldorado, and all the trade schools are rapidly being transmogrified into Disco Techs, but it hasn't changed the fundamental character of the people that live here. Even immigrants, *recent* immigrants, eventually get talked into assuming the WASP uniform (WASP: white anti-sexual Protestant).

Everywhere I go in gleaming Toronto I look around me and see replicas of the denizens of the '40s that I grew up with. I read about the brittle sophisticates in the Courtyard Café and Fenton's, but I see the same tight-mouthed and presumably tight-assed squares I grew up with, and of which I am undeniably part and parcel. The same ones who get up every morning, as I do, and repress a shudder when they look in the mirror.

What will be the preoccupation of the '80s? The Bee-Gees have said it all: Stayin' alive!

Don Harron, author, actor, broadcaster, host of CBC's *Morningside.*

Despite the rain close to 100 homosexuals demonstrated on Parliament Hill, 1971 August, demanding equal rights.
Peter Bregg/CP

Gay Lib

In mid-'79 hundreds of homosexual men and woman from all corners of Canada were in Ottawa for Celebration '79, the Canadian Lesbian and Gay Rights Coalition Conference. The delegates were experienced, articulate activists demanding nothing less than full equality in society and before the law. Only eight years before, in August 1971, a small band of 100 homosexuals came to Ottawa to march on an empty Parliament (it was not in session at the time). They wanted more than the freedom to do as they wished in the privacy of their homes (established by Parliament in 1969); they wanted, as they do today, full equality of rights. While the law has not responded to gay demands during the eight years since that rainy day in Ottawa, gays have come a long way on their own. Now there are nearly 200 different gay organizations across Canada and their number is growing as more men and women are "coming out" and declaring themselves as gays. Some represent a broad spectrum of gay concerns; others are minorities within a minority – such as Gay Academic Union in Alberta; Parents of Gays in Toronto and Montreal; the Community Homophile Association of Newfoundland.

In many of its tactics, the gay liberation movement in Canada has borrowed heavily from the women's movement, the '60s peace movement, the black movement and the gay liberation movement in the United States. The official public start of the movement was the founding of the University of Toronto Homophile Association in 1969, and it was firmly put on the map with the establishment of George Hislop's Community Homophile Association of Toronto (CHAT). During the '70s the movement spread across Canada.

According to the Kinsey Institute, about ten percent of the population, male and female, is homosexual. The vast majority of these two million people in Canada are still very much "in the closet." It still takes a great deal of courage to step out. But the closet door is becoming increasingly transparent. People are looking in. A recent cartoon showed a child saying his prayers, "God Bless Mommy and Daddy, Uncle Harry and his roommate, Joe, that we're not supposed to talk about."

One of the main objectives of the gay movement, at the end of the decade, is to have the words "sexual orientation" included in any and all documents dealing with human rights, as in: " . . . no discrimination on the basis of race, creed, colour, religion or sexual orientation." This is demonstrably important in relation to jobs and housing, two basic areas where discrimination is still widespread. One celebrated case is that of John Damien, a racing steward who alleged that he was fired by the Ontario Racing Commission because it was reported that he was gay. Only the province of Quebec has a "sexual orientation" clause in its human rights legislation, but the cities of Ottawa and Toronto, as well as some unions, have adopted that policy. Of the national parties, only the NDP has such a clause.

Anita Bryant and her Canadian counterpart, the Reverend Ken Campbell, have, unintentionally, done a great deal for gay rights. Bryant, who in the late '70s showed some political muscle, is now widely regarded as an embarrassment. When the Reverend Campbell attempted to have her speak at the 1979 Central Canada Exhibition in Ottawa, the city fathers turned down the proposition.

Campbell, however, had a couple of wins to chalk up for his side. He and his followers had a hand in having works by Margaret Laurence, Alice Munro and J. D. Salinger banned from some schools in Ontario and they stirred up some anger in Toronto against Mayor John Sewell in early 1979. The newly elected mayor had attended a meeting in support of *The Body Politic,* a national gay magazine.

The story began with the brutal and sickening sex murder in 1977 of a 12-year-old shoeshine boy, Emanuel Jacques, in Toronto. Four men were charged and three convicted and sentenced to life. A few months after the murder, *The Body Politic,* exhibiting a bewildering sense of timing, published an article called, "Men Loving Boys Loving Men," which contained interviews with men whose preferences were for young boys. Three members of the Pink Triangle Press, which publishes *The Body Politic,* were charged with "using the mails to distribute indecent, immoral and scurrilous material." The trial, early in 1979, became a media event. In the course of the trial, Sewell spoke at a rally in support of *The Body Politic.* He did not refer to the article; he was there to support gay rights. *The Body Politic* men were acquitted, but the attorney-general of Ontario asked for a review of the court's decision.

Sporadic police raids on gay bars and baths punctuated the news from time to time. The most dramatic raid was the 1977 raid on Truxx, a Montreal bar. One night police armed with machine-guns swept in and arrested 146 startled patrons and charged them with being found-ins in a bawdy house. A similar incident, without machine-guns, took place in Toronto at a steambath called the Barracks. Both cases are before the courts.

George Hislop, dubbed by the Toronto *Star* as the gay mayor of Toronto, was charged as a "keeper of a common bawdy house" in the Barracks raid. Hislop, a tireless worker for gay rights and gay pride, regards all the hassle as an expected part of the struggle for liberation. He smiles, "Now, it will all work out."

Norman Hay, writer, designer.

Reproductive Freedom

Family planning, birth control, contraception, responsible parenthood: No matter what this year's socially acceptable euphemism may be, reproductive freedom is what it's all about. The freedom to control one's own destiny. To decide whether and when to have children. And how many children to have. Even today, to a lessening degree, society continues to impose pressures on men and women to reproduce themselves. "You don't want children? How selfish!" Never, "You want children for all the wrong reasons – to keep a marriage together, to guarantee love and help in your old age, because *your* parents insist. How selfish and cruel!"

It changed in the '70s. There were new laws, reflecting, but not catching up to, changing social attitudes.

It's difficult to believe that it wasn't until 1969 that then Justice Minister Pierre Elliott Trudeau introduced omnibus amendments to Canada's Criminal Code which were to drastically affect some aspects of reproductive freedom in Canada.

For the first time, it was legal to dispense and obtain contraceptive information and devices. Sympathetic physicians, nurses and social workers who advised women on how to "limit" their families were no longer law-breakers. Women were now less dependent on paternalistic doctors, many of whom dispensed moral lectures along with contraceptives. "You should wait until you're married." "You're a fine, healthy girl. You can have half a *dozen* children."

Young men continued to obtain minimal information from their fathers and their peers. Condoms were more often regarded as "a protection against disease" than as an effective method of contraception.

Dr. John Rock's discovery, the estrogen-laden birth control pill, was hailed by physicians and their female patients as a panacea, the liberating end to years of anxiety and fear of unwanted pregnancy. Simultaneously, the prophets of gloom and doom predicted that the Pill would automatically transform women into sex-mad animals, promiscuous and irresponsible. The Pill would contribute, they said, to accelerated sexual activity at an earlier and earlier age.

It was left to a handful of cautious medical researchers and women concerned with their health as well as their freedom to voice fears of the medical implications of prolonged use of the Pill. Their warnings of possible side effects and of health hazards to women in high-risk categories were pushed aside. Society, blindly accepting the obvious benefits of the Pill, also, for a time, blindly accepted that women should take total responsibility for protecting themselves against unwanted pregnancy. The same society, which a decade before had pressured all young single women to remain virgin, at all costs, now tolerated, and even encouraged the *"Playboy* philosophy." And the pressure on women now was to be willing, eager sex kittens, always ready to respond. Men were pressured to collect scalps, to keep "score" and to be free of the "old hangups."

August, 1969, also saw passage of a "liberal" policy on abortion, an on-paper reform outmoded before it was passed. The new law made abortion illegal, except when performed in an approved or accredited hospital, after a therapeutic abortion committee of at least three doctors certified that continuation of the pregnancy would or would be likely to endanger the life or health of the pregnant woman. No hospital, however, was *required* to establish such a therapeutic abortion committee, no woman applying for an abortion had the right to be heard by the committee considering her application, or the right of appeal against a turn-down. Almost ten years after passage of "the reform that hardly was" fewer than one-third of publicly financed Canadian hospitals have even established committees. Access of Canadian women to the therapeutic abortion procedure varies widely, depending on location, socio-economic standing and, today, according to the composition of the hospital board of directors, which may or may not be opposed to abortion. There have been mammoth confrontations between anti-abortion and pro-choice forces in such widely separated communities as Scarborough, St. Thomas, Windsor and Vancouver.

Montreal physician Dr. Henry Morgentaler carried his personal battle against Canada's inadequate and schizophrenic abortion law all the way to the Supreme Court of Canada, and lost. Morgentaler, who had for several years operated a free-standing abortion clinic in a Montreal suburb, took on the Quebec political and judicial establishment by openly declaring his civil disobedience of section 251 of the Criminal Code.

He was charged in 1973 and acquitted in October, 1974, by a jury representative of the community he served. When that acquittal was overruled by the Quebec Court of Appeal, he was sentenced to 18 months in prison. And, in March, 1975, for the first time in Canadian history, the Supreme Court of Canada upheld reversal of a jury acquittal, and Morgentaler went to jail. Shortly afterward, he was tried on a second count, and again acquitted. Public outcry forced passage of the "Morgentaler amendment" which prevented an appeal court from reversing a jury acquittal. Morgentaler was freed in 1976 by then-Justice Minister Ron Basford, who ordered yet another trial in the first case. Again, a francophone, Catholic, working-class jury acquitted him of wrongdoing. The Lévesque government, elected shortly afterward, dropped the remaining charges against Morgentaler, declared the federal law "unenforceable," and called for repeal. Today, Morgentaler and other Quebec doctors operate free-standing clinics with the tacit acceptance of their provincial government. The Criminal Code, however, remains unchanged.

Several provinces have funded the establishment of birth-control clinics in public-health units. They are understaffed, underbudgeted and overworked. In Toronto, a family planning division operates under the direction of Dr. Peter Cole, and for the past three years, Toronto mayors have proclaimed "Birth Control Week," during which information is available to the public and high school students in their schools.

A noticeable and powerful backlash through such organizations as Renaissance has succeeded in blocking sex education programs, and in some communities banning books, but steady progress is being made.

The political decision makers have still to catch up with the rest of us. Family planning programs at the federal, provincial and municipal levels are underfinanced and frequently ignored by the people who created them. But our children have more information and more choices than we had. Perhaps, in a generation or two, the hope of reproductive freedom will become reality.

Eleanor Wright Pelrine, author, journalist.

Sexual Politics

Come Together was the siren song of the newly liberated 1960s.

But we didn't.

As any survivor of the 1970s knows, the real order of the day was coming apart, as men and women in the thousands lurched off to new mates, yoga retreats, singles' bars, disco binges, the Moonies, marathons, body awareness, gay lifestyles, mid-life crises, cocaine, God and celibacy, to name just a few detours from the Road to True Understanding promised by gurus a decade earlier.

"Next comes bigamy," says anthropologist Lionel Tiger. "It saves time."

Both sides, it seemed, had fought in the Sexual Revolution and lost. The 1970s did not bring men and women eye-to-eye, but hand-to-hand in combat fiercer and more deadly than ever before in history.

The battle of the sexes had spread from bedroom to boardroom. And as desegregation made it impossible for men and women to avoid each other, their anger, anxiety, tension and hostility had unlimited opportunities to explode. At the same time, the most intimate quarrels took on grave political significance.

In the 1970s the personal became political with a vengeance. And sexual politics became a banana republic of coups with very little billing in between (except through lawyers concerned with hard cash).

In the midst of this chaotic emotional sabre-rattling, neither side won more than a few minor triumphs, and the underlying power structure remained the same, unbalanced, but quivering from the onslaught.

The personal rage expressed by the two warring factions was no more than a scream of despair rising from the torn roots of power.

And why not? After thousands of years of familiarity and contempt, men and women were looking at each other with new – and sometimes blackened – eyes.

Women, used to getting "their way" by catering to men's stomachs and other easily satisfied organs, found themselves out on a limb when demanding their own piece of the action.

Men, who wielded the power of the pocketbook, were hurt, baffled and angry when their mates "mistook" protection for oppression and returned it unopened.

No longer perched on the happy hunting ground of mutual exploitation, male-female relationships now hung in mid-air.

Women had declared independence, but equality remained only a tantalizing rumour.

Men continued to control the wealth, government, law, religion, ethics and opinion of the liberated society.

Women – a step up from the Old Plantation of bed, babies and baking – were now the poor blacks of the new order. Free, but not quite Folks.

Gay lib apart, a man was a man for all that. But a woman was still the Other in a man's world.

Like newly freed slaves, women had sacrificed their traditional right to paternal care and concern; but they *were* at liberty to compete with the more advantaged for jobs, demand economic justice from those whose interests were threatened by it, and learn to win by gluing on the masks of the men in power. (Nor were the masks easy to remove. As the upside-down British Tory joke went, "Do you want an old woman to run the country – or will you support Margaret Thatcher?")

A woman might compete for power, but to win it, she risked becoming as unsexed as the murder-bent Lady Macbeth. Any "liberated" woman who slipped out from under man's domestic thumb could expect a few free backhanders.

"Democracy and feminism have now stripped the veil of courtly convention from the subordination of women, revealing sexual antagonisms formerly concealed by the feminine mystique," says that astute chronicler of the '70s, Christopher Lasch.

In the 1970s a man was forced to open the door for a woman in the marketplace – but he could slam it in her face with impunity at the supermarket. (A pertinent cartoon shows two suburban men watching an over-parcelled woman struggling out of a shop door: "I guess neither of us is pig enough to help her.")

It's no wonder that women who added up their relatively small material gains against their large emotional losses felt outraged and cheated. Some put on white boots and vinyl hairdos and tried to trip backward into the Total Womanhood of the '50s. Others walked an angry tightrope between "feminine" submissiveness and feminist revolt.

The death of etiquette, in fact, was no minor milestone in the new power struggle of the sexes. Disregarding Emily Post punctilio, courtesy can be seen as institutionalized caring, the public expression of concern for a fellow human being. But as public niceties were thrown aside, with them went private care, concern and commitment.

Freed from the "emotional debris" of love, marriage and children, sex was declared Fun and Good for You – and, lord knows, cheaper than tennis.

"Having sex," as columnist Russell Baker complained, replaced "making love" in the consumer-bent 1970s vocabulary. To turn down a helping was as impolite as refusing the host's homemade pâté.

The Pill, launched as the ultimate weapon in the sexual revolution, did nothing to balance the power between men and women. Rather, it widened the gap.

Men, resenting women's apparent freedom from the constraints of pregnancy (and thus traditional morality), handed over all responsibility for birth control – and for their partners. Pregnancy became a form of venereal disease affecting only women: easy to catch if you don't use the proper hygiene.

Able to wolf down man after man without fear of embarrassing procreative bulges, women soon lost their appetites. And by the end of the '70s, the *Hite Report* had effectively buried the myth of rapacious female promiscuity with hundreds of testimonies to a deeper need for trust, affection and intimacy.

Alas, too late was the cry. Not only the politics, but the game had changed. And neither side was very sure of the rules. Gone was the woman's scoreboard of commitment from a man (ten points marriage, five points going steady, one point red roses). And vanished was the man's score card of sexual conquest, the winning of something valued, guarded and sometimes forbidden.

Women, with no means of coercing commitment, handed over their sexual services for nothing (known by cynics as the Feminine Mistake). But men, who gained nothing very much from free love but cheap sex, felt empty and cheated.

The new score of the '70s was the elusive ideal of Love. ("Mention it first and you lost," says a disgruntled veteran of the decade.) A good score went to the most detached partner in a relationship; an outstanding score to the one who remained coolly uncommitted while basking in the emotional warmth of the other's wholehearted devotion.

But no amount of take versus give could put the Humpty Dumpty of traditional security back together again. Or remove sex from the harsh arena of politics, like the magical withering away of the Marxist state.

The fact is, the sexual revolution was only a quarter turn in the deeply held attitudes of men and women – a small disruption in a social caste system that has kept down half of humanity for 2,000 years, and which needs deep and fundamental changes to rectify.

If the sexual politics of the past ten years have been vicious and violent, they have also brought the slow cauldron of history to an unprecedentedly rapid boil. But pursuing solutions (other than bloodshed) at top speed can only change the order superficially.

If in the 1980s the voice of the turtle vanishes from the land, we can blame our own greed for turtle soup.

Olivia Ward, journalist.

One of the most disturbing books published in the '70s was Brenda Rabkin's *Growing Up Dead.* It reveals that suicide is the second largest killer, after accidents, of young people in Canada, and that for every suicide, there are an estimated 100 attempts. In the past decade the number of young Canadians who have killed themselves has tripled. "Adolescent suicide," says the author, "is very democratic, in that it knows no barriers of sex, religion, race, or economic or social standing. Any young person who desires it is an acceptable candidate."

Drug Busts

At the end of the last decade, in 1969, the federal Liberals responded to the growing phenomenon of adolescent drug use in the only way they knew how: they appointed a royal commission. A year later, in the spring of 1970, the LeDain Commission produced its "interim" report, in which it recommended that the penalty for the offence of simple possession of *any* drug be reduced to a maximum fine of $100. The government failed to reply, and in 1972, in its "Cannabis" report, the LeDain Commission took the next logical step, recommending the complete repeal of the prohibition against the simple possession of marijuana and hashish. There has been no such repeal. In fact, apart from a few procedural niceties, there have been no substantive changes in Canadian drug laws since 1961, each government reasoning that it's electorally more advantageous to continually promise drug reform than to actually deliver it.

In the decade since the LeDain Commission's first exercise of naive realism, more than 350,000 persons have been arrested and more than 250,000 convicted for cannabis – marijuana and hashish – offences. Simple possession accounts for about 90 percent of these cases. In fact, simple possession of cannabis accounts for about 25 percent of the increase in the official "crime rate" during the '70s. The typical cannabis offender is young, poor and, the way things presently stand, burdened with a criminal record for the rest of his or her life.

In light of official conceit, professional ignorance and public apathy, the "big" bust of the 1970s must be the bust that happens more than 100 times every day: your basic victim of official reefer madness. To these quarter-million martyrs to the cause of psychotropic self-determination goes the award for Bust of the Decade, just recognition of the role of the little guy in inspiring the expenditure of between $60 and $100 million a year in the ineffectual persecution of Victorian demons.

Shadowed by this extraordinary achievement are a small number of individual prosecutions of sufficient import to garner national interest. Five, in no particular order, warrant brief mention.

As an indication of the enormity of the market and the financial interests involved: the RCMP, in May, 1979, reported its largest dope seizure of all time: 30 tons (about 60 million joints' worth) of Colombian marijuana, officially "street"-valued at $50 million. Acting on a tip from the American Drug Enforcement Agency, 50 Mounties, 300 Canadian Forces personnel,

Members of the newly formed LeDain Commission were introduced by Health Minister John Munro at an Ottawa news conference, June 1969. CP

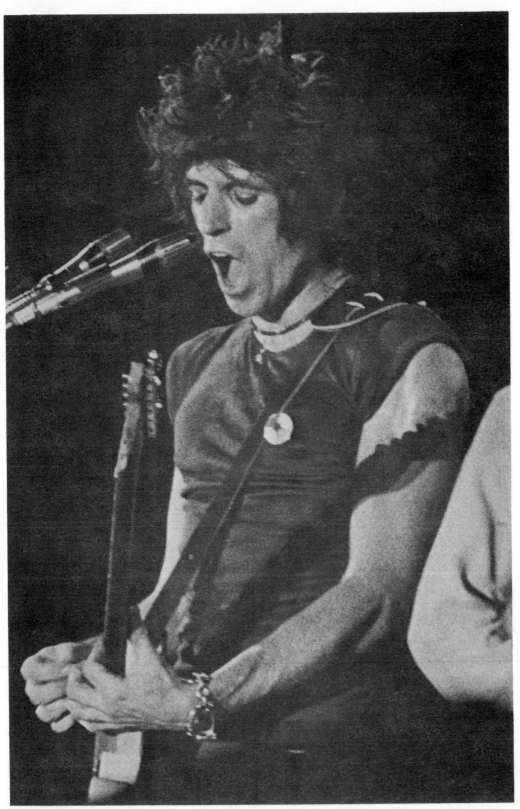

Keith Richards at his April 22, 1979 benefit concert for The Canadian National Institute for the Blind. CP

an Argus tracking aircraft, a destroyer-escort, two police boats and a Zodiac assault craft converged on the hapless importers at Sidney Inlet on Vancouver Island. Ten months earlier about 13.5 tons of marijuana, valued at $20 million, were seized about ten kilometres away. Interestingly, narcotics police estimate that they're able to intercept less than ten percent of the amount of cannabis annually smuggled into Canada.

For years Robert W. Rowbotham ("Rosie" to his friends) occupied a near-the-top spot on the RCMP narcotics hit list. Rosie, through the '60s, had become something of a folk-hero in the dope underground, at one time being the single major supplier of quality smoke to the inhabitants of once-notorious Rochdale College in central Toronto. When finally charged with conspiracy to import an alleged ton of Lebanese hashish, Rosie mounted a spirited defence which included evidence of illegal police wire-tapping, character witnesses of the caliber of Norman Mailer, and the claim that despite an extensive history of marijuana trafficking he had never sold so much as a gram of hashish. Convicted after a lengthy trial, Rosie was finally sentenced in June, 1977. Asked if he had anything to say before sentence was passed, Rosie refused to recant and, instead, compared himself to great religious leaders, spoke of his service to the people, and delivered a lengthy paean to the joys of cannabis. For his frankness he was rewarded with a 14-year term of imprisonment. Appeal papers were filed, but the price of justice being what it is (the trial transcripts alone were estimated to cost $25,000), Rosie continues to tread time from behind bars.

Despite some stiff competition, celebrity bust of the decade must fall to Keith Richard, lead guitarist of the Rolling Stones and world-class ex-heroin addict and general debauchee. In Toronto with the band to record some live tracks at the El Mocambo, Richard had the misfortune to be holding about an ounce of almost pure heroin when the local narcs dropped into his hotel suite one spring day in 1977. Subsequently, the Crown prosecutor agreed to drop the far more serious charge of possession for the purpose of trafficking in return for a guilty plea to the charge of simple possession, for which Richard was sentenced to perform two concerts for the Canadian National Institute for the Blind. Thanks chiefly to the political opportunism of the likes of John Diefenbaker and Ontario Attorney-General Roy McMurtry, the federal Department of Justice appealed the sentence (Canada being the only western society which permits the state more than one kick at the sentencing can), seeking a term of imprisonment. In the interim, Richard fulfilled the terms of his probation: withdrawing from heroin and performing two concerts, with the Rolling Stones, for mixed blind and sighted audiences at an Oshawa hockey arena.

In the late '70s, Calgary customs agents had an opportunity to really show their stuff. Keith Stroup, founder and director of the Washington-based National Organization for the Reform of Marijuana Laws (NORML) and the man probably more responsible for American "decriminalization" than any other single individual, had never been arrested for a drug offence before a Canadian NORML speaking engagement brought him to Alberta. During what is fancifully called a "routine inspection" at Calgary airport, his good luck ended as customs authorities discovered a couple of joints' worth of marijuana. Returning for his trial a few months later, Stroup was once again found in possession of a small amount of cannabis at the same airport, thus lending some credence to the hypothesized relationship between drug use and mental derangement. Not to be outdone by imperialist reformers, the founder of NORML-Canada, one George Baker, was sentenced to jail for cannabis trafficking in Vancouver in the spring of 1979.

Ever wary of the power of ideas disseminated by other than its own official organs, the government, in 1977, resorted to an obscure section of the customs regulations to prohibit the importation of *High Times* into Canada. *High Times* was, and still is for its American readers, a combination *Consumer Reports* and *Life* magazine of the drug culture. There are articles on hash smuggling in Nepal, international market reports, "High Witness News" accounts of the latest busts and scams, centrefolds of microscopically enlarged cocaine crystals and advertisements for everything from THC-extractors to nitrous oxide dispensers. American narcs are obviously embarrassed by the magazine (although they do subscribe), but it enjoys the same constitutional protection as such para-military advocates as *Soldier of Fortune* and such soft-core porn as *Penthouse*. Constitutional protection of civil liberties has never been Canada's long suit, so while *Soldier of Fortune* and *Penthouse* experience healthy Canadian newsstand sales *High Times* remains the victim of some anonymous bureaucrat's typically misplaced zeal. Drugs, it appears, constitute an even greater threat to the nation than terrorism or sex.

Finally, a single non-bust of the decade. In her best-seller, *Beyond Reason,* the sometimes-wife of Canada's recently deposed prime minister, Margaret Trudeau, confesses that the pressures of Sussex Drive were so great that she was driven to smoking several joints a day. Rather than arresting her, an observant RCMP – agent advised her to mask the odour with incense. Wise counsel that several million Canadians would do well to heed.

Mel Mezzrow, drugologist.

In 1962 there were 31,000 motorbikes registered in Canada. By 1974 this number zoomed to 320,000. In 1979 almost half a million of us are riding motorcycles.

Diets – Fad & Otherwise

Diets, diets and more diets. In the 1970s there were dozens of fad and reliable diets in vogue for weight conscious Canadians. The '80s will bring even more. Beware – be wise before you try.

Lacto Ova Vegetarian Diet, from *Diet for a Small Planet,* by F. M. Lappe

The lacto-ovo vegetarian diet is one that consists chiefly of fruits, vegetables and grain products but it does include eggs and dairy products excluding meat, poultry and fish. The diets of the lacto-ovo vegetarians can easily provide sufficient amounts of protein that is adequate in both quantity and quality. If the mixing of plant protein foods is done carefully, combinations of lower-quality protein foods (foods low or lacking in one or more essential amino acids) can produce mixtures of about the same nutritional value as high-quality animal protein food. With the careful choosing of foods rich in iron and B vitamins nutritional status will be maintained. The sample menu that was evaluated for nutrient content was suggested by the author in *Diet for a Small Planet.* This diet is not categorized as a reducing diet but as a meat alternative eating plan.

Nutritional analysis shows a reduction in the number of servings from the meat and milk groups. This omission may partially explain the deficiencies in thiamin (60-64 percent of need for men and 81-90 percent for women), riboflavin (72-76 percent of need for men and 100 percent for women 16-35), niacin (50-55 percent of need for men and 71-76 percent for women) and iron (78 percent of need for women). The sample menu, while not a weight reduction regimen, only provided 44-46 percent of the caloric requirement for men and 59-62 percent for women. The reduction in the total amount of food also contributes greatly to the vitamin and mineral deficiencies as well as to any ensuing weight loss. Additional servings may overcome nutritional deficiencies of this sample diet.

Difficulties may arise if this diet schedule is followed over an extended period of time, due to the inadequate supply of essential nutrients. This is not to say that this would be the case for all lacto-ovo vegetarian eating plans.

The Quick Weight Loss Diet, from the *Doctor's Quick Weight Loss Diet* by Irwin Maxwell Stillman, M.D., and Samm Sinclair Baker

This diet is designed to take weight off quickly. On the average, an overweight person should lose five to ten percent of his weight the first week. Dr. Stillman says this rapid weight loss should have no ill effects; however, fatigue can be expected. The diet consists mainly of boiled, baked or broiled lean meats, poultry and fish as well as eggs, cottage cheese and other cheeses made with skim milk. The dieter is expected to eat as much as he wishes of these specific food items. Coffee and tea without cream or sugar and diet drinks are allowed as desired. At least eight glasses (ten ounces) of water *must* be consumed every day. Dr. Stillman believes that this is an integral part of the specific internal process put into motion by this diet. He goes on to say that the burning of body fat leaves waste products that must be washed out of the system by the water. He recommends that a vitamin and mineral supplement be taken daily, although he claims that the diet is not deficient in these nutrients, and that sufficient vitamin C can be obtained from the seafood. (The amount of vitamin C in seafood has not yet been determined.)

Assessment of the diet pattern shows a complete absence of food from the bread and cereal, and fruit and vegetable groups. Only one milk serving is provided in Dr. Stillman's menu. The consequent inadequacy of nutrients associated with these foods is no surprise: carbohydrates (17 percent of need), calcium (76 percent of need for women 16-18 and 76 percent of need for all others), vitamin A (47 percent of need for men and 62-72 percent for women), thiamin (36-38 percent of need for men and 49-54 percent for women) and vitamin C (13 percent of need). The sample menu is calorically deficient (47-59 percent of need for men and 67-72 percent of need for women) and will result in the desired weight loss.

In view of the nutrient inadequacies, this diet might prove harmful if followed even for a brief period to time. The diet fails to teach users how to select the variety of foods necessary for good nutrition through sound eating habits. Because so few calories are prescribed, weight loss would be likely for anyone who could tolerate Dr. Stillman's Quick Weight Loss Diet.

The High Roughage Reducing Diet
from *The Save Your Life Diet,* by David Reuben, M.D.

The author claims that the "basic principle of this reducing diet is to normalize the functioning of the digestive system, not to derange it as most other weight reduction diets do." Dr Reuben goes on to say that "once the body is given a chance to operate the way it was designed to, it will automatically regulate its weight to within the normal range." The menu plan is simple and straightforward, eliminating all low-roughage foods, all ultraprocessed flour products and all refined sugar. The diet recommends eating high-roughage foods, including whole-grain cereal products, high fibre and raw fruits and vegetables, and nuts and seeds whenever possible and moderate amounts of low-fat meat, fish and poultry. He recommends moderate amounts of fats and oils and the substitution of molasses and honey for refined sugar. Other suggestions include the reduction of hot and spicy foods, avoidance of "synthetic" foods and all alcoholic beverages, as these will "under-

mine" the entire diet plan. An indispensable part of the diet is the addition of unprocessed miller's bran in the average amount of two teaspoons three times a day. Reuben emphasizes that no food amounts are specified, realizing that "anyone who really wants to lose weight will eat as little as necessary to feel full" and "as long as the diet is high in fibre an extra helping of meat and brown rice is not going to make that much difference." The final emphasis concerning the diet is that it is a lifetime menu plan designed to restore the body to its normal functioning and "incidently to its normal weight."

The Canada Food Guide evaluation of the diet shows a slight imbalance of food group choices – one meat serving is substituted for one milk serving. This could account for the inadequate supply of calcium and thiamin.

Overall, the diet prescribes a food intake that supplies a nutrient intake that is nearly normal. It proposes a diet pattern that leads to basically wise food choices. However, over an extended period of time, difficulties could arise due to lack of sufficient calcium. The diet is calorically deficient (48-54 percent of need for men and 69-73 percent of need for women). This decreased caloric intake in itself will result in weight loss. The author also advises the ample use of bran to promote rapid intestinal motility claiming that this, too, will result in weight loss.

Dr. Atkins' Diet Revolution
from *Dr. Atkins' Diet Reduction, The High Calorie Way to Staying Thin Forever,* by Dr. Robert C. Atkins

Dr. Atkins prescribes a high-protein, high-fat, low-carbohydrate diet, which tries to exclude as many carbohydrates as possible, actually approaching a no-carbohydrate meal plan. He believes that people who tend to gain weight are "allergic" to carbohydrates and eating carbohydrates causes hunger to increase. By eliminating carbohydrates from the diet, Atkins maintains that the body is forced to burn fat as a source of energy. Dr. Atkins goes on to say that each individual has a threshold level of body carbohydrate intake beyond which their body ceases to burn fat for energy.

Low carbohydrate diets force the body to use fat stores for energy. These fat stores are metabolized to yield two carbon units which are then used either for energy production or (if present in excess amounts) condensed into carbon fragments, called ketone bodies, which the body then excretes in the urine. Dr. Atkins says that the state of ketosis is highly desirable since it causes appetite depression. However he does not go on to explain the undesirable aspects of the ketotic state. These include calcium depletion, dehydration, weakness, nausea and kidney failure or stones, gout or gouty arthritis and possible artheriosclerosis in susceptible individuals.

There are five levels in the diet, each with increasing amounts of carbohydrate. The dieter begins at level one, a diet virtually carbohydrate-free, and gradually progresses from level to level, seeking the one that will allow him his maximum carbohydrate intake combined with continued fat burning capacity. This will be the dieter's lifetime maintenance regimen. Dr. Atkins recommends that megadoses of vitamin and mineral supplements be taken daily to help fulfill the nutrient requirements not supplied by this diet revolution.

The Canada Food Guide evaluation shows a complete omission of the bread and cereal group combined with a reduced number of servings from the milk, fruit and vegetable groups. In addition, a vitamin A source is provided. Omission of the bread and cereal group contributes to deficient intake of carbohydrate (10 percent of need), thiamin (80-85 percent of need for men) and niacin (80-88 percent of need for men). The milk group shortage causes calcium (75 percent of need) and riboflavin (72-76 percent of need for men) to be extremely low. The reduction in the number of fruit and vegetable servings results in the accompanying deficiencies of vitamin A (68 percent of need for men). Iron and vitamin A are barely adequate for women and vitamin C is at the base level for men and women.

In summary, this diet does not supply the needed amounts of nutrients to maintain proper health, and prolonged or intermittent use may result in hazards to health. The diet does not propose a diet pattern that leads to wise food choices.

Weight Watchers Diet

from the *Weight Watchers Program Cookbook*, Weight Watchers International

The Weight Watchers program has been designed to assist and educate the dieter in new and sound eating habits. The program provides reducing, levelling (ten pounds from goal weight) and maintenance (at goal weight) diets for teenage and adult men and women based on a food exchange system. The combination of social and educational stimuli has resulted in the successful loss of excess weight and the maintenance of desired weight for many people.

Evaluation of the sample meal plan shows a shift in food group choices. For women two meat servings replace two bread and cereal, while for men four meat portions are added. All nutrients are substantially provided for in the diet and the reasonable caloric deficiency will result in weight loss.

Joan Fielden, journalist.

The Faith Eaters:
Health Food as The Way,
The Truth & The Life

I can't remember exactly when I first contracted food guilt, but I think it was some time in the late 1960s. Food guilt is a common affliction, of course, among those who, trying to lose weight, eat that forbidden slice of pie. But my own food guilt had nothing to do with weight. It was a handbill that did it, a manifesto for some natural food outfit that I happened to be looking at one day, along with some other literature of the counter-culture. The first sentence read something like this: *So you enjoyed that hamburger you just ate, did you?* I hadn't eaten a hamburger for days when I read this ominous rhetorical question, but already I could feel vague stirrings of guilt. *Well, let us tell you just what was in that hamburger,* it went on, and then ticked off a horrifying list of chemical additives – along with their dire effects on the human body – which were supposedly in that innocuous patty of beef, and the soft white roll that covered it.

The point, naturally, was that you couldn't expect to remain healthy if you ate things like this. You wouldn't keel over or anything, at least not for years, but you could expect to catch every "bug" that went around, experience low energy and generally feel lousy. After I finished reading the handbill, I knew there were certain kinds of food I would never be able to eat from then on without feeling at least a little guilty. As time went on, the guilt increased every time I consumed any processed, refined or chemically treated food.

Of course, in one sense it was inevitable that the various anti-capitalist, anti-technological, back-to-the-land movements of the late 1960s would spawn a "natural food" movement. And yet the concern over the food we eat has out-lasted the counterculture. More and more people are beginning to look at the list of ingredients on the side of the cereal box with suspicion; to wonder whether they should really pick up that frozen pizza at the supermarket. This does not mean that people are necessarily eating better. It does mean that food guilt is spreading all the time.

I myself became something of a reluctant convert to health food. Reluctant because sunflower seeds were never my idea of a tasty snack. Raw salads did not excite me. But I had to admit that the people I knew who were on rigorous health food diets looked better. They seemed more supple, more lovely. Even though some of them were well into middle age they gave few signs of acquiring those traits our society associates with middle age – bodies that sag and wrinkle like half-deflated volley balls. Of course, there were more public examples, like the 81-year-old prime minister of India, a strict adherent of the "nutritional path" to health, who took over the government of the world's largest democracy at an age when North Americans are widely considered to be fit enough for little more than playing canasta.

Following are some of the varied tenets of the health food movement. People who heed them religiously feel that the improvement in their diet has given them a certain vitality, a certain spiritual lift that makes life appear brighter than it did before. They feel they have strengthened their bodies against ailments ranging from arthritis to arteriosclerosis. On this question conventional medicine, of course, has its own views and in many cases disagrees adamantly with the ideas of illness and healing presented by health food authorities. It is not the objective of this article to make claims one way or another. Some of the ideas are obviously sounder than others. The individual who is really concerned with finding out which make sense and which do not will obviously have to read and study far more material than can be presented here – and then make his own decisions about what he wants to eat.

Mr. Natural in the Raw

For people on the "nutritional path" to health, there is nothing more important than learning to love fruits and vegetables. It is true that civilization, which has developed the TV dinner, among other technological wonders, does not encourage us to love them (there's more money in onion-flavoured potato chips). But to acquire a real taste for them instead of "convenience" foods would be like acquiring a taste for Duke Ellington instead of the Bay City Rollers, if we lived on music.

Most health food enthusiasts eat their fruits and vegetables raw, following a basic rule of thumb that at least three-quarters of the foods they eat should be raw foods. Raw vegetables in the form of salads are considered excellent. Raw vegetable juices are even better. One gains nutrients without a lot of bulk. A spinach and carrot juice cocktail may not look appetizing, but to the person hot on the trail of natural food, it's a treat for the body and the soul.

When health food people do cook their vegetables, they almost never boil them because they feel a high percentage of nutrients simply dissolves in the water. They also consider peeling potatoes and vegetables unwise because so many mineral salts are located directly under the skin. Such cautions are observed particularly when eating fruits and vegetables from the supermarket, because people concerned about natural foods are convinced that the quality of this produce is not terribly high to begin with. Most of the produce is grown on huge farms – vegetable factories, as it were – complete with chemically treated soil and a variety of pesticides.

Anybody who writes about health food considers these "inorganically grown" fruits and vegetables to be a desecration of a basic good in life, like taking the classics of literature and rewriting them in the style of Jacqueline Susann. The label "organically grown" (grown with natural fertilizers, with no chemical pesticides, and on soil that has not been chemically treated) has now become almost a fetish for many people, who insist that the non-organically grown produce is tasting worse each passing year.

They will tell you about pesticide sprays that you can't wash off (they're absorbed into the food), and how the poisons in these sprays accumulate in your body over the years until perhaps one day the doctor tells you that some of your internal organs are now acting kind of strange. For your peace of mind you'll either have to tell these people to shut up, or else start shopping for produce at markets where they sell the organic brand.

Git Along, Little Dogies

Almost nobody who is serious about health food ever eats any meat. Some health food enthusiasts have been known to make themselves unpopular by talking about "warmed-over turkey corpses" when their friends sit down to their Thanksgiving dinner. Still, to these enthusiasts, meat itself is not as harmful as, say, the breakfast cereal so many kids eat every morning. The main trouble with most meat today, in their view, is that you don't know what chemicals are in it.

In any case, it is certainly untrue that you need meat as a source of protein. There are too many vigorous. and hearty vegetarians walking around who don't even think about where they're going to get their protein, to put much stock in meat as a protein source. Nuts, cereals, soybeans and cheese seem to provide them with all the protein they need – along with a steady diet of fresh fruits and vegetables. (Technically speaking, vegetarians who eat dairy products like milk and cheese are not true vegetarians, but "lacto-vegetarians." True vegetarians *do* need to exercise more care in making sure they get "complete" proteins, by combining protein foods like nuts and rice correctly.)

There are a variety of reasons vegetarians come up with for abstaining from meat, many of them quasi-moral or quasi-spiritual. One theory is that not eating meat forces our inner "astral" bodies to produce fat on their own, from within our physical bodies, instead of relying on the fat from animal meats. This activity helps the astral body come to full life, as it were. It's a hard theory to explain in a few sentences. Most vegetarians don't worry too much about the exact rationale for giving up meat, anyway – they just give it up, and don't seem to miss it.

White Death, Here is Thy Sting

If you're an average North American you're going to consume about 120 pounds of sugar this year, according to Dr. Emmanuel Cheraskin, in his book *Psychodietetics*. This is an interesting statistic, because if there is one thing that all health food advocates are agreed on, it is that sugar is one of the worst things you can put into your body. It doesn't matter if you deliberately avoid things like soft drinks, cakes, cookies and candy – obvious sources of sugar. If you eat *any* packaged breakfast cereal, consume *any* ketchup, bottled salad dressing or canned soup, you're likely eating sugar. Just check the list of ingredients on the can, bottle or package, and you'll probably find the presence of what is fondly known in health food circles as "white death."

The reason sugar is considered so harmful by health food proponents is that it's a refined product devoid of minerals or vitamins (I am not talking about sugar found naturally in fruits and vege-

tables, the sugar found in honey or molasses or maple syrup – this kind of sugar, of course, is accompanied by all sorts of minerals and vitamins).

Some health food disciples, such as Dr. Cheraskin, feel that refined sugar, because it does not come with these elements, may combine with minerals and vitamins in your own body, in ways that do your body harm. Jerry Green, a Toronto doctor who emphasizes nutrition in his practice periodically blasts the medical establishment, says flatly, "All the links of the chain are not known exactly – how sugar is harmful – but we know sugar *is* harmful." Many of Dr. Green's views are, however, strongly disputed by members of the medical profession.

Another reason sugar is bad for you, according to people like Dr. Green, is that it causes a condition called hypoglycemia, or low blood sugar. Refined sugar paradoxically lowers the sugar content of your bloodstream because it stimulates an over-secretion of insulin, the hormone that regulates the sugar content. Low blood sugar, or hypoglycemia, may often be responsible for such symptoms as depression, a sense of lethargy or listlessness, headaches, irritability, restlessness, muscle cramps and blurred vision. Again, all this would be hotly disputed by many orthodox nutritionists, who believe that hypoglycemia is comparatively rare. Dr. Green and health food proponents believe that it is very common indeed.

Table salt is another condiment frowned upon by health foodists. Even conventional doctors have steered people who have high blood pressure, or weight problems, away from salt. Health food advocates go further and maintain that you should not eat *any* table salt – mainly because of certain chemical additives in it. They feel that anyone can get along just fine on the natural salts found in fruits and vegetables.

The Drinking Man's Diet

An important part of health food wisdom emphasizes the need our body has for good clean water. Over half our body is composed of water, after all, and bodily fluids play an essential role, not only in digestion but also in circulation, respiration, the elimination of wastes, the maintenance of the correct temperature and even in the lubrication of joints and the preservation of muscle tone. Although we get a great deal of water from solid foods, people generally don't drink nearly enough liquids, say health food believers. They suggest, for example, that you drink a glass of water every morning upon rising. (They do not suggest, however, that you drink liquids with your meals, as they feel the liquid tends to dilute the digestive secretions of the stomach.)

Here we encounter a fierce controversy among these advocates over whether we should drink distilled water (water that is condensed from steam but pure H2O) or mineral water (water from natural mineral springs). They are unanimously agreed, by the way, that we shouldn't drink ordinary tap water – too many weird chemicals. Distilled water advocates argue that distilled water is utterly devoid of "ash" content – carbonate and lime compounds that hasten the aging process by hardening tissues and bones. According to such advocates, if these compounds aren't ossifying your bones and tissues they're probably off somewhere bothering your kidneys and your arteries.

Mineral water devotees such as Paavo Airola, a European naturopathic ("natural healing") doctor, answer right back that inorganic minerals *are* good for you, and point to people like the Hunzas, an isolated tribe in the Himalayas who drink mineral water all the time and are totally free of hardening of the arteries, as well as kidney stones and gallstones. Distilled water advocate Paul Bragg, a health food writer given to bathing in wintery seas when he was pushing 90, pointed to people like the South Seas Islanders whom he met in his youthful travels. These people, he assured us, drank only rainwater they collected, water that was reasonably free of minerals, and they were beautiful specimens of manhood and womanhood. This is probably one of those health food controversies that will last until the end of time.

The Mysterious Feast

The mystical wing of the health food movement views diet in the light of "Spiritual Science." Spiritual Science is more an art than a science. As with all arts, how much of it you accept depends on your personal taste. There are some people with a pronounced relish for it, and they accept such basic tenets of Spiritual Science as relating diet to personal temperament.

Writers Rudolph and Grethe Hauschka suggest that this can be done by determining whether one is a choleric, phlegmatic, sanguine or melancholic type. These categories, modelled roughly on the four basic temperaments of ancient Greek medicine, describe people who are variously affected by certain bodily fluids, or "humours" – yellow gall, black gall, mucus and blood. If you are a hot-blooded, quick-tempered individual, you may be a choleric, say the Hauschkas, suffering from a preponderance of yellow gall. If you are one of our heavy brooders, you may be a melancholic, suffering from too much black gall. A placid and slow-moving type, and you may be a phlegmatic, suffering from mucus. If on the other hand, you are scattered and unstable, you may be a "sanguine" type – not in the dictionary meaning of someone hopeful or confident, but in the Hauschka meaning of someone suffering from a predominance of the blood humour.

According to the dietary calculations

of Spiritual Science, fiery-natured cholerics should eat a lot of light-leaf and stem vegetables, and such watery vegetables as squash and cucumber. These tend to cool the blood, along with fruits, which are considered helpful to the circulation. Sanguine people could benefit from an emphasis on phlegmatic foods, like nuts and olives, and heavy cereals. Phlegmatics need fairly sharp foods like radishes, onions, chives and heavily acidic fruits. Melancholics could sweeten up on foods like tropical fruits, blossom teas and honey. These, by the way, are prescribed especially for children between the ages of 7 and 14, if they seem to be leaning too much in the direction of one type.

Astrology also links diet to personality. There are specific mineral salts, vitamins and herbs associated with each sun sign. For example, sodium phosphate, vitamins A, B1, B12, C, D, K and P, and dill, fennel and coriander go well with Sagittarius.

The Mad Hatter's Riceparty

The only time a clerk in a bookstore ever tried to stop me from buying a book on her shelves was when I happened to look at one on macrobiotics by the Japanese author, George Ohsawa. "I knew a couple," the clerk told ne, "who put their baby on a macrobiotic diet and he had to spend 14 months in a hospital. His bones were so fragile they'd just *snap* if he fell, or anything." I have no way of knowing if the story is true, but I added it anyway to the list of horror stories I've heard over the years about macrobiotic diets. The macrobiotic regimen, worked out by George Ohsawa, is more mystical than scientific in its emphasis, and some of its principles run counter to well-established precepts of healthy eating. I present the outlines of his theory only because it has had an impact on a lot of people, particulartly those receptive to religious lore from the Far East.

The heart of the theory can be sum-

med up in the Japanese words *san paku*, which means, literally, three sides.

If you have any white showing below the irises of your eyes – in other words, if there are three sides of white around your irises – you are *san paku*. Advocates of a macrobiotic diet consider this to be a sign of possibly the worst physical and spiritual condition you can be in, short of being dead. What it means, basically, is that the forces of Yin and Yang in your body are severely imbalanced. Yin and Yang, classic Eastern thought, are the two great forces of the universe, opposed to each other and yet complementary to each other. Yin is light, expansive, cold and female. Yang is heavy, constricted, hot and male. In nutritional terms, foods rich in potassium are Yin, and foods rich in sodium are Yang.

People who believe in the principle of Yin and Yang insist that the ideal food for a human being is natural, unpolished brown rice, because this rice has within itself the perfect ratio of five parts Yin, or potassium, to one part Yang, or sodium. Most people never attain this ratio of five Yin to one Yang in their diet. They eat far too many Yin foods and, the theory runs, thereby expose themselves to every illness and misfortune known to man. The best diet is one consisting entirely of raw cereals: rice, wheat, barley, buckwheat, millet and oats, with brown rice at the head of that list.

There are other principles involved in the macrobiotic diet – like the injunction to chew each teaspoonful of food at least 100 times before swallowing it – but eating only cereals is the heart of it. The diet downgrades vegetables, and insists that you avoid fruits, and cut out heavily Yin vegetables like potatoes, tomatoes and eggplant altogether. It advises that you limit your intake of liquids so that you don't urinate more than twice in 24 hours if you are a woman, or three times if you are a man. Here we leave the realm of the absurd and enter the regions of the preposterous.

Mixed Blessings

One school of health food thought, led by Dr. Herbert Shelton, of Dr. Shelton's Health School in San Antonio, Texas, emphasizes that it's not enough to eat healthy foods. If the foods you eat are to be properly digested, you have to take some care in the way you combine them. Shelton maintains that different kinds of foods require different kinds of digestive enzymes, or enzyme combinations. For example, the stomach secretes certain enzymes for starchy foods that are quite different from the enzymes it secretes for predominantly protein foods. If you eat a lot of starch and a lot of protein at the same meal you will only confuse your stomach, according to Dr. Shelton. Your stomach needs all the help it can get in these troubled times. Therefore, do not eat that baked potato with your steak.

What will happen, says Shelton, is that neither of the foods will be digested properly. They will only ferment and putrefy in your digestive tract. I don't like to get clinical about it, but when your food putrefies like this you have bad breath, indigestion and "gas." At least that's how Shelton and other food combiners see it, and if they had their way you'd never shop at the drugstore again for something to help your digestion.

Since few people are willing to stick to one kind of food at a single meal, most health food advocates simply abide by the general rule to eat as few different kinds of foods as possible at a meal. A balanced *diet* may be good for you, but balanced *meals,* in their view, are something else, and resolutely to be avoided. Also if you're sick, extremely tired, or emotionally upset, health food advocates maintain that you should not trouble your stomach with *any* food. The digestive enzymes will not cooperate. This is one rule of healthy eating that anybody can agree with.

Flours of Evil

White flour, the essential ingredient of our baked goods, including white bread, or what James Baldwin once called "blasphemous foam rubber," usually ranks with sugar at the top of the list of health destroyers drawn up by health foodists. One of these, Paavo Airola, a member of the International Society for Research on Civilization Diseases and Vital Substances that Albert Schweitzer founded, says of white flour and white sugar that "these two nutritionless monstrosities, disguised under the name of food, are responsible more than anything else for the deterioration of health in civilized countries." White flour, of course, is grain that has been refined. The refining process strips the outer bran coating and the wheat-germ kernel from the grain. This neatly eliminates over half the vitamins and almost 90 per cent of the minerals in that grain. "Enriched" bread is bread made from this devitalized flour with a few chemical vitamins put back in. If a bread is advertised as "enriched," health food proponents are always quick to ask, enriched compared with what?

One Grew Over the Cuckoo's Nest

Most health food authorities view disease as a kind of voice the body uses to inform us that something is wrong. What that something is may have nothing to do with the symptoms of the disease. In fact, it usually does not have so much to do with the body itself, or the sick part of it, as with the way we're living our lives. Perhaps we are not getting enough rest, exercise, clean air and water. Perhaps we are burdened with a troubled spirit or a dishonest heart. Then again, perhaps we are not eating well.

In any case, the thing to do, in their view, is not merely to treat the disease but to seek out the ways in which we are violating the laws of good living. Health food authorities, of course, tend to look first at the way we eat, and proceed from there. Some of them claim that everything from arthritis to baldness may be caused by inadequacies in our diet. Dr. Emmanuel Cheraskin in *Psychodietetics,* has claimed that even "mental" illnesses, such as schizophrenia, alcoholism, anxiety neurosis, and any other personality disorders you can attach a label to, are ultimately caused by poor diet. Alcoholism, for example, has been linked to low blood sugar, a condition caused by eating *too much* sugar. Researchers at Loma Linda University in California have induced a craving for alcohol among rats by feeding them a diet heavy on glazed doughnuts, hot dogs, carbonated drinks, white bread, chocolate cake, and similar foodstuffs.

Doctors like David R. Hawkins of Long Island, N.Y., who take this approach, favor megavitamin therapy for the "mentally ill" – in particular, feeding heavy doses of vitamin B3 (niacin) to alcoholics and schizophrenics. Ordinary neurotics may just have to cut out white sugar from their diet.

Philip Marchand, journalist.

The Jews in Canada

The Jewish faith cannot be completely considered aside from the Jewish people. Therefore, this reflects what happened to us both as a faith community and as a socio-political group.

Six positives:
  • A greater hunger for learning, among both the young and the old.
  • The establishment of small communities in large congregations ("chavurot").
  • The awakening of Soviet Jewry to its identity and world-wide Jewish involvement in its liberation.
  • The growing supply of rabbis, male and (in the Reform movement) female.
  • The growth of Jewish day schools and of departments of Judaica in North American universities.
  • Peace between Egypt and Israel – a watershed for confidence and security.

Six negatives:
  • The rising rate of gentile/Jewish (mixed) marriages, the apparent inevitable price of living in a free society.
  • The shrinking size of Jewish families.
  • The polarization between the ultraorthodox faith community and the rest.
  • The decreased emphasis on social action as a Jewish imperative and, with it, the growth of middle-class prejudice.
  • The inroads that various cults made among Jewish youth, highlighting, for many, the failure to find answers in their synagogues.
  • The rising rate of divorces.

The 12 problems delineated above highlight the difficulty for diaspora Jewry of living in two worlds at once: the Jewish and the general. In Canada, the uncertainty about Quebec's future has also affected Jews, highlighting the fraility of diaspora living. At the same time, Jews in Canada have, during the '70s, lived up to their reputation of being perhaps the most intensely committed Jewish community anywhere outside of Israel.

Rabbi W. Gunther Plaut, OC, JD, DD, LLD.

The Anonymous Canadians

Joe who? Two words portray two decades. Joe Who? We must still keep asking into the '80s. That '70s question must become a quest to identify and dignify Canada's socially anonymous Joes. Joe Who and What and Where.

Like Joe Zulgan. He is our most precious asset, a resource worker.

He is dying.

He has silicosis, a severe respiratory disease. He has served 17 years in the uranium mines. He suddenly, brutally learns what his X-rays show three years after they were taken. He is given $56.25 a month while he battles for full compensation.

Then he is socially cast out.

He is a disaster statistic in every sense. He is one of one million industrial workers injured *every* year in Canada. Half are disabled for a time, though long enough for the annual lost man-hours to be triple those lost through strikes. The annual revenue loss: $2 billion – and rising. The cost in social alienation can only be imagined. The permanently crippled (now 40,000 in Ontario alone) have for years endured double handicap: compensation unadjusted to cost-of-living. The seriously disabled become discards: Joe Zulgan, Joe Anywhere.

He is out of sight: his last service. He plays solitaire. On and on he plays solitaire. He has the strength to make the streets but not for what he sees there.

So he sits and sits, in a corner in a trailer home in a boom town he has built with muscle and blood; red vomit coming from blackened lungs; spasms and solitaire. Suddenly there is blood on the cards. There is for far too many Joe Whos.

Of all the varied human tragedy from my television world travels in the '70s, the fate of Joe Zulgan, pitiful and pitiless, screams incomprehension. Perhaps he is too hauntingly close to home, expendable if deemed in any way unfit, his face and sickness a visage of all this country's ills . . . a Canadian, kind of . . . a man dispossessed of fellowship in a country obsessed with unity. His eyes have the plea of a different hurt as he says, "I hide home. Nobody likes to see you around." His son, Rod, hides in another corner, sobbing, "Daddy, Daddy." His wife, Mary, can still worry for others, telling our cameras: "What is the future for the ones who come to this town." It isn't a question.

The town is Elliot Lake, Ontario's "uranium capital of the world," born in the '50s with a billion-dollar U.S. order, sudden heaven for unskilled workers ignorant of the hell below: the high silicate and radiation dust known to officials. Elliot Lake is a lovely cover-up, 18 scenic miles from the Trans-Canada Highway, migrant route of boom-and-bust company towns where a satanic-mills mentality governs the resource workers of the atomic age, where unbenevolent companies remain largely unregulated by the provinces, monitoring their own safety conditions, company doctors keeping employee health records and the companies actually financing the Workman's Compensation boards! Canada, 1980. True, there have been recent improvements (partly new boom expediency). An Ontario miner, at least, can now refuse without penalty to work in an area he considers hazardous, and there's an improved system for rating silicosis. But the *mentality* of our resource lands is the jungle, virtual survival of the fittest which is nationally suicidal.

And somehow it all surfaced in the '70s. Too many Canadians ceased to share or belong or believe. Perhaps it isn't entirely our fault as a people: as world problems loom larger, individuals everywhere feel inadequate, turn inward, even from neighbours. Perhaps at heart it isn't a lack of feeling for each other, more a lack of voice. Perhaps the jungle roots spring from long ago: too few of us in a land too vast, which we have never wholly known, nor even wholly owned – still a tenant nation, duly subdued. But in truth what we see (and read in this book) as our major problems – unity, productivity, youth morale – arise from this single crisis of community.

Elliot Lake is one small example. Medical data indicates that 80 percent of long-term miners (and most are) will develop silicosis. Acceptable? No one would say so if they broke their silence. But in this two-company town there is the muteness of fear and page after page of interview notes are headed "Prefers to remain anonymous." The silence becomes a general sentence of anonymity, and worse.

There's the silence about Joe Zulgan, fateful for him. "They talk around you," he says. "They say 'because of him or him maybe the mine is gonna close down.' " He looks down, at the cards on the table. "I'm proud – I was a miner." Routinely his hand reaches for the cards, then clenches. "That damn dirty doctor. 'Go back to work,' he tells me. 'Stop talking to reporters and go back to work,' he tells me." He starts to cry. His wife goes to him. "He can't even carry a shopping bag," she says.

Joe started talking after he began "spitting blood all over," when too weak to work he fought for compensation, waiting, waiting, while they checked his annual X-rays.

Joe never did see them. They went to the Workman's Compensation Board and months later a board doctor called him and asked "How did this happen?" The X-rays for three years earlier showed silicotic dust on his lungs. A year later, the dust had doubled. He was suddenly, at age 45, totally unfit for work: compensation fixed at $585 a month, less than half his income. A year later they discovered the lesion: lung cancer, inoperable. Silicosis can often hide cancer.

But Joe, dying, is still a miner, still an asset. "We gotta get uranium. We need that," he says, "but if they let men die the way they have we get disaster." Pull out every silicotic, retrain them? Why not? But in a drapes-drawn room off a pretty street an Elliot Lake widow explains why not: "Yes, there's a retraining school. They can learn to ski, or ice a cake, not that there's a bakery in town and anyway; learning that wouldn't have brought my husband even half a loaf."

"What we need is simple," she says. "We need people to say, 'We're with you,' so that somebody will do something in the end."

"I don't wanna die," says Joe, his arms around wife and son. "If I die they only get half the compensation, $290 a month."

We call him a few weeks later, but he is dead. Joe Who? Joe Reject. Joe Two-Ninety-a-Month. Joe Seventies. Joe Eighties?

Joe Who? Canadian, kind of. On the Identity Question still no I.Q. Joe Who? Keep asking.

Michael Maclear, broadcaster, journalist.

Pollution Probe
Reviews the Decade

Founded in 1969 by a handful of individuals concerned about environmental and energy issues, Pollution Probe grew to become one of Canada's most respected and well-known public-interest groups during the 1970s. Four Probe staff members present overviews of some of the decade's most pressing environmental problems.

THE GREAT LAKES

Water pollution in the Great Lakes Basin is not a recent phenomenon. For more than 200 years human activities have altered the appearance and quality of Ontario's lakes and rivers. The clearing of land for farming, the construction of water-powered mills and the dumping of wastes into waterways reduced fish species and numbers.

However, the pollution problems that have plagued Ontario waters since settlement began have been intensified by rapid industrialization since World War Two. In the past decade, three major crises have appeared.

Lake Erie was once the most prolific of fishing grounds, producing more fish than the other four Great Lakes combined. But by the 1950s beaches were closing and dead fish, strangled in green beds of algae, littered the shores. In popular mythology, Lake Erie was "dead."

The governments of the United States and Canada were moved to ask the International Joint Commission to study pollution in the lower Great Lakes and, in 1969, the commission advised both governments to reduce phosphates to a minimum practical level immediately.

Phosphorus was indicated as the principal factor in the excessive growth of algae that threatened to overwhelm Lakes Erie and Ontario. The one source of phosphorus pollution that could be most easily regulated was phosphate detergents. In 1970, despite protesting detergent manufacturers, the Canadian federal government passed regulations under the Canada Water Act limiting phosphorus in household detergents.

Today phosphorus levels in the lower lakes remain high, but the deterioration of the lakes from this problem has been temporarily stayed.

At about the same time, the dangers of mercury poisoning in Ontario waters were recognized.

During the 1960s six chlor-alkali plants operated in the province, discharging several tons of mercury into adjacent waters. Mercury was known to accumulate in the food chain, with the highest concentrations found in the largest and most prized fish.

151

In 1961, it had been revealed to the international scientific community that the Japanese victims of debilitating Minimata disease had been poisoned by eating mercury-contaminated fish.

Eight years later the Ontario Water Resources Commission sampled fish downstream from the chlor-alkali plants and discovered that the fish contained dangerously high levels of mercury. On March 26, 1970, then Minister of Energy and Resource Management George Kerr ordered the six plants to stop "discharging mercury into the environment."

In May, 1970, commercial fishing was banned on Lake St. Clair, Lake Erie and the English-Wabigoon River system.

The six affected plants included Dryden Chemicals, a subsidiary of the Reed Paper Company, whose mercury discharges threatened the health of Indians of the Grassy Narrows and White Dog reserves and destroyed their fishing economy. Also included was the Dow Chemical Company plant on Lake St. Clair.

In an unusual legal action, the Ontario government sued Dow for $35 million on behalf of the fishermen and bait dealers who could no longer earn a living. After seven years of legal wrangling, Dow agreed to pay the 40 fishermen a total of $250,000 in a private settlement with the Ontario government.

Though now stopped, much of the inorganic mercury that was discharged in the '60s and early '70s remains in lake and river sediments and is still converting to the deadly methyl mercury at a rate of one percent annually. The legacy of mercury contamination will be with us for another century.

The latest and probably most encompassing environmental crisis facing the waters of the Great Lakes Basin is acidification. Because most air masses bringing rain and snow into this region are contaminated with sulphur and nitrogen oxides, precipitation contains sulphuric and nitric acids. Some Ontario precipitation is hundreds of times more acidic than normal.

When highly acidic snows and rains fall in areas with substantial soil cover or limestone bedrock the acids are buffered or neutralized. But water bodies on insoluble Canadian Shield bedrock have little buffering capacity and are susceptible to severe acidification.

In the 1960s researchers from the University of Toronto discovered that fish were rapidly disappearing from the lakes in the LaCloche Mountains near Sudbury and that these lakes were becoming more acidic. In February of this year, Ontario Environment Minister Harry Parrott announced that 140 lakes are now dead and another 48,500 could become too acidic to support fish populations within the next 20 years.

Although the Great Lakes are not currently threatened because of their size and buffering capacities, some watershed streams and rivers where Great Lakes fish spawn are already affected.

Most of the sulphur and nitrogen oxides contributing to acidic precipitation in northeastern North America are emitted from coal-fired power plants in the United States. However, the International Nickel Company superstack in Sudbury is the largest single source on this continent.

Dr. David Shindler, a federal government scientist who chairs an International Joint Commission committee of experts, told the Ontario legislature's Standing Committee on Resource Development in February that, compared with the eutrophication problem affecting the lower Great Lakes earlier in this decade, acid rain presents a threat "certainly of the scale of 100 times more extensive and more important, both environmentally and economically."

There are, nevertheless, other serious problems: inadequately treated effluents from industries and municipalities, polluted run-off from roads and farms, contaminants seeping from abandoned and carelessly maintained waste disposal sites, remnants of past abuses lodged in the sediments of lakes and rivers.

The public concern that has grown over the last decade has prompted the discovery and study of many complex and unresolved problems. Finding solutions to these problems will be a challenge to the ingenuity and resourcefulness of the public, the scientific community and all levels of government.

Anne Wordsworth

PESTICIDES

After nearly 40 years of heavy insecticide use, the silent war against insects is far from over. Indeed, it may be entering a new phase. The pests are still prevalent, and increasing scientific questioning of the environmental effects and overall effectiveness of chemical insecticides has led to a search for alternative strategies, the most attractive of which are the more ecologically-based methods of integrated pest management.

For thousands of years, humans have been fighting the small but numerous and persistent insects that compete for our food, fabric and land. However, it was not until World War II that we entered the synthetic pesticide era and began depending on chemicals to wage the battle for us.

DDT marked the beginning. First used in Italy in 1943 (although it was first synthesized in 1874) to combat typhus, DDT soon inspired new hope that bugs could be eradicated.

As an insect killer, the chemical was a marvel. It was toxic and long lasting, killed with rapid and deadly efficiency, and was cheap. A massive industry was established to meet the ever-increasing demand for DDT and a wide range of other chemical insecticides and herbicides.

Nature, however, did not take to it. Although early reports of environmental contamination and occasional fish kills were taken lightly, it soon became evi-

dent (especially through the work of Rachel Carson, author of *Silent Spring)* that DDT and other chemicals of the organo-chlorine group posed serious human and environmental hazards.

When tests established DDT could cause cancer in laboratory animals, Canadian environmentalists called for a ban.

In 1969, 22 years after it was first introduced in Ontario, DDT was restricted to bat and mouse control. Since then, annual usage has dropped from 463,000 pounds to 3,839 pounds in 1977.

The use of other organo-chlorine insecticides – Heptachlor, Chlordane, Aldrin and Dieldrin – has also been curtailed and according to several reports there has been a marked decrease in organo-chlorine residues in human tissues, food and the environment.

Although DDT was the beginning, Ontario's ministry of the environment says 605 active ingredients are now being used in some 14,000 pesticide products. Growing worldwide population and resulting demands for more and better food have been blamed for the increase.

In Canada, 15 million pounds of insecticides were sold for agricultural use in 1977. Canadian pesticide sales that year totalled over $191 million.

Despite the regulations that now restrict use of certain pesticides and classes of pesticides, the public is still wary.

Peter Radonicich, who markets non-chemical bug controls in Toronto, says the debate is centred on human health considerations. Reports that certain pesticides can cause cancer, birth defects and mutations have added to the skepticism and, he argues, the chemical industry is becoming increasingly hard pressed to counter the evidence.

The Canadian Wildlife Service of the federal department of the environment confirms that Canada has not escaped environmental contamination from pesticides. Nearly all the samples of Canadian mammals, fish, fish food, marine invertebrates, migratory and non-migratory birds analyzed during a five-year study contained pesticide residues.

Participants in the pesticide debate have also noted that insects are now acquiring resistance to certain chemicals, necessitating progressively greater and more costly applications. Scientists have been trying to keep a step ahead of the insects in this escalating spiral, but their success has been limited.

At the outset of the synthetic pesticide era, when the U.S. used roughly 50 million pounds of insecticides annually, insects killed or destroyed about seven percent of preharvest crops. Today, under a 600 million pound insecticide load, 13 percent of preharvest yields are lost to insects.

Scientists refer to this as the pesticide treadmill, and are now looking at integrated pest management as a means of avoiding the escalating chemical war.

Based on ecological principles and aimed at maintaining pests at economically acceptable levels rather than trying to eliminate them entirely, integrated pest management methods could eventually reduce pesticide use by as much as 80 percent, while cutting crop losses to pests by 30 to 50 percent.

Integrated management can involve a wide variety of ecological techniques to control potential pests, but it relies mainly on natural controls – for instance, use of insect hormones to sabotage the pests' sex lives and physical development.

Biological controls, which use friendly organisms to prey on pests, have also been applied successfully. When cottony cushion scale began to ravage citrus groves in California about a century ago, scientists imported its natural predator – the vedalia lady beetle – from Australia and within a year the pest was subdued.

More recently, scientists have been studying a virus that kills major cotton pests but leaves other insect species and life forms unharmed.

Pheremones, the scents by which male and female insects tell each other apart, can be artificially produced. If the right pheremones are introduced in heavy concentrations into the atmosphere, the male and female insect pests should, in theory at least, become confused and fail to reproduce.

One of the benefits of using natural predators and parasites to control insect populations is that they are discriminating fighters: they only kill their natural enemies. In contrast, chemical pesticides often kill not only their intended victims, but their predators as well.

In the Canadian case of the spruce budworm, for example, the pest recovers from pesticide effects more quickly than its enemies and, because the natural foes are reduced, more spraying is needed to prevent further outbreaks. A vicious cycle of spray and more spray results.

Although integrated pest management has few critics, it will probably be years before chemical insecticide use declines in its favour. The bulk of research and development money is still devoted to conventional chemical pesticides and most observers see this as an indication that the bug war will continue for some time to be fought primarily with chemicals.

Debra Henderson

ELECTRICITY

In the last decade, blind and blinding use of electricity went out of style.

A newspaper article from 1969 began, "A sight for sore eyes awaited Ontario government employees when they first moved into their highrise offices at Queen's Park. Unused to such bright surroundings, some of them literally had to don sunglasses until their eyes adjusted to the new conditions."

The photo caption read, "Ten thousand civil servants will ultimately occupy this Ontario government centre where the window cleaners use two-way radio and the monthly power bill now tops $50,000."

Some readers in those days were undoubtedly proud of the progress we had made. Peak electricity requirements in Ontario increased 5.6 percent between 1968 and 1969. Electricity cost 0.8 cents per kilowatt-hour. And the airwaves were filled with Ontario Hydro's urgings to "live better electrically."

But not everyone was dazzled by the vision of an all-electric future. Environmentalists, concerned about air and water pollution, land-use conflicts and transmission lines, were gearing up for what became a decade of conflict over electric utility planning.

According to one utility executive, every effort to construct new generating stations in the U.S. was fought in the courts, and every tower line right-of-way got snarled in red tape.

In January, 1970, *Ontario Hydro News* declared the "spirit of negativism" to be public enemy number one. "Pessimism is shortsightedness . . . The future belongs to our form of energy, and we must not allow our immediate problems to grow so tall as to obscure the glowing horizon."

That glowing horizon became broader and less blinding in the ensuing years. Alarmed by soaring power costs and soaring debts, the Ontario government acted in 1975 to cut back Hydro's expansion program, and set up the Royal Commission on Electric Power Planning to investigate future electricity supply and demand.

Since then, electric growth rates have fallen far below those predicted earlier, and Hydro's critics have realized that growth itself is a debatable point.

Today, growth rates are still falling, and Hydro's program is still being cut back. But environmentalists have not gone away satisfied.

As the problems of radioactive waste and acid rain have become more urgent, environmentalists have begun attacking the regulatory and institutional mechanisms that encourage continuing electricity expansion.

They now call for rate reform, equitable access to capital, and building code revisions to encourage conservation and use of small-scale, renewable and environmentally benign energy technologies.

The last ten years have seen some advances. Electricity expansion is no longer taken for granted, commissions and inquiries have been set up, and attitudes towards energy have changed. Wasting electricity, we are now told, turns people off.

Changing the slogan from "live better electrically" to "wasting electricity turns people off" was a big step in the right direction. But it is just a beginning.

Jan Marmorek and **Chris Conway**

Voices from the Sea

It was during the past decade that we truly began to measure ourselves against the sea. Aided by satellites and international programs, we started to take stock of "planet ocean," focussing on its great largesse and many problems. In the process, we initiated a world-wide ocean consciousness.

Many events brought this about: the plight of whales, the Law of the Sea conferences, repeated and massive oil spills, the films of Jacques Cousteau, ocean photographs from Apollo and Skylab . . . these and other events brought the ocean into our living rooms. We began to see ourselves for what we were, the first "seaspace" generation.

In Canada we established a 200-mile limit and began to rediscover the importance of fishing. Thanks to able administrators and hard-working marine scientists, we continued to study the implications of the Canadian ocean legacy. In pursuit of elusive hydrocarbons we moved offshore, peering into such dark and difficult corridors as the Beaufort Sea and the Grand Banks.

For me, it was a decade of challenge and adventure. In 1970 I led my first expedition under the ice of the polar sea. Since then I've travelled over 75,000 miles to 30 diving sites, including three trips to the North Pole. The object of this work was to find out how well man could perform under the polar ice as a diver – and how to best equip him to operate safely in the world's most hostile environment.

Ten years and 800 dives later we have found only some of the answers. We explored waters that can kill within minutes if you are unprotected. We saw whales, shipwrecks and the other side of icebergs – and were excited, knowing we were the first human beings to do so. Under the ice of Resolute Bay we built the world's first polar manned station. During the decade we spent hundreds of hours underwater, some of it in quiet reflection, listening to the voices from the sea. In the cold mirror of the Arctic Ocean it is possible to discover who you really are, and to glimpse the future.

Dr. Joseph B. MacInnis, Undersea Research Ltd.

The Slick Decade

Big Lloyd Bourinot sits at the piano in the dining room of the Isle Madame Motel in Arichat, thumping out his song:

> While travellin' down to Isle Madame
> You'll find the sea is mighty ca'm,
> 'Cause a dirty oil slick's holdin' down the foam;
> But Ottawa don't seem to care
> 'Bout the Bunker C that's lyin' there,
> In that little oil-ringed island we call home.*

Lloyd wrote the song in 1970, when the tanker *Arrow* impaled herself on Cerberus Rock, almost within sight of the motel window, and spilled 17,000 tons of black, gooey crud on the beaches of Chedabucto Bay. But on Easter Sunday, 1979, the song is fresh again: the British tanker *Kurdistan* has broken in two off Cape Breton, and oil blotches disfigure the coastline from Big

*Song copyright Lloyd Bourinot, 1970. Used by permission of the author.

Bras d'Or to Halifax – 240 miles as the dying eagle flies, infinitely more as the ragged coastline meanders.

The diners, who live here, smile at the song in sorrowful amusement.

The '70s were a decade of quiescence in the face of brutal assaults on the biosphere, the decade of Harrisburg and Seviso, of the Love Canal, the *Amoco Cadiz,* and Minimata disease. For Cape Breton, the decade opened and closed with the most destructive oil spills in Canada's history. Why did we do so little about disasters so appalling in themselves, so ominous for our future?

"Turdistan," grunts Farley Mowat, glaring at the oil-spattered beach of his Cape Breton home.

I will remember the '70s as a decade of ruthless and self-centred prosperity, of mass Sunflight vacations while a million Canadians lay unemployed. The angry, hopeful passion of '60s rock has been replaced by the merchandized meat-market of disco. Fascist, irrational cultism dominates religion. Politics has been surrendered to media imagery and the shallowest forms of opportunism. Flacks paint supergraphics over our malaise, and for plummy fees tell us it is not a malaise at all.

But no one can PR the oil out of the sand.

In 1970, scruffy, fragile tankers under flags of convenience furrowed the Maritime waters. The largest ships on earth disgorged oil in Saint John and Port Hawkesbury. They had single engines and delicate cooling systems and no auxiliary power. Canada had not one single tugboat capable of towing one of these monsters away from the rocks.

In 1979, we have better traffic control in the shipping channels, and a $50 million oil clean-up fund. But unsafe tankers still infest our waters, and we still do not have a tugboat beefy enough to tow a supertanker. In 1974, the supertanker *Halcyon the Great* went adrift in Chedabucto Bay, its single engine dead. The weather, happily, was calm, and four tugs from the Gulf Oil refinery in Port Hawkesbury were able to tow it in. But if it had been stormy, we might have watched helplessly as the ship laid a carpet of oil several feet wide and several inches deep over every indentation of the coast from Cape Breton to Boston.

How can we stand, slack-jawed, staring at such dreadful prospects like cave men viewing an eclipse? We are not helpless. We could build the monstrous tugboats we need, and ban flag-of-convenience tankers and under-qualified officers. We could demand that no tanker move within our 200-mile limit except with an Environment Canada observation team aboard. We could insist that, as of 1982, say, all tankers in Canadian waters have double bottoms and twin engines.

And we could organize the world's major consuming nations – Japan, the United States, the Common Market countries – to take the same steps. Canada could, for once, initiate a benefit to mankind. In the process, we might even learn again the joys of directing our own lives, shaping our own futures, living as though we really wanted a clean and lovely world to leave for our children.

We might do that, if we chose to act like mature citizens of the planet. In the meantime, we can only sing along with Lloyd Bourinot, recalling the cargo of Imperial Oil's Bunker C which was consigned to the pulp mill at Port Hawkesbury, but delivered to 125 miles of beaches instead:

> So jump in your car and come on down
> And see our dirty little town
> That once a rural beauty did possess;
> You can gaze on oil as thick as fudge,
> Grease and grime and slick and sludge:
> Always look to Imperial – for the mess.

Silver Donald Cameron, journalist, author.

Energy

Turmoil has characterized the energy scene in the '70s.

The generation of electricity by nuclear power plants surged ahead amid catastrophic warnings from environmentalists who were successful across the United States in stopping the construction of many new plants and delaying others. Nevertheless, the number of nuclear installations built both in the United States and Canada during the decade was substantial.

At the end of the '70s controversy swirled around safety and the high potential for nuclear disaster whereby in some cataclysmic event deadly nuclear radiation sweeps over the countryside killing hundreds of people, rendering large areas uninhabitable and contaminating the atmosphere. The "unspeakable" happened on film at the same time it was happening at Three Mile Island in Pennsylvania. The film *The China Syndrome* and the Three Mile Island incident demonstrated clearly that regardless of the engineering perfection, human factors in handling of nuclear power plants play a major role in the safe/unsafe operation and that combined with mechanical defects and engineering deficiencies do, in fact, give good cause for concern for the safe handling of nuclear installations. The fact is, however, they are in place, producing urgently needed electricity to sustain the high level of American and Canadian civilization. Every indication is that there will be more of the same being built in the '80s with smaller and better computers taking over from error-prone humans many more of the day-to-day operations.

But it was oil that produced the major energy turmoil of the '70s. As the western world entered the decade, crude oil prices were low, the supply abundant and secure. No problems anywhere. Then came October, 1973, and with it the Israeli-Egyptian war. The Arabs of Saudi Arabia, Kuwait,

Qu'atar, Abadabi simply said to all nations supporting Israel in the conflict: "Either withdraw your support and renounce Israel or we'll put an embargo on the supply of oil to your shores." The embargo did go on. It was enforced against most western European nations and North America, although there was much evidence that oil was still seeping through. Use of gasoline became restricted in Europe.

At the same time the embargo was imposed by the Arabs, the newly formed Organization of Petroleum Exporting Countries (OPEC) decided that it was time to take the posted price of their crude oil and put it at a level they thought was fair. They started off by quadrupling the price in the fall of '73 to about $8 a barrel. By the end of the '70s it was at the $18 a barrel range with post-Iranian revolution spot prices as high as $30. The OPEC countries claim that the inflation that pervades the western world forces them to keep raising the prices in order to maintain their real return constant.

When one considers that western Europe obtains 93 percent of its crude oil from the Persian Gulf and the OPEC nations, and that its economy, industry and civilization are totally dependent upon crude oil, the impact of the high oil prices on the cost of production of goods and services follows in a parallel, dramatic, upward curve. In turn this leads to further inflation. And so the circle is joined.

Reeling under the unexpected crunch of both the Arab boycott and the OPEC cartel's massive price increases, the western world began its frantic look for alternative sources of hydrocarbon energy. For Norway, Holland and Great Britain a bonanza gradually surfaced from under the North Sea. Discovery after discovery was made of new fields of crude oil and associated natural gas. However, the value of the pound dropped into the $1.70 range against American currency in the pre-North Sea production days of 1975. But by the end of the '70s the pound had regained much of its world market strength, not on the basis of the nation's productivity or trade union stability, but rather on the crude oil and natural gas bonanza flowing in from the North Sea fields. By the end of the '70s Great Britain was energy self-sufficient, a factor that promised to put the nation in a strong geo-economic and world-trade position in the '80s.

Meanwhile, in the United States, frantic efforts were underway to establish new energy policies and to produce that elusive alternate fuel that would release the Americans from the clutches of the Arabs and their OPEC partners. The daily consumption of imported crude oil was edging up to 50 percent of the 14 million barrels per day required to keep the United States on the roads, in the air and its industry producing. President Jimmy Carter's first major policy package was energy. In brave, bold thrusts he laid before Congress a dramatic mountain of energy programs designed to cut foreign imports, increase domestic production, encourage exploration and the development of alternative energy forms.

Unfortunately, Congress did not get the message. After long, bitter battles in the Senate and the House of Representatives an eviscerated package of legislation was finally enacted at the end of 1978. It included a phased deregulation of the price of both crude oil and natural gas. Meanwhile, consumption of oil was increasing and the percentage of imports of crude, instead of being held and reduced, was enlarging. By 1979 the secretary of energy, Dr. Schlessinger, decided that there was no shortage of natural gas. He saw a temporary surplus so he advocated that industries switch from oil to natural gas. It was a strange decision in that the United States' natural gas industry predicts that by 1985 there will be a five-trillion-cubic-foot-a-year curtailment of natural gas out of a total demand of about 21 trillion. The frightening part of the industry's statistical analysis is that in that year and for the first time there will be a one-trillion-cubic-foot *residential* curtailment. However, the Americans are notorious for ignoring signs of impending disaster, being optimistic adherents to the principle that "it can't happen here."

In the '70s, up in that unusual land to the north of the Americans called Canada, the natural gas industry in Alberta and British Columbia was developing new fields of natural gas with discoveries being made almost on a daily basis. By the end of the '70s Canada has what is regarded as a substantial surplus of that commodity, although in 1979 its National Energy Board decreed that only 2.5 trillion cubic feet would be available for export. A wise decision because natural gas is usable as an alternative fuel in automobiles. This technology, although not yet used in Canada, represents the nation's opportunity to be totally independent of the OPEC countries or anyone else for hydrocarbon energy.

By the end of the '70s, Canada's export of crude oil to the United States had virtually ceased, there being no exportable surplus. All western crude oil was committed to supply the Canadian market west of the Ottawa River, while Quebec and the Maritimes were supplied by offshore OPEC oil. It is this longstanding government policy that has locked Canada into the merciless grip of OPEC, both as to supply and as to price of the commodity. And it is this policy that has required the Canadian government to subsidize out of the general treasury the importation of oil from the OPEC countries into Quebec and the Maritimes while keeping the price of western gas lower than the OPEC prices. The cost to the taxpayer toward the end of the decade was running at about $1 billion a year. Of course, the OPEC set higher prices of both crude oil and natural gas are totally artificial. Nevertheless, they apply in Canada, resulting in a devastating impact on the Canadian cost of living as well as the cost of producing goods in competition with those of other industrial nations.

On the other hand, the high prices of domestic crude oil and natural gas have also brought into economic reality production of oil from the Athabasca tar sands in Alberta. The enormous costs of the extraction processes required to take the bitumen away from the sand that bears it are now being met by the prices that the commodity brings. The first plant came into operation at the end of the '60s, Great Canadian Oil Sands. The second, Syncrude, with help from Alberta and Ontario, started up in 1978. Between the two they produce close to 200,000 barrels a day. Each new plant now ranges in the neighbourhood of $2 billion to build. At the end of the '70s plans were being prepared for a third plant, this one backed by Imperial Oil (Exxon). What is in negotiation is the matter of adequate federal and provincial government incentives. These must be resolved to Imperial's satisfaction before its 100,000-barrel-a-day proposed plant gets under construction.

Meanwhile, up in Alaska, the 1968 find of approximately 10 billion barrels of crude oil, with large volumes of associated gas, resulted in the construction of a crude oil pipeline from Prudhoe Bay to Valdez on the south coast of Alaska. That pipeline is capable of carrying up to two million barrels of oil a day into a west coast/U.S. market that can only take about 800,000, the balance being surplus. The United States owners are desperate to find a way of getting their precious commodity to the major market in the eastern seaboard without going through the Panama Canal. The plan most likely to succeed is that of building a pipeline from a fork in the Trans-Alaska pipe near Fairbanks and taking the surplus along the same route that will be used for the natural gas line that must be built from Prudhoe Bay into the lower 48 states.

There are huge volumes of natural gas available in Alaska associated with the crude oil as it is being taken from the ground or in independent pockets. It is urgent that the U.S. build a transportation mechanism to carry that natural gas to market, particularly to the lower 48 states as shortages build up toward the mid-1980s. The governments of Canada and the United States have come to an agreement concerning the construction of the gas pipeline. The successful bidders who want to built it are in place. What remains is for the department of energy in the United States to come up with a gas pricing proposal that would enable world financiers to decide whether the return is good enough for them to put up the money.

Down in the far reaches of Mexico word emerged in the late '70s that the Mexicans were looking at the potential of oil reserves in the range of 200 billion barrels of oil, which would put them in the same category as the Persian Gulf. With the Mexican crude oil comes associated natural gas. The Mexicans want to sell natural gas to the United States but the haggling has been enormous. The same applies to crude oil prices. President Carter and his advisors have been wooing and courting the Mexicans, who are hanging tough because of long-felt insults over countless decades from the people in the United States whom they consider to be arrogant.

Which brings us to the lesson of Iran as the street revolution took place and oil exports were cut off. Even though Iran accounted for only five percent of the U.S. imports, the shortages that developed brought tremors of gasoline rationing, higher prices from the OPEC countries and a disconcerting ripple through the entire American economy. A cutoff of ten percent or 25 percent of OPEC crude oil coming onshore the United States would clearly be a disaster. Turmoil would be a timid word to describe the fallout of that kind of catastrophic event. And yet the explosivity of the governments that control the Persian Gulf and, for that matter, most of the other OPEC countries provides the instruction that there can be a cutoff for a whole host of reasons: war, insurrection, revolution, strikes and even the lack of willingness to produce crude oil so that the treasure can be kept in the ground, thereby causing shortages and fetching higher prices.

Energy turmoil in the '70s has caused global upheavals of which more are to come, much more dramatically in the '80s.

Richard Rohmer, QC, best-selling author.

Nuclear Power
or Alpha Beta Gamma isn't a Fraternity Any More

From: P. W. Walsh, Director of Communications
       Public Interface Program
To: Howie Smyth, Deputy Minister,
       Canadian Reactor Advisory Commission
Re: "Advertising in the '80s – A Reaction"

Dear Howie:
Many thanks for your comments. As you are no doubt well aware, the problems faced by the commission after the excursion at Three Mile Island earlier this year have left us in a somewhat nonpositive position vis-à-vis our PI program here at Communications.

Let's face it – selling the idea of nuclear energy to the public these days is becoming increasingly difficult. Things have been going from bad to worse ever since the Chalk River reactor blew up when we first turned it on back in the '50s. On top of that, the Americans screwed it up royally when the Enrico Fermi installation almost took out Detroit in '62, not to mention all those dead fish in the Columbia River from the leak at Richland.

I think we're all in agreement that we've managed to maintain a reasonably low profile through all of this, but Three Mile Island's put a crimp in our plans for a slow educative process with the public. I don't think we're going to be able to call hard radiation "sunshine units" anymore.

We have that installation in Renfrew County, Ontario, leaking like a sieve, the one we're building in B.C. is right on a major fault line and the pilots are using the glow from Pickering as a night beacon on their approach to Toronto International. The reactor under construction in New Brunswick is a real winner, too – and they thought they had trouble with spruce budworm!

Frankly, the state of nuclear safeguards in Canada is on a level with putting a flaming can of gasoline into a paper bag. You know and I know that accidents happen. It's part of the price we have to pay to keep out from under the lads in the burnooses. We're also both aware that those accidents are going to happen more frequently as time goes by – you know the old saying: "You can't make an omelette without breaking eggs." What we have to do, and I feel it's part of my responsibility as PIP director, is to make those accidents as positive as possible.

The potential is certainly there. For instance, a radiation leak might sterilize all the mosquitoes and blackflies in a resort area – good news for the tourist industry. Year-round tans. Warmer winters. Giant strawberries and tomatoes the size of watermelons. We can probably even get something out of future birth anomalies (anomaly is a much better word that defects). How about something along the lines of "two heads are better than one"? A labour force of people with four arms would be a real economy stimulator, too. At the very least it would be a boost for the orthopedic prosthetic companies.

As I outlined in my paper, television should be our main focus. Saturation of viewers during prime time on all three networks would give us the widest audience participation. The boys in the psych office tell me the surveys show a strong "self" projection for the average viewer, and I think that's the way we should go – kind of a "if-number-one-is-okay-then-to-hell-with-every-one-else" tack . . .

EXAMPLE:

Master shot:
– middle-class living room – night. Macramé wall hanging. Benjamin Chee-Chee print over the fireplace. Good-looking woman curled up on the sofa, reading *Maclean's*. Two children in front of the TV. Man in early 30s in a repro Eames Chair reading Pierre Berton's latest. As the camera zooms in slowly, he looks up and smiles.

MAN: "Nuclear energy? It's the greatest. It lights my home and keeps my family warm. My food stays fresher longer because of it, too. Sure, there's a lot of talk about accidents and pollution. But at least it's a clean pollutant. You can't see it, or smell it, or taste it. It's almost like it wasn't there at all. Okay, it might make my life a bit shorter, but it sure makes my life better. To me nuclear is more than a source of power, it's . . . well, it's a lifestyle."

– Camera pulls back slowly. Man goes back to his book. Camera continues pulling back, dissolves slowly to an exterior of an Alcan Universal Home sitting in the midst of complete desolation (see Locations/Sudbury). As camera pulls back into a full crane shot we see that the entire countryside is pulsating with a faint bluish cathode light.

V/O "Nuke. Come on into the warm."

CUT TO: TITLE SLIDE:

NUCLEAR ENERGY – A GLOWING FUTURE FOR ALL OF US.

Christopher Hyde, journalist, author of *The Wave.*

Greenpeace

When they began the news media dismissed them as a bunch of West Coast crazies. But today Greenpeace can launch an anti-whaling vessel to confront Spanish and Icelandic whalers in the Atlantic, call Brigitte Bardot to help its cause in Newfoundland, and command the attention of *Der Stern,* the London *Observer,* and the New York *Times.* Greenpeace has made Vancouver a world centre of the environmental movement.

The chairman, Robert Hunter, can be forgiven his contented chuckle. Greenpeace has not only endured but gone global. It now has twenty branches in Canada, the U.S., Australia, New Zealand, and Europe, and about 30,000 members worldwide; it's still growing. "We're breeding like rabbits," Hunter says.

The first move in 1971 was to become characteristic: sending a ship, *Greenpeace I,* to sail into the Aleutian Islands blast zone and challenge the right of the U.S. to (as Hunter puts it) "trash the environment." Greenpeace went on to launch dramatic protests against France's nuclear testing at Mururoa Atoll and continuing confrontations at sea with Japanese and Russian whaling fleets. Its most visible recent campaign, led by president Dr. Patrick Moore, has been against the killing of seal pups in Newfoundland.

Greenpeace's tactical method is to choose the most dramatic, most *visual* issues and fight them through the world media. "It's McLuhanesque warfare," says Hunter, who quit the Vancouver *Sun* to join the movement full-time. "We're firing images rather than missiles at each other. That's the way change is going to happen now, by firing mind bombs at people through the delivery system of the mass media."

Greenpeace is still most successful in B.C., where there are now fifty-one environmental organizations; Greenpeace alone has 15,000 backers. An environ-

Greenpeace V escort grey whales off the West Coast of Vancouver Island. CP

mental alliance stopped in its tracks a proposal to start uranium mining last year. The company may try again, but it will have a fight: concern for the environment has become a crucial aspect of B.C. public affairs.

Greenpeace's gains have been fairly modest. The most dramatic was the recent sail-in protest by Greenpeace U.K. that forced a stop to killing seals in the Orkney Islands. In November, after two summers of work, Greenpeace Australia was able to get that country to withdraw from whaling. And Greenpeace takes some credit for keeping the Russian fleet more than 700 miles off the North American coast (to avoid Greenpeace protest vessels). "Now there's a *de facto* zone of sanctuary close to the North American coast, due to our protests," Hunter says.

Greenpeace intends to continue its campaign against killing Newfoundland seals. That one has been embroiled in controversy, and some ecologists regard it as an embarrassment. Hunter doesn't agree: "I don't think it can be an embarrassment to be trying to save those animals from slaughter. Only in Canada is there a groundswell of support for the slaughter of nursing animals." Greenpeace will be back on the Newfoundland ice in March 1980. Greenpeace just won't go away.

Inside Track, *Saturday Night.*

The Mackenzie Valley Pipeline Inquiry

Funny, but, looking back, it doesn't seem as historic as it did then, as historic as it was supposed to have been. The Mackenzie Valley Pipeline Inquiry surely ranks in the "top ten" stories of the '70s, but I am sure there are arbitrators paid to consider these things who don't know if it was about a gas pipeline or an oil pipeline or whether the damn thing was approved or not.

Those of us who were close to it felt there was something enormous about it, something that might change things. As Justice Thomas R. Berger kept saying: "The inquiry is not just about a gas pipeline; it relates to the whole future of the North." He even used to haul out that old poem by F. R. Scott:

An arena
Large as Europe
Silent
Waiting the contest

I never worked harder on a story, or as long, or cared as much about it. One sparkling northern night, all night under the sun that doesn't set, I travelled with Judge Berger in a freighter canoe from a Slavey fish camp to Fort Norman on the Mackenzie River. We ate dried moose meat and Dad's Cookies. We arrived at what would be dawn in most other places, then we told some stories, threw a softball around, went to bed in the bunkhouse and got up three hours later for the start of another community hearing. We listened to the old men and the old women, the chief, the children. They told stories of how fish hooks were made 100, 500 years ago. It got so weary some hot afternoons that the interpreter translated Slavey into Slavey and English into English and nobody noticed.

The Berger Inquiry moved on, to Fort Franklin, to Fort McPherson, to Fort Liard, way over and up to Old Crow in the Yukon, then further north to Holman Island and Tuktoyaktuk and Sachs Harbour and Paulatuk. There has never been anything like it. Berger even took the thing south to Vancouver, then across the country all the way to Charlottetown. It was the inquiry into everything and anything. Berger kept saying that the *process* of the inquiry was as important as the inquiry itself, that it was a massive consciousness-raising, an inquiry unique in the country's history. "This is the first time in Canada that we have a full-scale inquiry before we proceed with frontier development," Berger said. He asked huge questions. "How much energy does it take to run the industrial machine? Where does the energy come from? Where is the machine going? What happens to the people who live in the path of the machine?"

The analogy with the building of the first transcontinental railway was obvious, and even in the '70s it felt a bit like we were back there a century ago with Chief Piapot's Crees and Louis Riel and Gabriel Dumont and Craigellachie. The gas pipeline would be 2,600 miles long, carrying natural gas from Alaska's North Slope across the top of the Yukon to the Mackenzie Delta, then up the Mackenzie Valley to markets in the south. It would cost $5 billion, then $7 billion, then $10 billion and then we stopped counting. The standard description was that it would be "the biggest project in the history of private enterprise." The oil and gas companies wanted it so badly they spent $50 million just studying the impact a pipeline would have on the North.

In the end, however, what caught the imagination of the country was the story of the people, the land and the animals. The population of the North is not enough even to fill Montreal's Olympic Stadium but the area is one-third of Canada, the caribou migrate in hundreds of thousands and the Mackenzie Valley is where half of the bird species of North America breed. In the end, this is what stopped the pipeline, for at least ten years, which was the moratorium Judge Berger recommended.

It made sense to the native people because they think of people, land and animals as an interdependent whole. What seems ice-bound and barren to us is as rich and abundant as Manhattan to them. In June, 1975, Chief Harry Deneron of Fort Liard told the inquiry that one day he noticed a sign on the door of the Hudson's Bay store that said: "Do not drink from the river." He told the inquiry that it was okay for humans to have a sign like that, but what about the rest? "How can we get the message to the animals that are depending on this water, the fish and that?"

We were supposed to learn from them this time. I remember how Judge Berger picked up on the smallest, subtlest things. "One thing about the native people is that a pause in the conversation doesn't disturb them," he said. "They expect gaps in conversation. If you can't think of something to say, you don't say it. You often just sit there looking at the river." Think about it next time you are bombarded by the babble of a cocktail party.

We all came home to chase after other stories that didn't seem nearly as historic and now, only years later, the great inquiry seems remote and distant as the land itself. We read about the North when a satellite crashes somewhere on the permafrost, or when there is news of a big gas or oil strike that would inspire another pipeline to make bucks and jobs and keep the homes warm in Etobicoke. Sometimes the only tangible change seems to be that newspaper style books now call Eskimos "Inuit" (though they still don't use the singular "Inuk"). One more Northen Vision on the shelf, next to Diefenbaker's and the others'. Where's Paulatuk anyway? And what's a Dene? "We have an opportunity to make a new departure, to open a new chapter in the history of the indigenous peoples of the Americas," Judge Berger concluded his report. "We must not reject the opportunity."

I thought about it again at the federal election in 1979 when George Erasmus, the young president of the Indian Brotherhood of the Northwest Territories, ran for office in the new riding called Western Arctic. Erasmus was at the epicentre of all the drama back then in the mid-'70s. He was the new-style native leader, the new Dene: thoughtful, passionate, respected, courageous.

He came third.

Martin O'Malley, journalist, author.

Women in Society

The decade of the 1960s undeniably belonged to youth. Popular culture and the media eagerly copied the music, clothes and lifestyles of the exhuberant young. The 1970s, then, should have been the decade of women. But the 1970s have certainly not been labelled "Women's Decade." Far from publicizing the dramatic changes that have been happening to women, popular culture and the media have almost ignored them. Why? Because society, policymakers and some women themselves prefer to believe the thrust for change in almost every aspect of women's lives that occurred during the 1970s was temporary, or that it only applied to marginal groups of women, or that the whole movement was an aberration that would disappear in time.

The 1970s were characterized by conflict and dysfunction between the traditional expectations about women's behaviour and reality. Large numbers of women joined the work force. But this phenomenon was generally considered somewhat aberrant and perhaps temporary. The efforts of women to reach equality of pay and opportunity and to achieve other changes in society to accommodate their changing lives were, therefore, regarded as unnecessary. As unemployment increased, pressure from society and governments to persuade women to return to their homes increased. What society and governments seemed unwilling to face was that the "homes" depended wholly or partly on women's paycheques.

"I did . . . she just said 'Why not!'" Len Norris, Vancouver *Sun*

In the late 1960s the Royal Commission on the Status of Women began its hearings amid general derision and amusement from the press and a large segment of the public. But as the hearings went on, and women's hardships were chronicled, it became apparent that this report, which was tabled in 1970 with its 167 recommendations, was one of the most important royal commissions in Canada's history. The recommendations set down in clear, irrefutable terms a litany of all the ways Canadian society discriminated against women. Slowly the federal government began to respond with legislation, equal opportunity programs in the public service, etc. One of the recommendations of the commission was the establishment of an advisory council. This was set up in 1973.

The attitudes of feminists in the early 1970s were spontaneous, optimistic and even euphoric as many women realized for the first time that their experiences, as women, were not unique, but shared by women all over the country. Consciousness-raising was a tremendous release and learning experience for many women who had never before questioned or even tried to describe their role in society. Women's organizations sprung up all over the country to study and make recommendations to governments. Books about the history of women, their psychology, sexuality appeared. Women's studies programs were launched in university courses. Agitation to have less stereotyped textbooks in schools began.

All of these activities peaked in International Women's Year in 1975 at the world conference in Mexico City.

But after 1975, typically, governments that had responded with legislation for many of the more manageable recommendations of the royal commission seemed to forget about the female half of the population again. Women themselves seemed almost discouraged by the lack of progress, although they began to focus their energies on more specific issues, such as rape crisis centres and hostels for battered women. The media changed "Women's" pages to "Lifestyle" or "Family" pages. There was less coverage of the women's movement by the media, and occasionally the movement was even declared "dead."

But the realities of women's lives continued to defy traditional attitudes and expectations of society and experts. Although government statisticians continued to label women as "secondary workers" and base future labour shortages on that assumption, women continued to join the work force as permanent members. Many worked because their paycheques were necessary to boost family incomes over the poverty line. Many worked as single-parent heads of families. But the majority by far were still clustered in the low end of the pay scale in low-paid, dead-end jobs.

The long struggle for equal pay for work of equal value, the continued existence of female ghettos in the work force and the ever-widening gap between the average salaries of men and women were still very much with us. Women were still not being recognized as permanent members of the work force even though by 1979, 48 percent of all women worked outside of the home and 38 percent of the total work force was female. Women were still being cut out of special training programs. Cuts in unemployment benefits hurt women most. Seventy-one percent of all part-time workers were women and two-thirds of them were not eligible for unemployment insurance if they worked less than 20 hours a week. The value of housewives' work was not counted in the gross national product, although Statistics Canada estimated that it counted for one-third of the GNP. Poverty became synonymous with women, especially older women.

By the end of the decade some small measurable progress could be observed, however. In professional schools that had been overwhelmingly male, such as medicine, law, business administration, more and more young women were being admitted. But on the other hand, unemployment among women was still higher than among men. There was no guarantee that there would be jobs for all of the aspiring female lawyers, doctors and MBAS. All through Canadian society, women still had to be better educated to earn the same salary as men.

However, women themselves were becoming more realistic and better organized. Voluntary groups that had been formed to deal with the real problems women faced, such as rape crisis centres and hostels for battered women, still struggled along on inadequate funds because governments generally didn't recognize them as part of the regular social structures.

Women were beginning to recognize their own power as lobbyists. As 51 percent of the population, they were tired of being treated as a minority group. They were beginning to rebel against the entrenched and paternalistic medical-social services hierarchy. Signs that they were at least attracting the attention of advertisers and school boards in their efforts to eliminate sex-stereotyping could be seen. The whole subject of violence towards women was widely discussed and aired. The new family laws at least recognized the contribution of women as equal to men's contribution in the marriage partnership.

But the fundamental fact that women at the end of the 1970s are still economically disadvantaged at every level in society means the struggle for change must continue well into the 1980s and beyond. And the struggle continues to be about a change in attitudes as well as for an equal slice of the economic and social pie. Many women still believe what men say about them – that they are good only for a *Playboy* centrefold or work at the kitchen sink. Women who stay home to raise families are not fairly valued or represented in the halls of power. Those who work in the labour force have to continually defend their right to do so. It's perhaps symbolic, that, for Canadians, the 1970s has been a decade of facing painful economic realities after the boom of the 1960s. For women the pain has been the slowness of Canadian society to accept and adapt to their rights and needs, of being the lowest priority when austerity hits, and the scapegoats on which many economic and other problems in society are often pinned.

Doris Anderson, president of the Canadian Advisory Council on the Status of Women.

Women in the News

Women who have changed the course of the decade for other women:

Doris Anderson, for her persistent feminist editorials in *Chatelaine*.

Flora MacDonald and **Rosemary Brown,** for the courage and persistence to be the first serious candidates for leadership of national political parties.

Pauline McGibbon, for breaking new ground, and doing superbly as lieutenant governor of Ontario.

Laura Sabia, unreconstructed and noisy feminist, especially as chairman of the Ontario Status of Women Council.

Irene Murdoch, who suffered so unjustly at the hands of law that marital property laws were at last redrawn.

Marian Engel, whose novel *Bear* unabashedly showed that women too have odd sexual fantasies.

Betty Kennedy and **Isabel Bassett,** who showed that it is chic to work, even if financially unnecessary.

Maureen McTeer and **Margaret Trudeau,** who march to their own special drummer.

Shirley Carr, who broke the all-male CLC barrier.

Barbara Greene, who proved a single woman can be reelected after bearing a child out of wedlock.

Gloria Steinem, beauty, brains, *Ms* magazine – convinced feminists need not depend upon stridency.

Betty Friedan, seminal.

Margaret Thatcher, who made it (?).

Indira Ghandi, who blew it!

Judy LaMarsh, lawyer, author, former cabinet minister.

Something happened during the last ten years. I spoke to my mother. I spoke to my daughter. Each spoke to me. Each spoke to each other. Amen.

Helen Hutchinson, TV host

Margaret Thatcher, Prime Minister of Britain, 1979. AP

The New Woman: My Mom with Cats

Notes toward a definition of the New Woman, by a man old enough to remember when girls were the only people who wore ponytails:

1. The New Woman is astoundingly knowledgeable about all aspects of nutrition or *seems* to be. She knows three different recipes for granola. She knows about protein chains and essential amino acids.

She knows that sodium nitrite (or is it nitrate?) in bacon causes cancer. She knows what a wheat germ is and why it's good for you. She has a long list of proscribed foods which, she warns me, I will ingest at my peril: refined sugar; anything coloured red, like maraschino cherries; Coke; white bread; Big Macs; indeed, almost anything I like to eat.

The most interesting thing about the New Woman's obsession with Things That Are Bad For You is that *the list keeps changing*. The New Woman is exactly like my mother in that respect.

2. The New Woman has either had a brief, tender affair with a sculptor or guitar player who is several years younger than herself, or she is about to.

3. The New Woman invariably reflects her origins, no matter how hard she tries to transcend them. The Jewish New Woman, for instance, still can't bear to throw out a plastic shopping bag. The Central Ontario WASP New Woman knows in her heart that if she ever gets married, it will probably have to be in a church.

4. The New Woman always has at least three of the following on her bookshelf: *Women and Madness*; *Our Bodies, Ourselves*; *Sexual Politics*; anything by Doris Lessing; *Let's Eat Right*; *Recipes for a Small Planet*; *The Managerial Woman*; *The Joy of Sex*; and *Your Erroneous Zones*. The only one she hasn't read is *The Managerial Woman*.

5. The most crucial word in the New Woman's vocabulary is, "supportive."

Broadly speaking, she wants everybody to be supportive. The men in her life are supposed to be supportive. So are her relatives, although her mother seldom is. It is especially urgent that her women friends be supportive, but they frequently disappoint her by "getting into a funny space" or "going through some funny changes" or by stealing her man.

6. The New Woman talks excessively about her cat – cats, rather, since she more typically has two. She gives them cute names like Che and Sigmund and Nellie McClung.

7. The New Woman drives a Honda Civic. She is shocked every month by her Chargex bill. She wants to go to Mexico next January. She's either traded up to a Cuisinart from her Waring blender, or is about to. She confides in her masseuse instead of her hairdresser. She wants a better stereo. She also wants a baby, but she will get the stereo first.

8. The New Women is 27 or, at most, 28. If she is divorced, she is between 32 and 34.

9. The New Woman's cycle of self-renewal begins in September. This is when she enrolls in a night school course in automobile maintenance at Central Tech. This is when she starts shopping for a new lover or a new job. This is when she resolves that, *this* year, she's going to see all the new plays and buy a symphony subscription. This is when she does yoga three mornings in a row.

10. The New Woman's relationships must, of course, all be "meaningful." They must be based on "sharing" and, of course, "equality." The New Woman has great difficulty in finding men who measure up to these exacting requirements. She is, therefore, talking about (a) having a baby on her own; (b) cultivating more male friends who are gay ("They're so understanding") or (c) becoming asexual. Sometimes she fantasizes about truck drivers.

11. Things The New Woman is against: Kraft Cheez-Whiz; pollution; men in boxer shorts; typing; anybody who declines to regard Dr. Henry Morgentaler as a selfless hero of our time.

12. Things The New Woman is for: yogurt; garage sales; men with small, tight bums; Judy Collins and Sylvia Tyson; non-sexist children's books with titles like Jenny and Melissa repair Daddy's Tractor; Dr. Morgentaler.

13. The New Woman definitely wants to settle down with a man "with no hangups." But not now. And not, apparently, with me. This is the whole trouble with the New Woman.

Alexander Ross, from, The Toronto *Star*.

Future Goals for the Women's Movement

Is it Juliet Mitchell in *The Longest Revolution* who says that women are involved in a long, very long, battle and all, absolutely all, energies must be mobilized? So 1990, to a certain extent, seems so close to us and at the same time so far away . . . Women's liberation: an exhausting 20 year guerilla war, subversion and infiltration into men's world.

No price is too high to pay. Our daughters will be the main beneficiaries of our vast movement of protests and demands. They are the ones who will have a chance to form and carry out a collective plan or scheme for themselves.

What I mean is that for another decade we will still be fighting to obtain *specific* rights. By then, our daughters should be able to draw up wide collective social goals for themselves and, as a whole, women will take hold of *their* share of power. In ten years they should be able to say: "We women ..." instead of "I a woman." The idea is to become collectively "political."

Before women begin that type of fundamental action, we will have to pursue the more immediate battles to obtain full equality of opportunities and economic independence. And I think that it will take a few more years to accomplish the recommendations of the Byrd commission in Canada and those of the Conseil du Statut de la femme in Quebec.

Briefly, here are some of the most immediate objectives women must attain to reach the essential first step, which is, as far as I am concerned, equality of opportunity and economic independence:

The abolition of sexism aimed at small children, especially through the elimination of all stereotypes in schoolbooks, games, etc.

The recognition of the right to choose motherhood by giving women access to proper birth control and even to voluntary termination of pregnancy.

The genuine free access of women to the job market by intensifying programs facilitating the return to work of housewives.

The institution of paid maternity and/or paternity leave.

The creation of a complete network of day-care centres.

A complete reform of civil laws aimed at bringing spouses to an equal level: revision of marriage contracts, the right of mothers to transfer their maiden names to their children, etc.

An intense effort to force the medical field to be more respectful of women; for example, a more cautious attitude towards such surgical procedures as hysterectomies, mastectomies and caesarian sections.

Better preparation for and available information regarding women going through menopause, thus limiting psychological and physical consequences.

A fiscal system enabling women raising small children to be recognized as workers.

A substantial participation of women in the power structure, associations, trade unions, political parties, governments, etc.

Lise Payette, ministère des consommateurs, gouvernement du Québec.

A '70s Disaster:

The one good thing about disasters is that they happen to someone else and usually that someone else is a hell of a long way from where most of us live. Floods leave millions dead and homeless in Bangladesh or volcanos decide to spill their guts over a crowd of natives that are living on a far-off island that very few of us have ever seen.

As such, the word "disaster" loses much of the punch that was intended, unless, of course, we find ourselves watching one in a movie house or on television. The '70s have ended all that. The past ten years have seen half the world threatened with a fate far worse than death. Nay, death would be a blessing. With the '70s has come enslavement for half the world's population.

An M.I.H.

And, worse, the most important half (see preceding drawing): Man.

Yes, *Man.*

The very thought, I know, will send chills up the spine of every decent, loving and law-abiding creature. But what is this threat to God's own favourite being? *Woman.*

Giddy with joy at the generous gift of man during the '20s, the right to vote, woman has bounded on and clawed her way into a position of power during the '70s that threatens not only man but the way of life once chosen for millions of air-breathing, animated beings. Like a large monster from a Japanese movie, she has slithered her way into the hearts of man and now threatens to control the world.

How has this happened?

It is not hard to see how kind, gentle man has been bamboozled into handing over the reins of power. Occupied with a Wall Street crash swiftly followed by a World War, man found the '30s and '40s giant pits of problems that had to be solved. Never fearing, he packed up his troubles in his old kit bag and smiled, smiled, smiled. Once in foreign parts, the poor sod had little time to concern himself with the little woman back home hiding behind a set of knitting needles and a pair of half-finished socks. How could he know that the greatest army the world has ever seen was beginning to plot and scheme. Not the army ahead, but the army left at home.

Slowly, ever so slowly, this army began to move. Held to the cover of its homes, it took the Vietnam War of the '60s to move it into the open. Lost in the crowd of demonstrators, women were at last able to communicate with each other. At long last they ventured out and linked arms with others of their underground army.

With every beard seen venting its hatred on L.B.J, a heaving bosom pushed and shoved the poor bearded sucker into the fray. Urging the men ever forward, women shielded themselves from the gaze of suspicious men. Women were able to hold massive meetings on behalf of the cause of Women at the very centre of what appeared to be demonstrations against a war. Poor, easily deceived men hurled their bricks as the women at their sides quietly discussed what they felt were their rights and the time of the next day's meeting.

With the men at war and in the streets, important offices of the nations soon became short of staff. Women made their move. Slowly they inched their way through the corridors of power until it was impossible to enter an executive washroom and find the seat in the upright position.

By the time Vietnam and Watergate were a thing of the past, women were entrenched. The truth was out. Too late. We were into the '70s and the disaster known as Women's Rights was firmly in place.

By 1979 the greatest blow of all: God's chosen being, the Englishman, was forced to step aside and watch in horror as a woman accepted the role of prime minister of England.

A woman blowing kisses from the steps of 10 Downing Street as a poor, befuddled man urged her to hurry inside as her supper was on the table.

England will never be the same again.

Man will never be the same again.

Disasters of the '70s?

I give you a disaster of the '70s, '80s, '90s and ever more.

I give you . . .

The Women's Movement . . . please take it.

Ben Wicks, cartoonist, author.

Women's Year

I suppose it was inevitable that some sensitive soul at the United Nations would one day place a finger on the global pulse and decide it was time to proclaim International Women's Year. Women, after all, were fashionable. Refugees were fashionable in 1959, so the U.N. threw a special year for them. It was International Cooperation Year in 1965 (though it's tough to comprehend why the U.N. felt *that* was particularly fashionable) and it was the year for Human Rights in 1968. Then, in 1974, we had World Population Year. It never did get through to me whether we were being asked to celebrate the miracle of conception or the discovery of the Pill.

In 1975, though, women were up-front enough to achieve the same international status as Education (1970), Books (1972) and Action to Combat Racism and Racial Discrimination (1971). One reason women were visible and therefore fashionable, of course, was because of the highly vocal women's movement. Surely no one believes we'd have won out in the U.N.'s pick-a-year committee (over say, International Garbage Year or World Plastic Food Year – both of them long overdue) had not some of us been sassy. We were fashionable because of currently simmering guilts. Oh, come on – only an organization squirming with guilt could solemnly admit the aims of IWY were to "promise equality between men and women. Ensure the full integration of women in economic, social and cultural development. And to recognize the importance of women in the strengthening of world peace."

We were fashionable because of Germaine Greer, Xaviera Hollander, Golda Meir and motherhood. On second thought, strike out motherhood. We were fashionable because of new words and phrases that were so In, they were practically – or some fervently hoped – on their way Out. Male chauvinism and job stereotyping. Women's Work and Affirmative Action. Ms. The orgasm/fecundity split in the archetype of the temptress. Lesbian nation. Trust in God – She will provide. Total fulfillment. Future shlock.

So what did we think of International Women's Year? After some dedicated checking, I can tell you that we hated it, approved it, distrusted it, tolerated it. I've talked to Women's Libbers who feel it was a calculated attempt to divide the women's movement and diffuse energies for fighting the cause. I've talked to some activists who believe it angered those who failed to get grants. And others who say that those who were angered at least learned what it was like to deal with the bureaucracy.

I've talked to women who believe the plethora of IWY festivals, exhibitions and media publicity focussed the spotlight on issues and created a forum for discussion. I've talked to women who believe the discussion was hot air.

I stood on a street and asked both men and women what they thought of IWY. Some of the responses: "My husband didn't like it." "A lot of women who couldn't get jobs went out and got grants and now they're stuck with no more funding." "Well, at least it brought out the drip-dry crowd. I saw them at the Viveca Lindfors show during the Women's Festival of the Arts in Toronto. They were roaring with appreciation at all the brutal clichés about men." "The government doesn't want us to have equal pay – where would the corporations find their cheap labour?"

And something I heard more often: The only way to improve things for women in Canada is for the government to bring in legislation to set standards for affirmative action programs. They've done it in the United States. Governments and corporations must start training women and begin to think about quotas and selective recruitment. Then there has to be contract compliance. It would be against the law to deal with any company, government or institution that did not have an adequate affirmative action program.

I talked to Sharon Batt, editor of *Branching Out*, a woman's magazine published in Edmonton, who passed on some replies from a nationwide survey about IWY: "The government was willing to fund artsy-craftsy, discussion-type, personal development programs, but nothing that would encourage large numbers of women to enter the labour force." "I think it was fantastic – it gave women an opportunity to look at themselves and the job they're doing." "IWY should have made a greater impact – but then, women were not given the top jobs so they at least were not to blame for the mediocre publicity, direction and planning.

Personally, I'm inclined to be neutral about IWY, and this is not a cop-out. It's realistic. I'm not sure whether it had any real impact – good or bad – because even those who condemn it or praise it will waver in their opinion if you talk about the year for long enough. All I know for sure is that it had little real impact on me. I don't think the U.N. had any sinister motives when it proclaimed the big bash. I simply think its Events Committee thought it was doing something awfully clever. I don't think Ottawa was plotting anything more devious than a shot at breathing time – both during and after the party – in the hope that some controversial issues would either go away or be conveniently resolved. I do think that everyone who got us into IWY truly believed we would be flattered, pleased and diverted from our ceaseless bitching into being very, very busy.

I don't think anyone's expectations have come up to scratch and I don't think it matters. Women are a resilient gender. I'm not hopeful we will see immediate changes in attitude or even changes. The two World Wars and the Depression of the 1930s caused massive global changes and it is significant that in this century, they were the times when women themselves changed most.

It's a depressing thought that our effective advances have been linked with disaster and stark necessity. But the economic temper of the times seems to indicate that we are about to take our next long step along the yellow brick road.

Betty Lee, author, journalist. From *The Canadian*.

10 Best Jokes of the 70s

Whaddaya get when you put a canary in
  a Cuisinart?
Shredded Tweet.

Searching for Truth and Roots, a business exec quits his nine-to-five job and
decides to move back to the land as a
chicken rancher.

He goes into the local farm co-op and
buys 500 baby chicks.

A week later, he's back at the supplier
and picks up *another* 500 baby chicks.

A week goes by and the exec turns up
at the co-op again!

"I want 500 *more* baby chicks!" says
the exec-turned-farmer.

"Wow!" cries the local dealer. "That
makes 1,500 you've bought so far! Your
chicken ranch must be going great
guns!"

"Naw," sez the city kid sadly.
"They're all dead. I must either be plant-
ing them too deep or too far apart."

Two pin-stripe wheeler-dealers are having lunch at a private club. They're crying the well-known blues over a mostly
liquid lunch.

"So how are things *really*," asks one
broker after the second martini.

"Awful," sez his lunchmate, big tears
welling up in his eyes. "I just came from
my doctor: he says I've got VD. Me! I've
got VD at 40!"

"Hell!" cries his friend loudly. "You
think *you* got problems? I got INCO at
nineteen and a half!"

Pierre Trudeau has been campaigning
across the prairie farm country all day
long.

The sun is hot, the barnyards stink
and the farmers seem unresponsive.

Last stop of the day is what appears
to be a muddy farmyard, but as the Liberal organizers slog forward to 50 prairie
farmers, they realize it's wall-to-wall
manure and pig plops.

Trudeau is standing ankle-deep in the
shit, shaking hands and trying to smile
when a grizzled old farmer comes running up and grabs the prime minister in
mock horror.

"I'll save you sir!" yells the farmer to
his grinning colleagues. "I'll save you
from melting!"

Two city slickers decide to spend the
weekend ice-fishing at the cottage.

At the end of the second day, they are
huddled together wearing everything
they own, staring down a little hole in the
lake.

Not a nibble, not a bite and they've
run out of beer.

Suddenly, they see four snowmobiles
r-o-a-r across the frozen lake, the drivers
yelling and waving.

"Ya see?" cries the ice fisherman to
his buddy. "I told ya! That's what *we*
oughta be doing! Trolling!"

A giant Christmas party is raging on the
twenty-second floor office digs of the
town's biggest law firm.

A young comer in a three-piece-suit is
having a cozy desk-top drinkiepoo with a
young lady who seems *very* interested.

"Hey!" cries the young lawyer, stall-
ing for time til' he can manoeuver her
into the broom closet. "Whatever happened to Jack's secretary – that loonie
broad with the big boobs who kept yack-
ing all the time about women's rights?
Remember her? What happened to the
big blonde with the big mouth?"

The secretary eyes him coldly.
"I dyed my hair."

What do you do if you see Joe Clark
  coming with a pin in his hand?
Run like hell.
It means he's got the grenade in his
  mouth.

Have you heard that Robert Stanfield
says as soon as he's elected, he's buying

178

the Canadian Forces 500 brand-new septic tanks?

And as soon as the generals figure out how to run 'em, they're gonna attack Paul Hellyer.

MP Tom Cossitt was discovered running down the hallways of the Centre Block, yelling:

"Trudeau's a lousy leader! Trudeau is a lousy leader!"

Mounties grabbed the outspoken MP and locked him away in a basement dungeon.

It is well after midnight when Solicitor-General Jean-Jacques Blais arrives at Cossitt's cell.

"Why are you holding me?" demands Cossitt of Blais.

"For what you said about the prime minister," Blais explains. "You're going to be locked up for 20 years and ten days."

"Twenty years and ten days?" asks Cossitt.

"Twenty years for yelling in the Centre Block," sez the Solicitor-General, "and ten days for telling a state secret."

Times are so tough panhandlers on Yonge Street now ask for their small change in German marks.

10 Worst Jokes of the 70s

What's two shades of blue and lives in the cellar?
The Toronto Argos.

What do you get if you put a pirana and a puppy in a electric blender?
Pirana Dog Chow.

What do you call an octopus who puts safety pins in his tentacles, sings with a punk rock band, has a girl friend who's mysteriously murdered and finally dies himself?
Squid Vicious.

An Argo fan is sitting in the stands, trying to keep his eyes off the bloodbath going on at the game.

Suddenly, behind him, he spots a huge, blue-eyed sheepdog, tears pouring down its face as it watches the Argo game. The dog is crying its heart out!

"Is that your dog?" he asks of the guy sitting next to it.

"Yeah," sez the guy. "Rex is a real Argo fan."

"He's crying!" exclaims the first guy. "I've never seen anything like it!"

"Yeah, Rex always cries when the Argos lose," claims the owner.

"What does he do when they win?" asks the fan.

"I don't know," sez the owner. "I've only had him eight years."

What's the difference between a buffalo and a bison?
Have you ever tried to wash your hands in a buffalo?

Did ya hear about the sperm whale who fell in love with a submarine?
Every time the sub shot a torpedo, the whale gave his buddies cigars.

Have you heard about the rotten mugger who beat up a kid on the corner and stole 25¢ from him?
Police are looking for a quarter-person-pounder.

One out of four Americans owns a gun. That means that any *one* of the Lennon Sisters could kill you.

What does Ayatollah Khomeini tell people who ask why he wants to be head of Iran?
"If Ayatollah you once, Ayatollah you twice, Ayatollah you three times! Khomeini times I gotta tell you?"

Do you know that Great Britain has a

whole department to look after clones? Clonial Office? Where do clones go on vacation? Cloney Island? Who loans clones money at high interest to duplicate themselves? Clone Sharks! Where do you find the most clones in Canada? The Clonedike! Where do clones go when they die? Nowhere. They clonely live once.

Gary Dunford, Toronto Sun.

Education

It was the 1960s that concentrated man's attention on the concept that education was salvation. The school replaced the church, the teacher supplanted the priest, the diploma, certificate or degree became the mark of virtue and well-being.

And there was good reason. H. G. Wells had stated that the race was between education and annihilation, but the "balance of terror" had seen mankind through the '50s. Education was seen as synonymous with a high standard of living and the good life. "Stay in school" was the persuasive and pervasive advice given to young people by employers, politicians and newspaper editors.

Education, they said, would provide young people with the skills to assure a career in the age of computers, with its superindustrial system based on growth, production and waste. Education would blur the distinctions of rich and poor; allowing any person an opportunity to climb the ladder to power and affluence (assuming both ability and motivation). Education would raise the cultural and spiritual life of our society.

The '60s culminated in a supreme belief in the civilizing, humanizing features of individualized, liberal education. Even the expectations of the hardened businessman were borne out by the evidence that investment in educational activity could be proven to bring a 17 percent dividend. What more could one ask?

For those who unthinkingly and uncritically accepted the rhetoric of the '60s, the '70s were ashes in the mouth. To be fair, most of those propounding the exaggerated claims of "paradise found" were talking of schooling, not education. Before the decade began, Ivan Illich had analyzed with cutting clarity the weaknesses of schools and systems of education built on institutionalized learning. But in Canada, the emphasis was still on building more schools, community colleges and universities and additions thereto, adding more facilities to the community colleges that, by one name or another, began to spring up all over the country, and enlarging the extraordinary number of universities Canada had established by the centenary of its union. True, one or two provincial treasurers had ruminated about the percentage of revenues being drained off by the educational enterprise, but these were regarded as the bad-humoured observations that men of finance are at times prone to make.

Before long, indeed, before the '70s could scarcely be said to have settled in, the costs of education began to concern every government. For the economy was slowing down – inevitably – and the debts incurred through the massive expansion of the public sector since World War II (and increased schooling was only one aspect of the expansion) became an inflationary pressure and an embarrassment.

But leaving money aside, the idealism of the '60s had become tarnished. For it became evident that schooling did not create jobs – except for teachers and professors and support staff. Indeed, it became evident by mid-decade that another process had come into effect: the university degree had become debased coinage. Both in terms of status and income expectation, the bachelor's degree had lost its value. As well, it became obvious that Canada was training many of its professionals beyond levels at which the economy could provide satisfying employment. At the same time, the educational system was not providing skilled craftsmen, able tradesmen, effective middle managers or first-rate technologists in proper numbers. The country was simultaneously complaining about the high cost of education and disconcerted by the fact that companies were still importing their valuable employees from the UK and Europe.

Nor had the schooling of the young really solved the stratification of our society. The children of the well-to-do, or comparatively so, to a great extent, still filled the universities. The inner-city programs, indeed, all the efforts to raise by the bootstraps those defined as culturally deprived, had not brought the millennium. Many recognized the basic reason: that in most cases children can only be brought to a delight in learning along with their families and communities. But for others, it was apparent that not only had money been wasted, but also the school's role had been distorted. For now not only Johnny, but Janey, Jimmy, Susie and Ernie couldn't read – and they had come from "good" homes where books were collected and displayed.

Finally, Canada had come to realize at the end of the '60s how little care it had given to the transmission of its history, its culture, its victories and defeats, to its own children. Canadian history was given a "shot in the arm" and "CanLit" courses began to spring up on every campus. But it had come too late. In the '70s, as in most social revolutionary periods, it was not enough to give insight and perception to the children. No resolution of the basic question of Canada's future as a unified nation had been possible and the educational system was seen as culprit in the creation of a gulf too wide to comprehend.

Nor did schooling save us from the nasty eruptions of racism. As the mix of our people changed, and as more black people came from the Caribbean and as more brown people came from Uganda, the UK or more directly from Southeast Asia, there developed a tension in our cities not unlike that which had ultimately destroyed the decency of other North American communities. The schools had not been able to do more than reflect the prejudices and hatreds of the community around. Once more, the expectations of the community had been unfulfilled.

The schooling system in Canada had been greatly advantaged, when, in 1960, the federal government had made a significant contribution to the capital costs of vocational training in every province. Hundreds of millions of dollars were poured into facilities and equipment. Ironically, this investment had less influence on the provision of skilled workers for industry that it had on the provision of wider cultural options, particularly in the secondary schools. The extraordinary explosion of theatre, art and music across Canada since centennial year has at least some of its roots in the generous infusion of resources into schools and the rather imaginative use that was made of them. For the '60s had seen a virtual doubling of the percentage of students who could be convinced of the value of completing secondary school. Having increased the spectrum of interests and abilities of students exponentially by that process, the school found that it then had to serve those widening interests at several levels of natural ability. The "cafeteria-style" program of the secondary school was the answer. But it became the target of those who wished to criticize the costs in the late '70s, for these were the "frills" – along with trips, projects, heritage programs, English as a second language – that host of services that had grown beyond imagination throughout the decade. It was evidence of the complete lack of focus and direction that had infected the schools in the '60s and was to be eradicated in the '70s.

All in all, the schooling system was judged and found guilty. It had failed to support the economic goals of the nation, it had made little impact in providing social justice and economic equality, it had played no role in keeping Canada united, but had, instead, succumbed to collecting cultural enthusiasms and academic ambitions that were seen to have little to do with the basic task of training the young.

The effect of these negative perceptions of schools and teachers, colleges, universities and faculties was dramatic.

First came a demand for a return to the basics. With the "Hall-Dennis Report" as a national scapegoat, the hue and cry for better reading and numeracy skills became deafening. There was evidence of short-fall – as there always has been. There was little recognition of the inevitable diluting effect of mass education and less willingness to concede the value of other forms of communication. It was "back to basics" – and as the '70s depart, those convinced of the importance of other understandings and sensitivities are struggling to keep the schools tolerable for many students whose interest in a narrow academic path is questionable.

These collective disappointments of the citizenry as they related to the schooling system most certainly affected the priority of education in budgets, both provincial and municipal. Other priorities emerged – health care and environment most certainly. By the end of the decade all these concerns had joined schooling as objects of budget restraint, in the realization that the public sector must be a lesser burden in an economy no longer growing with vigour and dynamism. The linkages between school-board budgets and the cost of oil, inflation, unemployment, the falling dollar were clear and direct. Canada was not just leaving an old decade, it was entering a new era. John Robarts, the man who dominated the '60s and fashioned the '70s in Ontario, admitted we would never see the buoyancy and consumerism of post-war Canada again. Most observers agreed with that analysis.

These outside pressures have led to divisiveness and frustration within the system. In place of increased salaries came restraint and, even more shocking, the spectre of redundancy. As the '70s close, with falling enrollments, elementary teachers by the hundreds are being phased out; fewer in the western provinces, but even there the fear exists. As important in terms of morale has been the loss in mobility. During the '50s and '60s teachers, especially those in secondary schools, could expect to move from school to school, from area to area and, more significantly, up the ladder to chairman of a department, to vice-principal and ultimately to principal and into the central administration. The frustrations and disappointments that teaching inevitably bring to the idealist could be sublimated within the hopes of new surroundings, new colleagues, new responsibilities and new rewards. That world is gone and the fury of those who have been forced out is only slightly more than that of those who have to stay!

The college and the university saw only minor deviations, downward for the university sector to be sure, but the restraint was largely financial – driven doubtless not only by macrobudgetary considerations but also by government preparation for the enrollment disasters projected for the '80s. Capital support in some provinces dried up in the early '70s, but in all provinces the year-to-year increase in operating funds no longer matched the inflationary trends. The effects have been electric. Faculty unrest and unionization and evidence of academic deterioration abound. Federal support for research, never considered adequate in the '50s and '60s, has been even more distractingly absent in the '70s.

The '70s began with expectations that the "community school" would be the bulwark of educational progress in the future. There was considerable difference of opinion as to whether this designation meant opening the school gymnasium and arts and crafts rooms for parental participation – or whether it meant that parents would have some real interchange on curriculum and learning methods with principals and teachers. In any case, the objectives of both groups were only minimally met. The cost of an overtime caretaker so often frustrated the former, while professional fears and jealousies in a period of fiscal restraint limited the success of the latter group in many jurisdictions.

The decade has seen a substantial shift in imagination from east to west. As the CGEPs (college d'enseignement general et professionnel) in Quebec were a leap forward in the '60s, the most exciting developments in Canada in the '70s, I suspect, will be the continuing education councils spread throughout Alberta, the community based college system in Saskatchewan, the new commitments in the universities to research on the one hand, and the outreach through an enhancement of noncredit education on the other in the most western provinces in our country.

Thus a decade begun in the glow of idealism (misguided as it may have been in some cases) has concluded in the cynicism of destroyed expectations. The chanting of angry demonstrators, the sit-in, the disruption of unpopular lectures or even convocation ceremonies may be the memory of the '60s, but budget cuts, redundancy, basics, raw accountability will focus the nostalgia of the '70s. With some confidence in the pendulum theory of education, welcome to the '80s.

Walter G. Pitman, president, Ryerson Polytechnical Institute.

The Russians Are Coming...

Although it was the most famous Canadian sporting moment of the decade – there are few people who can't remember precisely where they were, and with whom, when it occurred – the goal Paul Henderson scored on September 28, 1972, at the Luzhniki Sports Palace in Moscow scarcely serves to sum up what happened to hockey in the '70s. Henderson's goal was a winner, the third winning goal he had scored in that unforgettable first series between Team Canada and the Soviet Nationals. When he scored it, with just 36 seconds left in the eighth and deciding game, Canadian hockey fans were ecstatic. Our system, our players, had triumphed, albeit over a system and a team that had been given little chance against us when the series had first been arranged.

That, however, was the last series a Canadian team was to win in the '70s over the Russians' best, and by April of 1979, when a team composed of the best players from the National Hockey League's worst clubs went to Moscow for the World Championships, the Russians' superiority was clearly established; they had taken over the game that had evolved on the frozen rivers and the sloughs of the Canadian outdoors, and had gradually declined in its excellence at home.

The biggest spur to that decline had come in 1967, when the NHL expanded suddenly from six teams to 12. There simply weren't enough players of the top rank to man those teams. When the World Hockey Association was launched a few years later, and waved large enough cheques to bring over such NHL stars as Bobby Hull, Gerry Cheevers and, indeed, Paul Henderson, the dilution grew worse. Conn Smythe, the man who had built one of the greatest dynasties in all of sports, the Toronto Maple Leafs, but who could not by 1979 remember the names of all the cities that had professional teams, summed it up: "I don't drink whisky," he said. "But I know that when you put too much water in it you ruin it. And there's too much water in hockey now."

Paul Henderson scored the winning goal in Canada-Russia series, 1972. Toronto *Star*

With the players of superior skills spread so thinly, more and more professional teams tried to follow the pattern that the post-expansion Philadelphia Flyers – the Broad Street Bullies – had used to win two Stanley Cups. Lacking accomplished skaters and stick-handlers, the new-style teams concentrated on defense and, at their worst, intimidation. Offense became increasingly a matter of throwing the puck into the opponents' corners and sending in the big guys to fight for it. Finesse was scarce.

At the same time, the Soviets – and to a remarkable degree, the Czechs – continued to hone the skills of their international teams. Their systems were elitist, reaching into (in the Russians' case) their vast numbers of potential athletes to find those best suited for hockey, and offering them the best facilities and training the state could provide. To many fans, the skills the Russians exhibited in their rise to the top recalled the best of the earlier Canadian game: quick and accurate passing, deft stick-handling and a reliance on accuracy in shooting instead of the awesome but often erratic power of the Canadian slap shot. A few voices – notably that of Howie Meeker, a former NHL player and coach who rose to such prominence as a hockey analyst in the '70s that Canadian radio and television artists presented him with their highest award for "outspokenness and integrity" – cried out for the need for a radical readjustment of the Canadian game. The cries went unheard. By the end of the decade, even the mighty Montreal Canadiens, the preeminent North American team, had added rugged checking and size in the corners to their arsenal of weapons. Though the Canadiens were still the quickest team in the western world, their moments of what their articulate goalie, Ken Dryden, called "prettiness" were fewer.

In January of 1979, the Soviet National team beat the best of the NHL six-zero in New York. The collection of players who went to Moscow that spring played gallantly but without hope. As Ed Staniowski, the goaltender who had been – with meaning – the outstanding Canadian player in a nine-two loss to the Soviets, said: "They're better athletes playing a better system." Paul Henderson, the man who had lifted so many hearts seven years earlier, was in Alabama, playing out the final season of a team called the Birmingham Bulls.

Peter Gzowski, journalist, broadcaster, author.

The Ten Greatest Tennis Players

Bjorn Borg	Guillermo Vilas
Jimmy Connors	Ilie Nastase
Rod Laver	Ken Rosewall
John Newcombe	Adriano Panatta
Arthur Ashe	**Dr. Robert Bregman,** head professional,
Stan Smith	Downtown Tennis Club, Toronto.

The Big Hockey Deals

The Guy Lafleur deal: The Montreal Canadiens obtained Oakland's first-round draft pick in the 1971 Amateur Draft and François Lacombe, in return for Montreal's first choice in the 1970 Amateur Draft and Ernie Hicke. The choice made by Montreal in the 1971 Amateur Draft was Guy Lafleur. I consider this to be the most outstanding deal of the '70s.

Bobby Orr set the National Hockey League buzzing when he agreed to a five-year $1 million contract with the Boston Bruins in the summer of 1971. This was the first $1 million contract in the history of hockey and made Orr one of the top-salaried players in all sports. This was one year before the World Hockey Association came into being.

Bobby Orr. CP

Bobby Hull signed a contract for ten years for $3 million with the Winnipeg Jets of the newly formed World Hockey Association in 1972.

Marcel Dionne signed with the Los Angeles Kings in 1974 as a free agent and received $1.8 million for six years.

Wilf Paiement was chosen in the under-age draft in June of 1974 and signed a contract with the Kansas City Scouts that made him the highest-paid draft pick in hockey history. He earned approximately $800,000 for the four-year contract.

Darryl Sittler and **Lanny McDonald** signed seven-year contracts in 1977 with the Toronto Maple Leafs, each of which was in excess of one million dollars. The outstanding aspect of these negotiations was that Sittler and McDonald took 40 percent less than they were offered elsewhere in order to stay and play with the Toronto Maple Leafs.

The Big Hockey Events

The 1972 Canada-Russian eight-game series was the most outstanding event in Canadian sports history – Team Canada defeated the Soviet Union on Paul Henderson's last-minute goal in the eighth game. Canada won four, lost three and tied one in the eight-game series.

The 1976 Canada Cup of hockey tournament involved six countries: Canada, USA, Czechoslovakia, Soviet Union, Sweden and Finland. Darryl Sittler's overtime goal won the Canada Cup for Team Canada over the Czechoslovakian national team. Bobby Orr was named the outstanding player of the tournament, which was his last major hockey series.

The 1979 Challenge Cup saw the Soviet national team defeat the NHL All-Stars in February, 1979, two games to one. This victory by the Soviet Union stimulated amateur and professional hockey authorities to reassess our attitudes toward minor and professional hockey.

R. Alan Eagleson Q.C., executive director of NHL Player's Association.

Andy Donato. Toronto *Sun.*

The Fitness Boom

If you're looking for someone to praise – or blame – for the whole thing, for the colossal explosion in fitness that drove several million North Americans to sleek good health in the 1970s, and drove millions more to boredom and distraction, then consider Seymour Leiberman. Good old Seymour, an attorney out of Houston, Texas, happens to be the man who conceived the activity that lies at the centre of the New Fitness. This takes us back to 1953 when Seymour was 45 and when his pals in Houston were dropping with heart attacks at a rate that seemed alarming, at least to Seymour. In panic and self-defence, he took up an activity he called simply and accurately "slow running" and he discovered that it brought him such fresh pep and energy that he rushed to spread the gospel. At first not many people listened – "What kind of nut has Seymour turned into anyway?" – but Leiberman persisted, and 20 years later, when "slow running" had caught on, when roads and parks, highways and byways were clogged with folks in Adidas and track suits, the International Council of Sport and Physical Education got around to acknowledging Seymour's contribution to our culture. The council officially pronounced him "the founder of the jogging movement."

Of course, it wasn't *just* jogging. The 1970s fitness boom also brought prosperity to other participatory sports. In the sudden pursuit of blooming health, North Americans in staggering numbers took to handball and racquetball, to swimming, cycling and golf, even to plain old walking.

Jogging into the '80s. CP

Some statistics? In 1972, according to the Dominion Bureau of Statistics, 700,000 Canadians played tennis at least one and a half times a week; by 1977, the figure had zoomed to 2.2 million Canadians. There were exactly 30 squash courts in Toronto in 1971; in 1979, there were almost 400 courts kept in steady use by 50,000 players with another 75,000 squash devotees spread across the rest of the country. So it went – sales in bicycles in Canada quadrupled from 1975 to 1978 – with every conceivable physical activity that called for a little healthy pressure on heart and muscle.

But, ah there, Seymour Leiberman, it was jogging that captured the attention and the legs of by far the majority of the '70s exercise fanatics. And why not? It's the most basic of physical activities and, what's more, it had science on its side.

Just ask Dr. Kenneth Cooper, who emerged as the guru of gurus in the fitness movement. Working out of the Institute for Aerobic Research in Dallas, Texas, and acting as an indefatigable proselytizer through his best-selling book *Aerobics* – "aerobics" has to do with the promotion of oxygen through the body in rich enough supply to develop a hardy cardiovascular system – Cooper devised a meticulously calculated series of physical exercises that almost guaranteed a sound body and a long life. His programs took in every conceivable sport, but he left no doubt that running and jogging qualified as the blue chip events.

"If you ask me, finally, what exercise can be used most effectively," he wrote, "I'd have no hesitancy about recommending running. As one of my runners put it, 'It's like a dry martini. You get more for your money – and quicker!' "

Thus, by 1979, the Boston Marathon was registering the staggering number of 7,877 official entrants; James Fixx's tome, *The Complete Book of Running,* had spent 18 months on the *New York Times* best-seller lists; sales of Adidas, Nikes and all the other running-shoe conglomerates were, for the third straight year, headed for sales that topped a half-billion dollars; a California psychiatrist named Thaddeus Kostrubala had declared that "running is a new and powerful way to reach the unconscious"; and it seemed as if the whole continent had gone bananas for running and jogging.

Well, not *quite* the whole continent.

"One thing I really hate," Richard Nixon told the U.S. Sports Advisory Council in 1973, "is exercise for exercise's sake."

Sure, if Watergate hadn't got Nixon, joggers would have, but the facts are that many North Americans shared Tricky Dick's antifitness animus. Some were turned off by the sheer ennui of listening to runners, who emerged as the 1970s classic braggarts, proclaim the dogma of running as ultimate salvation. "Runners are bores," said Frank Deford, a New York writer who specializes in sports books, "and the refuge of the bore is self-righteousness." Other antirunning critics offered more valid, more medical points. "All that banging of the foot on the hard pavement," said Dr. Charles Godfrey of Toronto's Wellesley Hospital, "damages the runner's back, his hip, his liver. What jogging is doing is creating a generation of people with heel problems."

Such medical quibbling hardly discouraged the waves of part-time athletes who preferred to believe that there is something not merely physically blessed about running and jogging but something, well, *spiritual*. They subscribe to notions expressed in ways like this: "The runner creates out of instability and conflict something that gives pleasure to himself and others because it releases feelings of beauty and power latent within us all." This passage comes from a 1955 book called *First Four Minutes* written by Dr. Roger Bannister himself, the English neurologist who first ran a mile in under four minutes. To nonrunners, the words may strike the ear as slightly silly. To runners and joggers, true believers, they make eminent and surprising good sense.

Jack Batten, journalist, author of *The Complete Jogger.*

Sports Heroes

The Top Ten

Bobby Orr
He revolutionized hockey, literally. Defencemen became offensive players in his time because of his vast skills as skater, stick-handler, shooter.

Phil Esposito
He set scoring records that may go unsurpassed in professional hockey: 76 goals in one season, 152 points in one season.

Abby Hoffman
Best middle-distance runner Canada has produced and the woman who led amateur athletic administration before, during and after the 1976 Olympics. Broke the world 1,500 metre record at 1972 Olympics in Munich (though lost the race).

Sandy Hawley
Outstanding jockey. North American champion three times in 1970s (won more races than any other rider). Frequent winner international stakes in California and Maryland.

Graham Smith
Edmonton's human fish, winner of six gold medals at British Commonwealth Games in 1978.

Diane Jones Konihowski
Saskatoon's human projectile of track and field. Winner of the 1978 Commonwealth Games pentathlon gold medal, all-round star.

Sandra Post
One of the world's best women golfers. Two-time winner of the Dinah Shore-Colgate tournament in California (the top money event on women's pro golf circuit), 1978 and 1979, and the only player ever to win back-to-back titles.

Tony Gabriel
Outstanding Hamilton-born footballer with the Ottawa Rough Riders. He won the Schenley Award as best player in the country in 1978; caught the pass that won the Grey Cup game in 1977 on the last play of game.

Susan Nattrass
One of the world's finest trap shooters, international champion, Olympic competitor.

Paul Henderson
Well, he's the guy who scored the winning goals in the final three games of the mind-blowing Canada-Russia Game summit hockey in 1972, including the goal that won the series: sort of like first man to walk on the moon.

Trent Frayne, sportswriter, author.

Abby Hoffman. Toronto *Star.*

Toller Cranston. CP

Ferguson Jenkins. CP

Sandra Post, top woman golfer. CP

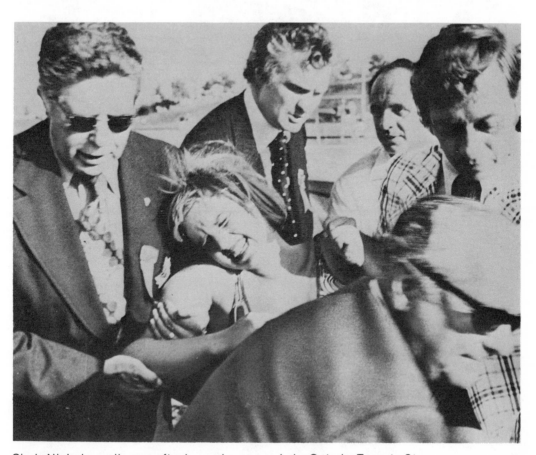

Cindy Nicholas collapses after her swim across Lake Ontario. Toronto *Star*

Gordie Howe—still going strong. CP

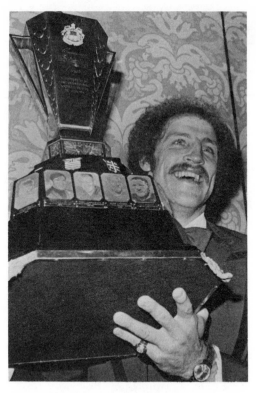

Ottawa Rough Rider, Tony Gabriel accepts the Schenley Award as the CFL's most valuable player in 1978. CP

Hooded Arab terrorists seized and murdered members of the Israeli Olympic team, Munich, 1972. CP

Romanian gymnast Nadia Comaneci, Montreal, 1976. CP

The Montreal *Gazette*

The Olympics – Canadian Winners

1972
Winter Games – Sapporo, Japan
Karen Magnussen
    Figure Skating-Women (*Silver*)

Summer Games – Munich
Leslie Cliff
    Swimming-Women (*Silver*)
    400 Metres
    Individual Medley
Donna Marie Gurr
    Swimming-Women (*Bronze*)
    200 Metres
    Backstroke
Bruce Robertson
    Swimming-Men (*Silver*)
    100 Metres
    Butterfly
Bruce Rob
Eric Fish
Willi Mahony
Rob Kasting
    Swimming (*Bronze*)
    Four x 100 Metres
    Medley
David Miller
John Ekels
Paul Cote
    Yachting (*Bronze*)
    Soling

1976
Winter Games – Innsbruck
Kathy Kreiner
    Alpine Skiing (*Gold*)
    Giant Slalom
Toller Cranston
    Figure Skating-Men (*Bronze*)
Cathy Priestner
    Speed Skating-Women (*Silver*)
    500 Metres

1976
Summer Games – Montreal
Greg Joy
    High Jump-Men (*Silver*)
John Wood
    Canoeing (*Silver*)
    G1, 500 Metres
Michel Vaillancourt
    Equestrian (*Silver*)
    Grand Prix
    Individual Jumping
Cheryl Gibson
    Swimmng-Women (*Silver*)
    400 Metres
    Individual Medley
Clay Evans
Gary MacDonald
Stephen Pickell
Graham Smith
    Swimming-Men (*Silver*)
    Four x 100 Metres
    Medley Relay

Nancy Garapick
   Swimming-Women (*Bronze*)
   100 Metres
   Backstroke
Nancy Garapick
   Swimming-Women (*Bronze*)
   200 Metres
   Backstroke
Shannon Smith
   Swimming-Women (*Bronze*)
   400 Metres
   Freestyle
Becky Smith
   Swimming-Women (*Bronze*)
   400 Metres
   Individual Medley
Gail Amundrud
Barb Clark
Anne Jardin
Becky Smith
   Swimming-Women (*Bronze*)
   Four x 100 Metres
   Freestyle
Robin Corsiglia
Wendy Cook Hogg
Anne Jardin
Susan Sloan
   Swimming-Women (*Bronze*)
   Four x 100 Metres
   Medley Relay

Pentathalon champion, Diane Jones-Konihowski. CP

Graham Smith set the world record in the 200 metre, 1977. CP

Kathy Kreiner won the World Cup Giant Slalom in 1974. CP

There will be a tendency, I believe, to dismiss the '70s in a negative way: that would be a mistake.

The decade has been a worrying one in economic terms and we have had to absorb some rude shocks, but most responsible people would agree that we had become profligate with energy and excessive in our demands on the economy.

On the other side of the ledger, our system demonstrated one of its greatest strengths: that it will not long endure abuse before imposing discipline upon us.

If the '70s have done nothing more than remind us that real productivity comes from individual initiative and enterprise, it will deserve more than the bad press it got.

Thomas J. Bata, Bata Limited.

Wild Rose Country

For Alberta, the most striking development of the '70s was the drastic increase in world petroleum prices by the OPEC countries, and the resulting changes in the value of our petroleum. Of special significance, the vast Alberta oil sands became economically attractive to develop. Because the petroleum resources are nonrenewable, Alberta established the unique Heritage Savings Trust Fund to convert present petroleum revenues into projects which will give a long-term stability to the economy.

A healthy agricultural sector, in combination with the petroleum industry, gave the province the most prosperous period in its history. Other sectors, including tourism and forestry, also did well. For the first time in decades, Alberta's small towns started to thrive and actually grow, reflecting our determination to encourage balanced growth through all regions.

The '70s, unfortunately, have also been a period of real frustration for Albertans in explaining our province's position on energy matters. Some national and provincial leaders as well as the "national" media have continually presented a picture of selfishness on Alberta's part. The truth is that we have kept our petroleum prices substantially below world prices and, in fact, have subsidized the other provinces to the extent of billions of dollars by phasing in negotiated price increases.

The Western Economic Opportunities Conference held in Calgary in 1973 raised expectations in all four western provinces. In the long run, Canada cannot restrict itself to one small industrial corridor for the whole nation. This Calgary conference – by coming to important agreements between Ottawa and the four provinces in such areas as transportation – appeared to set the stage for bold new opportunities for the West. I must say that the agreements have not been fulfilled, but if they ever are, the benefits for Canada will be enormous.

Alberta took a distinctive position in the constitutional discussions which concerned the country, particularly following the election of a separatist government in Quebec. We argued that Canada needed to pay more attention to the original spirit of Confederation; much of the authority that provinces enjoyed in 1867 has gradually been eroded. We recognized the need for a strong federal government – but a federal government that does not insert itself into areas of legitimate provincial jurisdiction.

The '70s were a period of many stimulating developments for our province. The first-ever urban provincial parks in Canada were established in Edmonton and Calgary. Efforts were undertaken to make Alberta a major research centre – in such divergent areas as environmental and cancer research. The arts flourished in an unprecedented manner.

Perhaps no event was more symbolic of the initiative and spirit of Alberta in the 1970s than the Edmonton Commonwealth Games in 1978. Private volunteers, not governments, were the essential component in putting together these games – and while the games were well managed and facilities were constructed under budget, the end result was a spectacular success for Canada.

Peter Lougheed, Premier of Alberta.

Some Hopes for Canada: Notes for an Address

Our fault is that our sectors are concentrating on their narrowest self-interests within a country which must enjoy concerted effort to maintain a valid nation.

Our strength is to produce leadership to convince our sectors that we just can't afford overprotection directed against each other but must accomplish less jealousy, greater tolerance and a valid national patriotism.

Although politicians and academics will contribute, some of that leadership must occur from the lifeblood of national economic health, which is business (and necessarily from the Canadianized business more than from subsidiaries of foreign business). Maybe some of that leadership from the professionals, too.

Canada is a swell place to be despite knowing all of:

unemployment (sickening);
stagnant business investment (timid or greedy);
noncompetitiveness (colonialized and timid);
currency doubts (mainly confidence problem);
hesitancy between sectors (our biggest error);
fat-cat privileges (we can't afford).

Our nation is totally valid, on reflection. It contains:

jigsaw of minorities, whose pieces have locked;
tolerance of minorities, fair but growing;
one of the world's superior records in past investment in social improvements;
most everything everyone else is short of (water, food, energy sources);
shortage of money, which can keep us all awake;
potentially cooperative attitudes.

Some of the current strengths include:

new investment in production of service plant which we know about;
labour attitudes;
growing self-reliance in industry;

new era of attitude in government services.

Some traps are still to be got out of, such as:

smugness within management;
professionalism among professionals: "professional" shouldn't mean hire out to all comers;
the fallacy that mechanical and economic perfection equals integrity;
hesitancy to fight for this very valid Canada.

Robert Blair, President and Chief Executive Officer, Alberta Gas Trunk Line.

Foreign Control of the Economy

More than 60 percent of our largest companies are controlled by corporations based outside of Canada.

Foreigners dominate the Canadian oil industry through their controlling interest in Imperial Oil, Shell Canada, Gulf Oil Canada, Texaco Canada and BP Canada. They dominate the automobile industry through the subsidiaries of General Motors, Ford and Chrysler.

There is no question that foreign direct investment in Canadian industry in the early days – and the technical, scientific, and management skills and, in many cases, the assurance of markets that came with them – helped to develop the Canadian economy more quickly than would otherwise have been possible. But for this we have paid a price.

In my view, the most serious of the problems resulting from such extensive foreign control of the economy are the following:

Our branch-plant system restricts the opportunities for Canadian management, scientific and technical personnel. The effect on the whole economy is debilitating, and it is also discouraging to the graduates of our universities seeking work in Canadian industry.

Foreign-controlled companies in the manufacturing field tend to import parts and components from their parent corporations and associates instead of developing alternative sources of supply in Canada. In many cases also, they are restricted from developing export markets that might compete with their parent corporations. Both these tendencies militate against greater employment opportunities in Canada.

Canadian subsidiaries are frequently required to rely on their foreign parents for research and new product development, which is a restriction on Canadian managers, scientists and technicians. Such key decisions as expansion of markets, the location of new plants and the promotion of senior personnel are made at head office, usually in the United States. This is surely not the best way to develop management and scientific talent in Canada. And it reduces the number of job opportunities for younger Canadian management personnel.

In our society, rightly or wrongly, businessmen wield a not-inconsiderable influence over public policy. When these businessmen are foreigners, or the Canadian managers of Canadian companies that are controlled by foreigners, this may not be in the best interests of our country. The influence wielded by the Canadian representatives of the international oil companies is a case in point.

It should be obvious that we cannot regain control of the Canadian economy unless the ownership of the foreign-controlled Canadian companies (or at least the larger ones) is acquired by Canadians or by the Canadian government.

Walter L. Gordon, co-founder of the Committee for an Independent Canada, chairman of Canadian Corporate Management Company Limited, from his book *What is Happening to Canada.*

In 1978 an average of $845,000 *an hour* flowed out of Canada – mostly to the United States – in payment for our total services deficit. In 1979, we will exceed $1 million an hour.

Non-Canadians control over $110 billion in Canadian assets at *book value.*

Today foreigners control:

65% of all of our combined manufacturing, mining, petroleum and natural gas;

98% of our rubber industry;
82% of chemicals;
46% of pulp and paper;
61% of agricultural machinery;
74% of the electrical apparatus industry;
59% of transportation equipment;
96% of the automobile and parts industry.

Mel Hurtig, publisher, from a speech to the annual convention of the Liberal Party of Ontario, March, 1979.

In my opinion, when people look back on the '70s, the most important event will not turn out to be any of the matters that seemed most important at the time or that earned the headlines. In retrospect, future generations may well decide that what the '70s were memorable for was for the way they ended – and just as the '20s closed with a massive crash, so I think the '70s will end with a massive inflation.

The '60s were a time of relative economic stability and we ended that decade with inflation of less than five percent, but through gross government mismanagement and overspending, we have managed to push the inflation rate up to double figures in just ten years. As our government, and that of the U.S., struggle with this now-unconquerable giant in the '80s, I am sure that many thinking persons will look back to this decade and say, "If only we had done something then."

Dr. Morton Shulman, author, broadcaster, journalist.

Prices are almost exactly double what they were in 1970. The 1970 dollar is now worth 50 cents. The rate of inflation went from 4½ per cent to 10 per cent. Food is two and a half times as expensive as it was in January 1970. In the supermarket the 1970 dollar is now worth 40¢. (You need $2.40 to buy what a 1970 dollar could buy). From 1969/70 food was rising about 2 per cent a year, now it's going up almost 17 per cent a year. Housing and Health care have doubled. Unemployment rose from 367,000 in 1970 to 853,000 in 1979 (from 4½ per cent to 7.7 per cent). If you add unemployment and the inflation rate in 1970 you get a discomfort index of 9, in 1979 it's 18.

Ed Broadbent, Leader of the New Democratic Party.

FLQ kidnap-victim, British Trade Commissioner, James Cross. This photo was received by the Associated Press in New York in a letter bearing a Montreal postmark, November 7, 1970. AP

Canadian Armed Forces

For the Canadian Armed Forces the decade of the '70s brought with it an uphill fight for an adequate slice of the government's budget; for an image of credibility and *raison d'être* in the mind of the public; and for a resolution of the aftershocks of the integration of the navy, army and air force imposed at the beginning of 1968.

At the opening of the 1970s support for the newly integrated Canadian Armed Forces in their unique emotion-arousing green uniforms was at a low ebb. The people of Canada had a pervasive perception of no direct military threat, a view that still thrives, notwithstanding the massive escalation of Soviet military might and capability since the Cuban missile crisis of 1962. Furthermore, the open, bewildering wound of Vietnam that so poisoned the American attitude toward the military spilled its emotional antiwar, antimilitary blood across the border into Canada. The result was a severe diminution of the credibility of the military that emerged in a cutback in the size of the Canadian Armed Forces from 147,000 in 1963 (125,000 regular and 22,000 reserves) to 100,000 (78,000 regular and 22,000 reserves). At the same time and for the same reasons, urgently needed programs to reequip the military with vehicles and weaponry, tanks, ships and aircraft were withheld.

Questions were raised. Was there a bomber threat? Could Canada really defend itself? Why not let the Americans do it? Why have a navy? Why should we have troops and fighter aircraft in Europe supporting NATO?

These are questions that are still being asked by a nation remote from the living reality of the people of Western Europe sitting next to the highly polished and visible Iron Curtain. They are our partners in the North Atlantic Treaty Organization providing mutual deterrent defence from the high Arctic through to Turkey. None of them could defend themselves individually. But in partnership they are able to.

Vietnam came to an end in the mid-'70s. From that time the perceived reputation of the military in Canada has been restored. At the same time, the public awareness of the necessity to have our forces adequately equipped to do the myriad tasks assigned to them began to increase. In particular, Canada's NATO allies let it be known that they expected the country to carry its military weight and meet its obligations. The result has been the acquisition of more than 100 Leopard tanks for our army forces in Europe; a program to purchase 18 new long-range patrol aircraft, the Lockheed Aurora, which will replace the ancient Argus; a new fighter program to procure a modern aircraft that can meet the role required under our North American Air Defence (NORAD) agreement with the United States and the role that our air force in Europe must perform. A new Armoured Vehicle General Purpose (AVGP) is rolling out of General Motors, London, Ontario, plant for use by the regular as well as reserve army. And the Canadian navy has six new frigates on the drawing board to replace aging destroyers.

There has been a turnaround in the equipment acquisition for the regular force. There will have to be a comparable approach to equipping the militia, naval, air and communications reserves in order that they can inexpensively backstop the regulars.

But what about unification and the green uniforms 11 years after the event? It is almost impossible to assess, let alone to quantify, the results of unification because the Canadian Forces are now quite different both qualitatively and quantitatively from those that existed in the early 1960s. Unification has brought about many economies of scale. For example, the number of basic training camps has been reduced from 11 to two and 30 specialized training schools now do the work previously carried out by 91.

Against the many advantages, there has been a considerable loss of individual service identity and of single-service perspective and expertise. As well, there has been a loss of healthy single-service rivalry and competition for resources at the highest staff levels.

The facts are that the support systems of administration, supply, finance and transportation are producing more with less than in preintegration days. From a functional viewpoint, the department is getting a more efficient peacetime force than ever before. In this context, the country is better served than before; the military is able to field a larger proportion of combat personnel than would otherwise be possible, but whether the field command structure and support systems would stand the test of war is, in some eyes, still an open question. On the other hand, one of the advantages of unification is that cooperative arrangements required for the three services to fight a war can be worked out and, indeed, are lived day-to-day in peacetime.

In the more emotional areas of morale, esprit, dedication and identity, some problems remain as irritants. Again the "green" classifications feel somewhat like "second class citizens" in such matters as adequate representation at NDHQ in personnel and career matters, uniform embellishments and adequate recognition at the staff colleges – *the price paid for unification was identity*. While the operations classifications can now identify with at least a command if not always with a unit, the support classifications feel no such identity.

The final act of unification was but a culmination of a long-term historic trend in Canada. It has been more than 13 years since the decision was taken and almost half of the officers and men know nothing but the unified Canadian Forces. The transition clearly was an emotional experience for some members whose allegiance was given completely to a particular service. The public outcry was most often associated with the navy, although the army and air force certainly had their share of adherents to the separate-service concept. However, as is so often the case, time resolves many things and it has done much to mold the new Canadian Forces.

It continues to be suggested in some quarters that unification has led to a loss of professionalism because it is not possible to be knowledgeable in naval, army and air force activities without the loss of expertise. Experience has not borne this out and with the rebalancing of the forces – such as the formation of Air Command – this factor is much less an issue. Moreover, the scope of understanding of operational considerations and the degree of empathy toward the needs of other environments, gained particularly by officers at senior levels, has by and large brought to the department more flexibility and fewer parochial attitudes than would likely have existed under separate services. Another criticism often levelled is that the morale of the forces would be adversely affected. It is true that change affects morale, but this is less and less of a factor with the passage of time. Moreover, problems of morale have less to do with unification than with such problems as overtasking and aging equipment. Finally, the readjustments which are now in the "fine tuning" stage, such as slight uniform changes to promote identity, have done much to lay this factor to rest.

Criticisms such as loss of professionalism and morale have to be viewed against the real accomplishments of unification. The forces can better act as a entity in terms of the politico-military realities that face us today. Command and control have been streamlined. Operations to date have all been successful. Economies of scale have been achieved in the support and logistics field. Automation has been possible on a large scale in personnel and financial administration. Thus, there are real and solid gains attributable to unification, even if we have yet to face the acid test of war.

How can the process of unification be further improved? First, it is doubtful that much more can be achieved in terms of economies of scale. However, there are adjustments that can be and are being made in certain problem areas described above. As noted, some of the problems are organizational and procedural, others are related to personnel. At the risk of being repetitive, the solutions to these problems are a matter of "fine tuning" rather than further radical and disruptive change.

In retrospect, unification, with the subsequent balancing adjustments which have taken place over the past decade, has been a success in the '70s.

Major General Richard Rohmer, CCM, DFC, CD, QC, the Chief of Reserves of the Canadian Armed Forces.

By the '70s young Canadians had outgrown their adolescent rebellion of the '60s. Faced with growing economic and political problems, they began exchanging doing-their-own-thing and knocking-the-Establishment for the seeming security of traditional values and beliefs.

And so, by the end of the decade, finding a job had taken over from finding oneself; Conservative governments had taken over from Liberal governments in both provincial and federal arenas; and, while it hasn't taken them over, nostalgia has at least coloured all our tastes.

John Bassett, chairman, Baton Broadcasting.

From Organized Labour

Looking back at the '70s . . . I remember, a few years ago, when I was director of the United Auto Workers union in Canada . . . one day there was a knock on the door of my office, and in came a man who introduced himself as the director of a new Swedish car assembly plant to be opened in Canada.

He said they were just about to start operations and he'd come to ask me whether the UAW would negotiate a collective agreement with his company on behalf of the employees in the plant.

I just about fell over. This was the first time in my long years in the labour movement where an employer would actually make an approach to a trade union about representing his employees, rather than fight tooth and nail to "keep the union out."

A few days later he came back to my office, all dejected. "I've been called all kinds of names by my Canadian colleagues in the business world," he said. "I didn't know that to be proper employer in Canada one has to hate the unions and fight them. In Sweden we find it quite natural to have the best possible relationship with the union that represents our workers."

I remember that incident because it illustrates the difference in outlook between North Americans and Scandinavians. In Scandinavia, they have just about the most peaceful, constructive labour relations climate in the world. Not because unions love employers, or vice versa. They bargain just as energetically as their Canadian counterparts. But they are both strong and they respect each other.

In Canada, during the '70s, we have made some advances toward a similar, more sensible relationship, but we are still far from the Scandinavian model.

Many trade unionists still have to fight for the most elementary rights, such as the right to be recognized by the employer when a majority opts to join a union, or the right to have their union dues deducted directly from the payroll.

Take for example the bitter strike in 1978 by some 90 employees (mostly women) of the Fleck Manufacturing Company in Exeter, Ontario. The women were fighting for just those basic rights. Instead of recognition, they had to walk the picket lines for five months, watched by up to 500 policemen with menacing dogs.

And take the increasing number of "seminars" by so-called management consultants, who for a handsome fee offer to teach employers how to thwart union attempts to organize their employees.

With this kind of a climate, is it any wonder that many trade unionists tend to adopt similar negative attitudes toward their employers?

Too often in the '70s, collective bargaining was based on unnecessary confrontation rather than on genuine attempts to come to an agreement. On the unions' side, this negative attitude could be attributed to a profound

sense of insecurity as they found it necessary to remain on guard to protect the shaky rights they had struggled to establish.

To achieve some sense of security, unions have been pushing for legislative measures to facilitate trade union organization. These included giving unions access to employees at work, the possibility of having a first collective agreement imposed upon recalcitrant employers on the request of newly certified unions, and stronger provisions to protect unions from unfair labour practices.

But during the '70s management has become more receptive to the idea that trade unions are a natural partner in the country's economy and in their plants. As for the trade unions, they have grown not only in memberships, but also in strength, unity and maturity.

A major factor in the growth of these qualities was undoubtedly the treatment workers received from the Liberal government in the second part of the decade. I am referring to the wage controls, slapped onto wage earners by then Prime Minister Pierre Trudeau only months after he had run on a platform opposing such controls. From 1975 until 1979, wages were effectively controlled, while workers saw the cost of living soar.

As a result, organized workers realized that they cannot count on collective bargaining alone to defend their interests, but that they must get actively involved in politics. That's why, during the 1979 election campaign, the Canadian Labour Congress and its more than two million members threw themselves heart and soul into a campaign to increase the strength of the New

Democratic Party in the House of Commons. They saw the NDP as the only party that would bring the country back on its feet without double-crossing the workers in the process.

As a result, Trudeau's Liberal government was defeated and the NDP strengthened. In addition, the CLC campaign helped the labour movement become a closer-knit community and pull Canada's workers further into the country's decision-making process.

But that was only the beginning. Look for the next installment in *Farewell to the '80s.*

Dennis McDermott, president, Canadian Labour Congress.

Business

The biggest deal of the 1970s was the decision of the OPEC countries in 1973 to raise the price of oil. That decision sent the economy of the western world into a tailspin from which it still hasn't recovered. And it had important repercussions in Canada. For one thing, it helped trigger a boom in western oil and gas that should continue until the end of this century. For another, it helped cool off the stock market, which in turn helped trigger a wave of mergers and takeovers that provided the biggest business stories of the 1970s.

Stocks were cheap, and the risks of launching new business ventures seemed harder to assess than ever before. For many large companies, the conclusion was obvious: instead of starting something new, let's buy a piece of a going concern. Many companies even decided that the best possible investment they could make would be to buy back their own shares from the public – usually for less than those shareholders had paid.

The cheapest, least risky way to grow was by swallowing other companies – even your competitors'. That's why the Hudson's Bay Company, under Don McGiverin, snapped up Zeller's and soon afterward, Simpsons. That's also why two rich men's even richer sons, Galen Weston of the grocery empire and Ken Thomson of the world-wide newspaper group, decided in 1979 to go after The Bay themselves. It was a multimillion-dollar bidding contest, conducted by phalanxes of high-priced lawyers, brokers and PR men. Thomson won.

In 1978, two more rich men's sons, Conrad and Montegue Black, inherited a minority interest in Ravelston Corporation, the holding company that controls the legendary Argus Corporation, which in turn controls about $4 billion worth of assets, including Dominion Stores, Domtar, Hollinger Mines, Standard Broadcasting and Massey-Ferguson. After the death of J. A. "Bud" McDougald, the former Argus chairman who was widely regarded as the dean of the Canadian financial Establishment, the Black brothers demanded a bigger say in running the empire. Argus' 70-year-old chairman, Colonel Maxwell Meighen, thought that would be rushing things a bit; Conrad Black, after all, was only 33 at the time, even though he'd already built a million-dollar newspaper chain, Sterling Newspapers, quite independently of his family's wealth.

The Blacks, to the considerable astonishment of Bay Street, responded by suddenly invoking a buy-out clause in the agreement between Ravelston's four partners. With the backing of McDougald's widow and the widow of another deceased Argus chairman, Colonel Eric Phillips, the Blacks forced Meighen (the son of a former prime minister) to sell them his 26.5 percent share in Ravelston. The transaction cost only $11.8 million, but it gave the Black boys undisputed command of one of the country's largest corporate empires. "Any suggestion that we are callow youths who must wait is wrong," Conrad Black later explained. "We are in a position to say we don't have to accept that."

The Ravelston buy-out signified more than a simple transfer of control from one set of shareholders to another. It also represented a transfer of financial power to a new generation. Canada is widely assumed to be an egalitarian society, but the extent to which rich men's sons dominated the financial news in the 1970s is absolutely astonishing. It was almost as though control of major portions of the Canadian economy (those portions not already controlled by foreigners) were being *passed on*, like family memberships in the Granite Club. Sometimes the succession was polite and gentlemanly, as with the genteel struggle for control of The Bay. Sometimes it was vicious, as with the Bronfman takeover of Brascan. But nearly always the struggles involved younger editions of familiar names: Eaton, Thomson, Weston, Bronfman, the Black boys. Few interlopers were involved. In Canada, we like to keep it in the family.

The Brascan battle, like the Argus takeover, involved a noisy collision of generations. Brascan's chairman was Jake Moore, 63, a canny, ambitious executive who'd begun his career as an accountant in London, Ontario, and who'd gone on to transform a small, regional brewery, Labatt's, into one of the industry's leaders. Now he was presiding over a company that had $425 million in cash – payments for the sale of its Brazilian power utility – and hadn't decided what to do with it.

All that cash in its treasury made Brascan a tempting takeover target. By the beginning of 1979, Moore knew he'd have to use that money to swallow some major company – or run the risk of being swallowed himself.

The expected challenge came in April. Edper Equities Limited, a powerful alliance of two of Sam Bronfman's sons, Edgar and Peter and the Patino mining group, announced that it planned to make an offer for 50 percent of Brascan's shares. Brascan countered almost simultaneously with an astonishing offer of its own: it proposed to use its own cash, plus a $700 million loan from the Canadian Imperial Bank of Commerce, to buy F.W. Woolworth, the century-old U.S. five-and-dime chain, for $1.3 billion.

That triggered a furious three-way fight between Brascan, Edper and Woolworth's that dominated the financial pages for weeks. The legal costs for all three parties totalled at least $1 million as lawyers, PR men and stock-brokers worked around the clock to checkmate each other's strategies. Woolworth's challenged the Brascan bid before the New York State attor-ney-general's office. Edper – which also opposed the Woolworth's takeover – undermined Moore by buying $174 million worth of Brascan shares in two days of frenzied buying in New York. Moore tried to get this Edper pur-chase disallowed by the U.S. courts, but failed. The Woolworth's bid was then withdrawn, leaving Edper apparently in charge of Brascan, and Jake Moore out in the cold. The rich men's sons had triumphed again.

The great pipeline battle of the 1970s wasn't won by a rich man's son, exactly – although Robert Blair of Alberta Gas Trunk Lines Limited (AGTL) went to the right eastern schools and knew all the right eastern people. But the multimillion battle over the route of a pipeline to ferry arctic natural gas to markets in southern Canada and the U.S. had the same generational char-acter. It was a collision not only of old and new corporate styles. It was also a dramatic assertion of the new sophistication and economic clout of west-ern Canada.

It began in the early 1970s as an orderly exercise in capitalist expansion. A consortium called Canadian Arctic Gas was formed to pull together the manifold details of a pipeline down the Mackenzie Valley. The line was expected to cost close to $10 billion, and the consortium included corporate giants like Exxon, Imperial Oil and Canadian Pacific. It might all have pro-ceeded in a quiet and gentlemanly fashion – except that Blair of the Calgary-based AGTL, irked at the eastern arrogance of the consortium, withdrew from membership and started pushing an alternate pipeline proposal of his own: the Maple Leaf route.

In the 1950s, pipelines were built by *diktat:* C. D. Howe would give the word and the bulldozers would move in. But this was a new and more com-plex world: a world where huge companies had to spend far more time and money mollifying native peoples, environmental groups and government regulatory agencies than they used to spend arranging loans on Wall Street. It was a new kind of arena, where the weapons were public relations, politi-cal savvy and environmental sensitivity.

The appointment of a socialist judge, Tom Berger, to investigate the competing proposals and their impact on the fragile arctic environment made the contest costlier, more urgent, more subtle. Simple, bottom-line economic feasibility was no longer the sole criterion. The interests of the Inuit, of migrating caribou herds, of arctic lichen, of tiny northern hamlets, were balanced for the first time against the interests of an energy-hungry southern economy.

It was an unfamiliar arena for the multinationals that supported Cana-dian Arctic Gas, but it was a congenial environment for Robert Blair. While CAG lobbyists tried to influence mandarins in Ottawa, Blair himself was stumping the arctic, learning firsthand the concerns of the Inuit whose lives would be most dramatically affected by the pipeline.

Although Blair's proposal probably made less sense in conventional economic terms, the Berger report, the National Energy Board and the federal cabinet ended up supporting it. The decision was regarded as a triumph for the West, for native rights, for Canadian nationalism and for Bob Blair's generation. In the euphoria that greeted AGTL's victory in 1977, it hardly seemed to matter that Bob Blair's pipeline might never actually be built. Cost estimates were escalating. A temporary gas glut materialized in Alberta. The barriers to raising the money in the U.S. seemed insurmountable. By the end of the 1970s, the future of the Maple Leaf Line was in doubt. It seemed likely that construction would be postponed until late in the 1980s, or perhaps postponed indefinitely.

Nevertheless, it was one of the genuine Big Deals of the 1970s in Canada. Like the Argus takeover, the Bay mergers, the Brascan-Edper-Woolworth's catfight, the battle over the arctic pipeline was about something more than money. The real question in all those contests was: Who's going to control the future? As always, youth won.

Alexander Ross, editor, *Canadian Business.*

Don McGiverin of The Bay. Toronto *Star.*

Conrad Black. *Horst Ehricht*

Lotteries

Lotteries used to be against the law in Canada. If you wanted to invest a couple of bucks in a million-dollar dream, you had to find a friend who could slip you a ticket on the q.t. for the Irish Sweepstakes.

Then suddenly, the laws were changed. What had been a sin was suddenly a virtue. Governments from coast to coast got into the act.

Today, Canada has ten major lotteries, nine of them government-operated. Collectively, they rake in almost $1 billion a year and shell out more than $410 million in cash prizes.

But are they a con game? Some critics think so. According to the Consumers' Association of Canada, lotteries are far from a good investment: "Like so many products of dubious value that sell well, they depend on hype and clever, unceasing advertising."

Bryan Elwood, a management consultant and an authority on lotteries, says that Loto Canada and its offspring have the lowest payoff of any form of gambling.

In the horse races, he points out, 83 percent of the money goes back to the players. In casino gambling, it's 75 to 95 percent. In lotteries, it's a maximum of 50 percent – and often it's only 40 percent.

"Let's face it: winning a lottery is a long shot or, depending on how you look at it, an incredible stroke of good luck," he says in his self-published *Whole World Lottery Guide,* which compares the odds against winning prizes in 25 countries.

If you're wondering how our lotteries compare to others, they're about average. The best payoffs were found in the Netherlands (66 percent) and the worst in Delhi, India (28 percent). Like half the countries studied, Canada's lottery winnings are tax-free.

Your chances of winning a million dollars in Loto Canada are one in 271,429, compared to one in 800,000 for the Provincial. But since you pay half as much for a Provincial ticket, the comparative odds per $10 expenditure are actually one in 400,000 for the Provincial, compared to one in 271,429 for Loto Canada.

In the *Whole World Lottery Guide,* Elwood ranks the ten Canadian lotteries in terms of expected cash payoff – meaning the percentage of ticket costs you could expect to recoup in prize money if you played the same game a very large number of times. The higher the expected payoff, the better the game for the player.

The expected cash payoffs (as of February, 1979): Loto Canada, 56 percent; Lottario, 50 percent; Loto Perfecta, 48 percent; Western Express, 47.4 percent; the Provincial, 43.4 percent; Wintario, 43 percent, Inter-Loto, 42.8 percent; Mini-Loto, 41.5 percent; Cash for Life, 39.9 percent, Atlantic A-1, 32.8 percent.

The debate about lotteries will undoubtedly continue.

Ellen Roseman, consumer reporter, *The Globe and Mail.*

There was some good news and some bad news. First, the bad news. Canadians grew ever more cynical and sceptical about each other, about themselves, about Canadians. It was the decade in which Canadians opted for self-interest and mediocrity.

Now the good news. A more honest morality (except at the fringes), bright, bright kids and, for me, an immensely satisfying personal life including, finally, baseball in Toronto.

Keith Davey, senator.

Issues for the Next Decade

The gay '20s. The sober '30s. The fearful '40s. The buoyant '50s. The liberated '60s. The turbulent '70s. What next? The fragile '80s.

The 1980s are in fact bringing Canadians, attention to bear on portentous decisions concerning their economic, social and political future. I will merely list those issues that I consider the most important, saving the reader from a detailed analysis of their causes or likely unfolding.

On the economic front, stagflation continues to elicit the strongest concern. Economic growth in the 1980s is not expected to reach the record rates achieved in the 1950-73 post-war period. Higher energy costs, increased regulation and new sources of competition portend intensified economic adjustment pressures, which could be more difficult to achieve in a context of slower growth. Thus, economic policy will walk the tightrope of inflation – and its cumulative effects – and the perils of higher unemployment. Canada *does* have a future, especially given her relatively privileged situation compared to many industrialized countries. Yet Canadians, if they are to adjust to new world economic conditions, will be asked to make important decisions and perhaps adopt new perspectives on the future of the welfare state, trade strategy and industrial policy.

On the political scene, the $64 million question remains: Will Canada survive? As much as political rhetoric of the late '60s and early '70s focussed on the quality of Canadian life, the very continuing of Canadian life will dominate the debate of the 1980s. Constitutional conferences and crises, the risks of intensified regionalism and the erosion of whatever exists of a Canadian national identity are very much in the cards, at least in the first half of the decade. The outcome? Breaking up? A constructive catharsis? Much will depend on the compromises that Canadians are willing to accept, and in this sense the 1980s are a pivotal decade between the threats and promises of Canada.

Of course, these economic and political conditions will both reflect and affect social trends. De Tocqueville said that revolutions were the product of unemployed intellectuals. Nightmare scenarios of various sorts have been written to illustrate the potential impact of a major constitutional crisis. Nevertheless, an important issue that is less well articulated pertains to the assimilation of the narcissistic culture.

On a broader front, the other very important issues to be faced in the 1980s relate to the international context. Questions that need to be dealt with on a priority basis pertain to nuclear proliferation. How will the world prepare itself for this eventuality? The United States-Soviet Union strategic balance is certain to emerge as a key question in the next decade. The Third World, particularly the poorest countries of that bloc, will also gain more attention and exacerbate pressures for more effective adjustment and assistance. Rapid growth in other less-developed countries also raises the possibility of political and social unrest.

Doom and gloom? No. Though an array of difficult issues are likely to arise in the 1980s, such is how the world operates. The crucial question is whether or not we will accept adjusting to these new conditions. Limits-to-growth cassandras would suggest that the 1980s will set the tone for troubled times, if not apocalypse. Yet, as far as Canada is concerned, the situation more accurately illustrates the problems of a rich society that can afford to preoccupy itself with issues other than standard of living. The fragile '80s may, in the end, force us to recognize the roots of our problems.

Marie-Josée Drouin, executive director, Hudson Institute.

The Retail Industry

The past few decades have seen a technological explosion in the retailing industry. Electronic gear – used in such areas as accounting, credit transacting and billing, payroll, inventory management – has made it possible for retailers to do a substantially increased volume of business and provide better service.

There have also been changes in the business environment brought on by government, by social pressures, by world events and by evolutions in lifestyles. These have all had their effects on the retail industry.

The past ten years also brought on many changes that were the result of actions by retailers and developers – changes that innovators and risk-takers put into action. The mushrooming of climate-controlled malls in the suburban areas as well as the inner cores of major cities have altered the shape of retailing.

Canada has also been experiencing high levels of inflation and unemployment for such a long period of time that many young people believe it is the norm.

Other important trends have emerged – slower population growth, small families and households, a shortage of energy resources, increased labour strife and international troubles and uncertainties.

The pessimist looking at these trends might have closed up shop. But retailers are optimists. They're resilient and innovative in reacting to change. Most have seen new opportunities in the merging trends.

In Canada, the retail industry is aggressive. We have great national and regional department stores, strong and vigorous chain stores, many of which are so successful that they are looking for new worlds to conquer.

Retailing during the past decade has been healthier than in previous years and reasonably prosperous. I look forward to an exciting and ever challenging next decade.

John C. Eaton, chairman, Eaton's of Canada.

No Name, No Frills

The time has come for no-name products and no-frills merchandising. These two ideas in their various manifestations will revolutionize your way of life in the 1980s.

Any individual who rejects that hypothesis is doomed to see the real value of his income seriously eroded by runaway inflation during the 1980s.

Any company who rejects that hypothesis is doomed to see the market share of its traditional products decimated by value-oriented no-name products.

Any people who do not force their government to adopt and implement a no-frills economic philosophy will find their country's economy and their personal jobs unproductive, uncompetitive and totally untenable.

Let me give you ten predictions on what the influence no-name and no-frills will have on your life during the 1980s:

1. North America will be forced to reject its current "cost-plus" mentality.
2. North American consumers will demand no-frills politicians during the 1980s.
3. Consumer marketing of "me-too" nationally branded products will be rejected as unjustifiably wasteful.
4. During the 1980s retailers will be forced to redefine their role.
5. As North American businessmen respond to the value needs of inflation-bombarded consumers there will be a dramatic improvement in the public image of free enterprise.
6. In the next five years 25 percent of grocery sales will go through no-frills and warehouse-type outlets.
7. In the next five years 25 percent of grocery sales in North America will be no-name.
8. No-name's success will soon begin to bring national brand prices down and thereby provide a positive force to slow down overall food price inflation.
9. No-name products will become a major export item of North America.
10. Greater creativity will characterize the next wave of no-name products.

David Nichol, president, Loblaws Limited.

The Wackiest Inventions

Flag-waving pole
A special flagpole for true patriots and people everywhere who like to celebrate! When there isn't enough wind to keep the old flag from drooping, *this* flagpole actually waves back and forth, so that no matter what the weather, *your* flag is always flying!

Flashlight shoes
Double-purpose shoes that promise you'll never have to carry a flashlight again! They have built-in lightbulbs, batteries, and on-off switches to light your way for every step! They're even great for finding a dropped earring!

Cold-puddle sunbathing
An inflated mat to lie on when you're tanning that always keeps you cool! Water flows over it from a hose connection so that a constantly renewed stream of cold water runs down the back of your body as you lie in the sun!

Sneaky-look eyeglasses
Special eyeglasses with mirrors and prisms built right in so that you can lie on your back and look straight up – and still see all the pretty girls on the beach! Or, if you're naturally nervous, you can watch the people *behind* you as you walk along, just to check if they're watching *you!*

Home-style log roller
An indoor log-rolling device, like a huge paint-roller on a stand! It features a non-slip surface and an adjustable rate of spin so that lumberjacks can practise their fancy footwork among all the comforts of home!

Dog-vacuum dog
A small vacuum cleaner hidden inside a toy dog, so that you can vacuum your own dog without frightening him! The hose attachment works as a vacuum – or as a blow-drier! – and it simply pulls out through the tail!

One-at-a-time toe holder
A special foot support for everyone who finds his toes getting out of range when it's toenail cutting time! A little pedestal takes turns fitting under each toe and lifts them up, one at a time, so that you can actually reach them without any unnecessary strain!

Love socks
A pair of socks with space-age technology built right in so that even when you *wash* them, they end up together! A miniaturized gold-thread transistor in each toe signals to ensure each sock always finds its proper mate!

Walking sleeping bag
A special sleeping bag for the outdoorsman who is too darned lazy even to *unroll* a sleeping bag! It has *built-in* arms and legs so that he can *wear* it, all day long – and when he gets sleepy, he can just lie down!

Sinking ceiling
A motorized ceiling that *lowers* itself to where you can *reach* it, for painting, or light-bulb changing, or spider-swatting, all at easy arm's length!

Talking bathroom scale
A bathroom scale that really *cares* about your weight-watching! If you're losing pounds, it compliments you in a clear, loud voice! And if you've gained again, it announces to the world that you look like a *blimp!*

Vacuum-grip golf tee
A golf tee that holds onto your golf ball *until* you hit it, no matter how hard the wind is blowing! Inside the tee a tiny vacuum device pulls the ball down against the tee so that it can never roll off again!

Two-fisted popcorn
A long, thin popcorn box that lets *two* people munch at the same time! It fits across *two* laps and has a hole at *each* end – and when it's empty, you can even hold hands without anyone knowing!

Dump-a-bed

A totally reliable way to get you up in the morning! – a tilting bed that's triggered by your alarm clock every morning! As soon as the alarm sounds, the bed *collapses* on one side and dumps you right onto the floor, to really get you rolling!

Telescoping pipe

A special pipe for every man who likes to look in shop windows! If the bowl of the pipe hits against the glass, instead of driving the stem down the smoker's throat, the *whole pipe* collapses, like a miniature telescope – and it doesn't even go out!

Robber-trap toes

A new way to *stop* bank robbers! It's a plastic container six feet high that suddenly *drops* from the ceiling, trapping the thief inside! And how does the bank teller trigger the trap? – she sets off an alarm that's built right into her *shoe* – just by wiggling her toes!

Michael Spivak, President of Science International, creator of *What Will They Think of Next!*

Science

Few historians and social critics today recognize the most explosive force for change during the decade of the 1970s. Entire cultures and ways of life are rendered extinct or altered forever – not by the exigencies of economic fluctuation, charismatic despots or leaders, or ideological conflict, but by *science* when applied by industry, the military and medicine. The cornucopia of technological innovation seems limitless: spray cans, liquid crystals, digital watches, microwave ovens, foam insulation, pocket calculators, CT scanners, foetoscopy, tape cassettes, videotape recorders, cruise missiles, SSTs, video games, fibre optics, laser telephones, Trident submarines, prenatal screening and recombinant DNA. There is no end to probable developments extending to the end of the century: giant space colonies, cancer pills, oral contraceptives for males, detection of signals from extraterrestrial intelligence, intelligent computers, earthquake prediction methods, genetic engineering, controlled nuclear fusion, cloning, weather modification, home computers and complete mood control. No doubt future scientific progress will also be accompanied by technological horror stories that characterized the '70s: dieldrin, dioxin, lead, cadmium, PCB, asbestos, radon, mercury, arsenic and PVC poisoning; Reyes Syndrome from pesticide spraying; oil spills from supertankers; ozone destruction by aerosol sprays; energy shortages; nuclear accidents; and the arms race.

The most exciting and far-reaching developments in science during the '70s took place with explosive force in fields connected to *information*: genetic, electronic and neural. As well, two other areas merit honourable mentions: energy and space.

The '70s witnessed the first spasms of a great upheaval, the impending exhaustion of petroleum supplies. While the concentration of global oil reserves in Third World countries and escalating prices have created economic havoc, in the long run the crisis signals the end of an entire way of life built on cheap, plentiful energy. The dilemma facing industrialized nations is whether the solution to the energy crisis will be high technology (and, therefore, high risk), such as nuclear fission or fusion reactors, giant solar satellites or coal gassification, or a radical transformation to a more labour-intensive, conserving, appropriate technology society.

In the same period, satellite and telescope technology have revolutionized astronomy. More than 4,000 satellites now circle the globe, delivering hourly weather maps, global environmental information and military surveillance data. The American lunar-landing missions have been superceded by the spectacular success of explorations of Mars, Venus, Jupiter and Saturn. The '80s will witness routine trips to outer space in the space shuttle while SETI, the search for extraterrestrial intelligence, will use extremely efficient telescopes to probe for other civilizations. The use of X-ray, infrared and radio-wave telescopes has revealed entirely new phenomena, such as quasars, which emit enormous amounts of energy at the very edge of the universe. Pulsars have now been explained as dying stars, while black holes resulting from the death of giant stars have captured the imagination of scientists and the public alike.

Decade of the Chip

If the '60s witnessed the supersession of the radio tube by the transistor, the '70s were characterized by the revolutionary technology of microcircuitry: tiny circuits of semi-conducting material sandwiched in a silicon matrix. Contained in a single chip the size of a baby's fingernail is all of the information in the most complex computer ever built before the age of transistors. Each year, the information content (referred to as bits in a binary system) of a chip has increased by 35 percent while the cost per bit has decreased annually by 21 percent. Today, the entire contents of the 20 million books in the Library of Congress in Washington can be stored in less than 20 IBM 3850 computers.

The chip, or microcompressor, is like a ganglion (cluster of nerve cells) that can do a lot of thinking for us. Already it has revolutionized society with the enormous storage capacity and speed of information retrieval for private and government agencies (anyone who has tried to book a flight while an airline's computer "is down," knows how dependent we've become). Electronic games, televisions, pocket calculators, automobile sensors, missile guidance systems and automatic supermarket inventories are only a few of the changes brought about by the magic chip. The '70s mark the period when very sophisticated computers have become accessible to virtually all members of society; the ramifications of this we can only speculate upon.

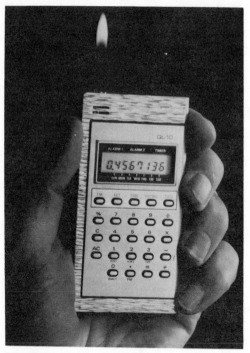

The Calculighter gives the time, date, and lights a cigarette. It weighs 3.68 ounces. AP

IBM memory chip can hold up to 64,000 pieces of information. It's dwarfed by the fingers holding it. AP

A tiny electronic interconnection circuit is overwhelmed by the eye in the background. It's used to automate assembly of other microelectronic devices. AP

Decade of the Brain

It is said that nothing in the universe is more complex than the human brain. The many branches of neuronal cells interlink to form more than ten trillion synapses, or junctions. While electronic computers can race through operations at millions of times the speed of a nerve impulse, nothing comes close to matching the brain for its amazing versatility. We have still to see a computer that can beat a master chess player. While memory, emotions and creativity remain mysteries to the scientist, an astounding insight into brain function heralds a revolution in behavioural science. The effects of drugs such as opiates on the brain suggest that there are cellular receptors to which the chemicals attach. When this was demonstrated, it had to be asked whether the brain itself normally makes opiatelike molecules. This paved the way to the discovery of brain hormones called endorphins and enkephalins, which attach to receptors and induce states of euphoria, painlessness, sleep and intoxication. The brain acts on the body by producing hormones! Now scientists are searching for hundreds of brain hormones which act on the body in countless ways. This will undoubtedly open a new area of pharmacology and neurochemistry for the treatment of psychiatric and physical problems.

Perhaps the most intriguing thing about the discovery of brain hormones is that it now provides a potential insight into the biochemical mechanisms underlying phenomena that hitherto seemed to lie outside of traditional Western science: mystical experiences, altered states of consciousness, psychosomatic problems, placebo effects, hypnosis, acupuncture, mind over body. Translated into more familiar situations, brain hormones may explain the absence of pain in times of severe stress such as war or car accidents, control of heart-rate and pain by fakirs, sudden occurrence of pregnancy after years of infertility upon adoption of a child, cessation of menses when a girl goes to college and its commencement when she returns home.

Decade of the Gene

At the moment of conception, a chemical blueprint, half from the mother and half from the father, begins to direct the development of that egg cell into a baby and eventually an adult made up of some 60 trillion cells. That incredibly complex process is dictated by a chemical substance called deoxyribonucleic acid, or DNA. During the '60s, the code contained in DNA was deciphered and found to be analogous to human language. The language of life is written in a linear sequence (like this sentence) with a four-letter chemical alphabet. The words in the biological dictionary are all three letters long (called triplets); hence, there are 64 different words. Sentences begin with a capital letter and end with punctuation marks with an average of about 300 words per sentence. Each sentence corresponds to a gene. In order to turn an egg into a person, it takes the DNA equivalent of 1,000 volumes of the complete works of Shakespeare!

The '70s have witnessed the development of tools for isolating and manipulating specific genes, and their insertion into totally unrelated organisms. This technology is referred to as recombinant DNA and already, the entire DNA content of the fruit fly has been chopped up and inserted as individual pieces into bacteria. Genes from humans have been inserted into monkey cells, from plants into bacteria, from bacteria into frogs, and so on. Indeed, entire genes have been constructed by sticking one letter at a time together in proper sequence. Thus, the gene specifying human insulin was made artificially, and upon its insertion into bacteria, was read properly and human insulin made!

Recombinant DNA technology promises enormous benefits, including the production of human growth hormones, insulin and blood clotting factors by bacteria; plants that make fertilizer from nitrogen in the air; microorganisms that degrade environmental pollutants; and the correction of hereditary disease.

Recombinant DNA also raised public concern about potential hazards. Insertion of DNA sequences of one organism into another species transgresses biological barriers to such interchange and thereby creates totally novel organisms whose biological properties may not always be predictable or benign. The ensuing uproar raised the consciousness of the public concerning the vested interests, ambitions and blind spots of scientists, of the scientist about the need for public information and safety, and of the politician about the need to enforce social responsibility of scientists. The double-edged potential of scientific knowledge as evidenced by nuclear energy has been confronted with recombinant DNA.

In summary, the '70s mark the clear delineation of revolutionary insights into information in the blueprint of life, the messages of the brain and the function of computers.

David Suzuki, scientist, host of CBC's *The Nature of Things.*

Best Television Commercials

Birth, London Life Insurance Co.: Goodis, Goldberg, Soren

Golfer, Speedy Muffler King: Goodis, Goldberg, Soren

Pumpkin, Government of Canada (Ministry of Transport): Richmond Advertising Assoc.

Near You, Trans-Canada Telephone System: McKim Advertising Ltd.

Tastes Great, Ontario Milk Marketing Board: Ogilvy & Mather Ltd.

Quartet, Trans-Canada Telephone System: McKim Advertising Ltd.

Working Man, London Life Insurance Co.: Goodis, Goldberg, Soren

Train, Philips Electronics Industries Ltd.: McCann-Erickson Advertising

Jerry Goodis, vice-chairman, MacLaren Intermart Inc.

The Buildings We Built

Four of Canada's leading architects, **Arthur Erickson, Raymond Moriyama, John C. Parkin** and **Ron Thom** each compiled a list of what they considered the finest buildings designed or constructed in the 1970s. This is a selection from those lists, in alphabetical order:

Church, Red Deer, Alberta: Jean-Paul Cardinal

Winnipeg Art Gallery: Gustavo da Roza

Student residence, University of Alberta: Diamond & Myers

Museum of Anthropology, University of British Columbia, Vancouver: Arthur Erickson

Bank of Canada, Ottawa: Arthur Erickson

Scarborough Civic Centre, Scarborough, Ontario: Raymond Moriyama

National Gallery of Canada, Ottawa: Parkin Partnership Architects Planners

Pavillion Soixante-Dix, St. Saigeur, Quebec: Peter Rose

Pearson College, Vancouver, B.C.: Ron Thom

Transformer station, Regina, Saskatchewan: Clifford Weins

Arthur Erickson's The Museum of Anthropology. UBC

Scientific Problems

It is fitting, in a dispiriting way, that the Three Mile Island nuclear accident occurred just before the tenth anniversary of the first moon landing. The two events provide capsule images of the '60s and the '70s, both epitomizing the scientific and technological tenor of their respective decades and underscoring the startling contrasts between them.

The '60s were a time of unparalleled scientific and technical expansion and success, a decade symbolized by the achievement of the seemingly impossible: flying to the moon. Regrettably, it was also a time of overweening technological optimism, a time that fostered the deception that science and technology could, given half a chance, solve all our problems, *especially* the impossible ones. This was, of course, a false and fatal cockiness. Going to the moon, it turned out, was an inherently solvable problem and, in fact, a simple one in its fundamental aspects, if not in execution.

The problems of the '70s were not in any sense simple and it's not obvious that they're even inherently solvable. The '70s humbled us. The first hard lesson was that throwing money and manpower at a problem is simply not enough if we don't sufficiently understand the basic nature of that problem. For all our cleverness, we have yet to unravel some of nature's most fundamental secrets. The war on cancer comes to mind as the prime example; the assault here was every bit as vigorous as that on the moon but, while advances have been made, we still don't know how to cure or prevent most cancers.

The second hard lesson was that scientific advances carry risks as well as benefits and that both are difficult to predict. We have always acknowledged the two-edged nature of science intellectually, but only in this past decade have our noses really been rubbed in its real-world consequences. We learned to splice together the genes of widely different organisms – and began to worry about creating strange new diseases. We produced millions of tons of fluorocarbon spray-can propellants – and began to worry about damaging the ozone layer that shields us from the sun's lethal ultraviolet radiation. We built more and larger nuclear plants – and began to worry about disposing of long-lived radioactive wastes for millions of years.

We were forced onto a see-saw, trying to weigh often-speculative benefits against equally speculative risks. Even if you accept that most people want to do the Right Thing, it was rarely clear what was the Right Thing to do. The "experts" were no help, arrayed as they were on all sides of each question. Never was the two-armed scientist ("On the one hand . . . but on the other hand . . . ") more in evidence. And since in many cases the day of reckoning might be years, decades, even centuries in the future, decisions taken now were in reality decisions taken for many succeeding generations.

The third lesson of the '70s was more subtle and even more disturbing: Scientific and technological advances may

Dr. Gerhard Herzberg, Nobel Prize winner for Chemistry in 1971, was the first Canadian to receive the Prize in either chemistry or physics. CP

have negative side effects that we not only can't predict, but that we may not even perceive until it's too late. The ozone issue provides a salutary model. The recognition that hair spray and underarm deodorant propellants might seriously harm the upper atmosphere was a casual, almost accidental, discovery – one, incidentally, that eluded all of the scientists who might logically have been expected to stumble on it. That we could be sitting here today blithely ignorant of this potentially devastating global environmental threat raises nagging questions: What have we missed? What are we doing to the earth's environment, even now, that we don't know about?

If the '70s gave us no answers to those questions, they underscored the urgent need for such answers. Galloping population growth, food and resource consumption and rising energy demand put an end to the naive contention that human activities were too minor to have a global impact, too puny to threaten the planet's ability even to sustain life. The '70s taught us that we do not have license, as one scientist put it, to "put out as many pounds of junk as there are pounds of water or air to foul up."

As we enter the '80s, we are forced to reconsider a basic human imperative: that what can be done, must be done and, in the end, will be done. We are forced to consider choosing not to do things that technically can be done: building nuclear reactors, splicing genes, burning fossil fuels, and myriad others. We are driven by events, and by the miscalculations of the past, to rejecting facile "technological fixes" and considering instead social solutions to our problems – solutions such as limiting our population growth, reducing energy consumption, abandoning polluting technologies, changing our eating habits, with all the adaptation in lifestyle that these things imply.

In its own way, the next decade will be as fascinating as the two that went before it.

Lydia Dotto, science writer, columnist, author.

Medicine

The 1970s will go down in history as the decade during which the government of Canada presented a radically new interpretation of the health problems of the nation and how to approach them. To be more precise, a landmark document, *A New Perspective on the Health of Canadians* was published in 1973, under the imprimatur of the Honourable Marc Lalonde, then minister of the department of health and welfare. Here's the gist of the new approach to health as expressed in *A New Perspective*, as well as in subsequent statements by Lalonde:

In times past, the most important causes of sickness and death were epidemics of communicable diseases, infections, poor nutrition and low standards of public hygiene. But, because of advances in medical science, the situation has been changing during the past four or five decades. Plagues of communicable diseases have been eliminated by programs of immunization; most infections can be controlled by powerful antibiotics; higher standards of public hygiene have been introduced; nutritional habits have improved;

and a variety of new drugs and diagnostic and surgical procedures have made it possible to cope with hitherto untreatable diseases.

All of this has put a new face on morbidity and mortality tables. The leading causes of death are now the so-called "lifestyle" or "self-inflicted" diseases. In rank of importance, they are diseases of the heart and blood vessels, cancer, accidents and respiratory ailments.

They are referred to as "lifestyle" diseases because, to a large extent, the individual can protect himself against them by altering his daily habits. These diseases are claimed to be the end product of an unwise diet, smoking tobacco, the immoderate use of alcohol and other drugs and a lack of regular periods of exercise and relaxation.

The full extent to which lifestyle contributes to disease can be gauged by comparing the health records of the general population with those of certain health-conscious groups, such as members of the Seventh Day Adventist Church. The Adventists claim a world-wide membership of some two million people, of whom 20,000 live in Canada. By religious stricture, they abstain from tobacco, alcohol and meat. They are also exhorted to exercise regularly. A comparison of the health histories of 11,000 adult male Adventists with those of the general male population in California revealed the following:

Cancer of the mouth, larynx and esophagus was ten times less common among the Adventists. Death from respiratory diseases was only three percent, as compared to 12 percent in the general population.

Adventists suffered heart attacks 40 percent less frequently, and the attacks came ten years later. The death rate of the Adventists was one-half that of the general population.

The impact of lifestyle on health is also documented by medical studies of members of the Church of Jesus Christ of Latter Day Saints, more commonly known as Mormons. Like the Adventists, they too lead prudent lives. The death rate from all major diseases among the Mormons is almost 50 percent lower than non-Mormons living in Canada and the U.S.

Government health officials have recently realized that they can no longer avoid recognizing the link between lifestyle and disease if they want to avoid future bankruptcy. Since the introduction of the health plans into the various provinces in the early part of the '60s, billions of dollars have been expended, yet the health of the Canadian people has not appreciably improved. Health costs continue to climb. In Ontario, for example, between 1974 and 1979, the cost of operating the Ontario Health Insurance Plan (OHIP) has skyrocketed from $2.2 billion to $4 billion. It's predicted that the OHIP budget will approach $11 billion by 1984. The experience in the other Canadian provinces has been similar.

These sobering statistics have fathered the view that the practise of medicine, in the future, must concentrate on preventing disease rather than treating it. The medical school, henceforth, must graduate doctors who possess the skill to help patients abandon a destructive lifestyle. Even more important, the physician should be equipped to identify the pressures in the patient's life – past or present – that cause him to persist in habits that cause disease. It's also essential to review the present fee structure of the health plans so that doctors, in the future, won't be penalized for practising preventive medicine.

I recently interviewed a doctor who may very well be the prototype of the 21st-century physician. Dr. Michael Smith, 40, is a graduate of the University of Toronto medical school and practises in Smith's Falls, a city of 10,000 situated 60 miles southwest of Ottawa.

After 10 years in general practice, Smith realized that he was doing nothing more than treating the same patients with the same symptoms (usually drugs) without giving them permanent relief. About 90 percent of his patients, he found, suffered not with serious organic defects but with such run-of-the-mill symptoms as fatigue, depression, insomnia, backache and skin disorders. He could usually trace these symptoms to one or more unsatisfactory situations in the patient's life: marriage to a selfish, insensitive spouse, a tyrannical boss, interfering inlaws, worries about children, income or housing.

In some cases, the patient had entered adulthood bearing emotional scars from his or her past. Some had been physically abused by their parents. Others had been psychologically scarred to the point where they were ridden with fears about older people, about sex, about authority and held themselves in low self-esteem. Smith told me, "The two most frequent complaints of my patients were fatigue and pain. Yet, 99 percent of pain is caused by muscle tension and most fatigue stems from emotional depression."

In most busy conventional medical practises, the physician spends a few minutes with the patient and sends him away with a prescription for a drug – tranquillizing, energizing or sleep-producing – that temporarily alleviates the symptoms. But, in a few days or weeks, because the root cause of the symptom has not been dealt with, the patient returns with his old complaints.

By contrast, Smith will spend 60 to 90 minutes with his patients, carefully exploring their past and present life, trying to identify the sources of their symptoms. Once he has diagnosed the origins of the illness, he will use one or more of several forms of therapy. These may include relaxation exercises, hypnotherapy, self-suggestion, bioenergetics, psychotherapy, acupuncture, group therapy, special diets and exercises. Smith describes his brand of medicine as "holistic medicine" – an approach that realistically deals with all the factors in the patient's life that affect his health. "Many patients claim that holistic therapy has helped them get rid of uncomfortable physical symptoms they've suffered with for years," said Smith.

Apart from the occasional use of cough medicine, antibiotics or heart stimulants, Smith seldom prescribes drugs for his patients. "Too many drugs only mask the symptoms," he said. To many informed observers, Smith is today practising the medicine of the future. He does not dispute the scientific logic of treating medical emergencies – such as heart attacks, infections and fractured limbs – in traditional ways. But, he points out, patients with such gross medical problems are in the minority. The indicated approach to the vast majority of patients, he says, is a holistic one. Relieve the symptoms by identifying the inner or outer pressures that cause them, and, in the process, "immunize" the patient against a return of the symptoms by helping him acquire a new lifestyle.

Sidney Katz, author, feature writer, the Toronto *Star.*

Underground Medicine

The intriguing snatches of talk buzz at you from all directions. On the bus. *"Then the guy told me he'd been Rolfed. . . . "* In the elevator. *"I mean, can you imagine curing the screaming-meemies by dosing yourself with the life-essence of the rock rose?"* In the checkout line at the supermarket. *" . . . I had this rotten pain, so I used glove anaesthesia. . . . "* Behind you in the theatre foyer. *"She was into G-Jo and shiatsu – now it's colour therapy and aura balancing."*

Aura balancing, radionics, psychic healing, foot reflexology. Never has there been such widespread interest in alternate, unorthodox or esoteric medicine. Never has there been such curiosity (among physicians, churchmen, psychic phenomena investigators, turned-on members of the public) about healing techniques and therapies that seem as new and as far-out as man on Saturn. Yet, basically, are older than the recorded history of man.

There is so much serious interest in alternate medicine, in fact, the signs are that the *orthodox* could be moving closer to the unorthodox all the time. For one thing, it's becoming common talk at medical and psychiatric conclaves that Chinese acupuncture has produced a lot of establishment MDs into Thinking Holistic. Holistic – a very with-it word right now as evidence grows that much of human disease is psychosomatic – means "whole" as opposed to "part," and medics who are boning up on the Taoist energy-balance philosophy behind acupuncture seem to be realizing that patients could be Total People rather than grab bags of isolated symptoms. Realizing, too, that all individuals could be linked by some kind of natural force. Not only to each other, as Carl Jung told us years ago when he wrote about the collective unconscious, but to the universe and its elements as well.

It's a theory that more and more of the interested and curious are finding more and more fascinating. If there *is* a bonding force, could it be the same life-energy that the Yogis call *prana*, the Polynesians know as *mana* and the Chinese call *Ch'i*? Is there some connection between the curative power said to be transmitted by herbs and herb-related homeopathic remedies and the Force-X that parapsychologists claim is transferred between faith healers and their patients? Does all of this somehow tie in with researcher Cleve Backster's communication experiments with flowers and vegetables? After all, if there is a flow of information or *thought* energy between humans and plants, could this mean that all living cells are hooked into the same massive switchboard?

Certainly the common theme of energy and harmony (of body and mind with nature) seems to thread through and link all of alternate medicine. Acupuncture is related philosophically to Japanese finger-pressure massage, to the yin-yang teachings of macrobiotic diet gurus, to the beliefs of naturopaths, herbalists, magnetic healers. Austrian scientist-mystic Rudolph Steiner spoke early in this century of illness being an "imbalance" of ego-astral – or physical, mental and universal – forces. Edgar Cayce, the celebrated American psychic, believed in the "attuning of vibrations," within and without the body, for the restoration of health.

Strangely similar ideas turn up in the ancient writings of Oriental healers and Indian swamis and in the passed-along lore of African medicine men. Albert Einstein made a life study of energy and its mysteries. And his Field Theory really parallels the thinking of Taoist teachers, psychics, Yogis, even Backster and Jung. Nothing exists by itself. Everything is, in its deepest truth, related to Everything.

The following therapies are all related to each other in some way, and they are all a part of alternate medicine. I make no recommendations and offer no endorsements. I am not suggesting that you taste or try. The exercise here is to define the terms and explain the methods. I simply want to put you in touch.

Homeopathy: "Like cures like," according to Samuel Hahnemann, the 18th-century physician who founded homeopathy. The idea is to treat a sick individual with a substance – animal, vegetable or mineral – that would cause identical *symptoms* of the illness when taken by a healthy person. Homeopaths say, for example, that the symptoms of malaria are produced by large doses of natural Peruvian bark. *Minute* or diluted doses of the same substance (the theory is that a sick body is more sensitive to medication than one that is well) have been found to cure the disease.

Hypnotherapy: Medical hypnotism uses the same techniques as theatrical hypnotism. Today, however, the "spasmodic sleep" demonstrated by the 18th-century German physician, Franz Anton Mesmer, has achieved considerable establishment status. Hypnotism is used to treat allergies, nervous disorders, and as a substitute for anesthetics. There's nothing mysterious about the technique. Hypnosis is merely a relaxed, detached state of mind. Some hypnotists say that many people walk around in a light trance for much of their working day, anyway.

Chiropractic: Deals with subluxations, or partial dislocations, of the spinal joints. Practioners make adjustments to the spine and claim to cure or alleviate a wide variety of physical problems. Asthma, neuralgia, neuritis, lumbago are most often mentioned in connection with chiropractic treatment, but some patients insist they have been cured of more serious diseases. Some chiropractors also practise naturopathy and magnetic healing.

Yogic healing: In Yoga, there is an integration of body and mind (*yoga* means "union" in Sanskrit) and the use of various healing systems. The most widely practised in Canada are the exercise techniques of Hatha Yoga, involving the "positions" or *mudras* and *asanas*, the meditative techniques or *dhyana* and the breathing techniques or *pranayama*. But then there are also the *satkarmas*, or cleansing techniques, involving internal washes or enemas. And Ayurvedic Medicine, which uses special diets and natural remedies.

Magnetic healing has been around for at least as long as the time of Franz Anton Mesmer, who believed that magnets could be used to correct disease-producing distortions or "tides" in the physical and psychic flow of human energy. Groups of Mesmer's patients would sit in a "magnetized" garden, absorbing good vibes from a tub of water filled with magnets and iron filings. These days, magnetic healing devices are more sophisticated and there are a number of different gadgets being used in Canada, many by naturopaths and chiropractors. "Unbalanced magnetic fields" in the body are diagnosed with magnetic probes or scanners (some practitioners claim they can also spot disorders from "off-colour" auras) and energy is then directed to the affected area. Success has been claimed in cases of high and low blood pressure and among patients with cholesterol problems. "Magnetic energy," says one therapist, "seems to affect the body's pH (acid-alkaline) balance."

Christian Science: The Christian Science Movement was founded in Boston almost 100 years ago by Mary Baker Eddy, who preached that illness is an error because man is made in the image of God. "Man is incapable of sin, sickness and death," she insisted, and so disease originates in the mind. The Bible is an important tool in Christian Scientists' healing of sin and believers find cures through the regenerative power of prayer. Christian Scientists are expected to ignore the orthodox medical establishment but as one Church primer explains: "If in extreme circumstances or under heavy family pressure he resorts to material means, he won't be treated as an outcast."

Acpuncture: Needle power from China, based on Taoist philosophy: all things in man and nature are related. Man, in fact, is one with the universe and its elements (earth, fire, metal, air, water, wood) and all are governed by the opposite forces of yin (passive, cool, night) and yang (active, hot, light). The purpose of the needles is to stimulate life-energy flows along the body's meridians or power lines and to bring yin and yang into balance.

The thing you need to remember about **Zen Macrobiotics** is that it is a diet based on the oriental principle of yin and yang – the principle, too, of acupuncture. Soft is yin and solid is yang. The late Dr. George Ohsawa, who spread the gospel of macrobiotics from Japan, believed that a balanced, yin-yang diet of soft and solid foods not only maintained health but healed all kinds of disorders as well. Ohsawa claimed to have cured cases of cancer, tuberculosis and heart disease with macrobiotics. Meat, fish and fowl are on the yang list. Many fruits and vegetables are yin. Whole brown rice is a revered macrobiotic food. According to Ohsawa's teachings, it is ideally balanced, yin-yang.

Dr. Bach's Flower Remedies are loosely linked with homeopathy, psychotherapy and magnetism. Maybe with autosuggestion as well. The late Dr. Edward Bach was a British physician who quit his practice in 1930 to explore the idea that the Vital Force of flowers could cure negative states of mind. Bad moods cause illness, believed Bach, and he classified 38 offenders (among them: fear, self-distrust, indecisiveness, anxiety), then experimented to match the destructive mood with the healing blossom. Sweet chestnut, for example, he found to be an antidote to mental anguish. Agrimony to restlessness. Cherry plum to despair. Methods for preparing his medicines are unique. Flowers are floated in spring water and exposed to sunlight, then the water is poured into large jars and drops of the "mother tincture" are mixed with more spring water in smaller bottles. Minute or homeopathic doses of Life Force *Impatiens Balsamina* (known as the touch-me-not in North America) is Dr. Bach's prescription for mental stress. The remedies are sold in most homeopathic stores.

If you understand something about dowsing or divining (for water, oil, even information), you have a better chance of grasping the principles of **Radionics.** To put it simply, radionics is presented as a way of diagnosing human disease by dowsing and interpreting electrical vibrations transmitted by the human body – or samples such as saliva or hair. It is also a way, claim radionics practitioners, of curing disease by transmitting a mental signal back to the patient. Radionics, in fact, might be called Instrumentized Psychic Healing. The instruments used are plain black boxes fitted with numbered dials. These dials are "tuned" as the operator dowses a blood or saliva "witness" (all that happens to be in the box) then checks the result against figures that refer to specific diseases or disorders (50, say, for cancer, 600 for arthritis). Healing Thought transmissions – which one also "turned" by the dials– have been described as "jamming signals," programmed to cancel out the damaging vibrations of the disease. Or to unclog personal receivers so that patients can absorb instructions about how to heal themselves.

Shiatsu or **Japanese Finger-Pressure Massage** is really acupuncture without needles, and practitioners in Canada claim they have cured a long list of ailments, including migraines, allergies, undefined backaches, lumbago. The Shiatsu practitioner "feels out" the quality of Life Force energy coursing through the 49 meridians of the body, then applies pressure to stimulate and balance the flow. **G-Jo** and **Do-In** are two do-it-yourself spin-offs from finger massage. There are illustrated books on the market now that claim they can show people how to rid themselves of headaches by pressing strategic spots on the head and neck. Or how to combat fatigue. For instance, press both temples with the first three fingers of each hand, then quickly release.

Naturopaths across Canada offer all kinds of alternate medicine: herbal treatments, homeopathy, heat and sun, routines that involve rugging up to your ears and walking barefoot in the snow. Sand therapy for rheumatism and arthritis is popular among naturopaths in Italy and the Canary Islands. Patients are buried up to the chin in hot sand that has been "vitalized" with seaweed. Then, there is healing with water – cold baths, sponges, compresses. American hydrotherapist Jeanne Keller says that the best bet for an earache is to go to bed wearing wet socks. On your feet, not your ears.

Don't try to sort out the differences between **zone therapy, reflexology** and **reflex therapy.** They are all loosely related to finger-pressure massage and they all claim that every organ and muscle in the body is connected by "invisible electrical currents" to a corresponding area in the feet. Massage or pressure at these strategic points appears to help such diverse health problems as bronchitis, bladder disturbances, high and low blood pressure. There are a wide variety of foot charts around. But one used in Canada shows, for example, that a spot just under the little toe is linked with the sinuses. Another area on the ball of the foot is connected with the lungs, and so on.

Chromotherapy or **Colour healing** is a combination of Yoga (treatment is focussed through the seven Yogic *chakras* or psychic inlets to the body), magnetism (therapists speak of colour as a "vibration" or a "cosmic force"), clairvoyance (the healers diagnose disease by checking the shape and colour of the human aura – the super-physical mists that are said to hover around all matter) and the occult (the chromotherapist says he can treat a patient on the spot or at a distance through meditation and concentration). Basically, the healer works to correct "disharmony" in the physical and "etheric" (spiritual) body by the use of coloured lights and healing thoughts. Prescriptions span the spectrum. Blue is said to heal pain. Rose-red is said to help anemia. Green is for irritabiity. Purple is prescribed for paralysis.

Individuals who have been **Rolfed** say they felt at the time as though they had been given a message by a wringer washer. But many who have submitted to this technique also claim they have been cured of back pains, prostate trouble and other physical problems. Their bodies, according to practitioners, were "restructured" by drastic pummelling and twisting. This, apparently, altered body chemistry and stimulated energy flow. Ida Rolf, the American biochemist who invented the therapy, once explained that she used the force of gravity to achieve "posture release." Disease, she has written, can be the result of bad memories. "And memories are stored in the body as well as the mind."

The believers in **Pyramid Power** are proliferating all the time. A pyramid, insist the addicts, can cure headaches, improve meditation, preserve food, sharpen razor blades and turn vinegary wine into something resembling Pouilly Fuissé. One way of checking out the claims is to build your own pyramid from metal or cardboard (you get the headache while figuring out the instructions), buy some cheap wine, then sit inside the pyramid to meditate. Eric McLuhan (son of Marshall), who has studied pyramids, says they are somehow related to gravity, magnetism and resonance. The chambers of Egyptian pyramids, he has found, are "resonant cavities" – enclosed spaces in which electromagnetic energy is stored or excited. Something like hi-fi speakers. Another theory is that the pyramid shape acts as a lens that directs cosmic energy to a point one-third from its base. Pyramid sales boom while the controversy continues.

Biofeedback has been called the celebration of the marriage between machine and mind. Understand how to use biofeedback equipment, say those who are pushing it, and you can relieve migraines, back pains, epilepsy, asthma and other chronic ailments. Disciples of biofeedback systems make them sound like so many personal survival kits. Basically, though, biofeedback training gadgets are monitors that pick up bioelectric signals transmitted by the body and feed them back in ways we can see or hear. If we can learn to control these signals – through concentration, meditation, we can control physical processes. Advanced students have been taught what was once thought beyond mental command – control of the involuntary nervous system. Through mastery of the relaxed Alpha state of consciousness, say BFT experts, individuals can train their hearts, blood vessels, visceral muscles to obey orders. And to banish disease.

"Psychotherapy (hexing): In young children, suggestion accompanied by impressive but meaningless manipulations, such as painting the [wart] lesions or touching them with unusual objects or exposing them to heat lamps is often remarkably successful." From the current *Merck Manual of Diagnosis and Therapy,* a handbook for physicians "aimed at supporting the latest and best in medical education and practice."

Mind Control, Mind Awareness or **Mind Development** courses in Canada all have their roots in the teachings of José Silva, an American pioneer in the Human Potential-ASC (Altered States of Consciousness) movement. Mind Control trains the students to achieve ASC levels through Alpha (relaxed, aware, a state close to extrasensory perception), Theta (slower, deeper) and sometimes Delta (dreamless sleep) without biofeedback equipment, and to use these levels to control their own health problems. Even to heal others. Students learn about glove anesthesia (how to touch an injury and stop pain), how to sharpen memory, improve eyesight, stop smoking or drinking. How to build a Mental Laboratory in which (through ASC) one can examine one's own joints, arteries, organs and fix problems if necessary ("if you see gallstones, crush them"). How to "view" the bodies and health problems of other individuals, how to diagnose and how to cure. Observers of Mind Control say that Silva and his imitators have borrowed many of their ideas from Zen, Yoga, religion and hypnosis.

What do **onions, garlic** and **ginseng root** have in common? Well, for one thing, they're all part of the herbalist's medicine chest – a chest that includes such ancient remedies as motherwort, nettle, echinacea and mistletoe. For another, onions, garlic and ginseng all emit "mitogenetic" or m-rays, an ultraviolet radiation that has been found to stimulate cell activity and rejuvenate the system. Ginseng (called the "elixir of life" by the Chinese) is expensive in Canada, though. Disciples of folk medicine are just as enthusiastic about the frequent use of the less-aristocratic onion and garlic bud for good health. This is a popular herbal remedy for a "streaming" cold: dunk a slice of raw onion into a glass of hot water for a mere second or so. Then, sip water from the glass throughout the day.

Psychic and **spiritual healers** are everywhere – there is a Federation of Spiritual Healers (Canada) Inc. – and they claim to do exactly that. Heal the sick, either psychically or spiritually. Spiritual healers use religious faith in their work. In other words, they believe the "warm energy" they feel flowing through their hands (sometimes directly to the patient, sometimes in the patient's absence) is Divine Power. Psychic healers are more inclined to speak of Cosmic Energy, Odic Force or n-rays, although some claim to be directed by spirit guides. Most healers, though, will agree that individuals who come to them for help really heal themselves through their own, natural, self-healing mechanisms and that healers merely act as metaphysical bridges between the Power and the Patient. Healers who have been observed and questioned by parapsychologists admit they were in an altered state of consciousness when they "merged" or "united" with the individual they were trying to help. Science, too, has been able to track the Energy that Unites. Kirlian photography (a process invented in the U.S.S.R.) has revealed spectacular auras or coronas surrounding the fingertips of healers in the act of healing.

Betty Lee, journalist. From *The Canadian.*

Boom Years in the Therapy Business

A generation ago, almost no one was treated by a psychotherapist of any kind. Almost no one *knew* anybody who was treated by a psychotherapist. But today, in many parts of Canadian society, "my shrink" is a more common phrase than "my butcher." In 1960 there were 611 practising psychiatrists in Canada. In 1971 there were 1,700. In 1978 there were 2,169. No one knows where it will stop.

And those are only the MDs licensed to practise as psychiatrists. Behind them, and around them, are legions more of psychologists and psychotherapists, trained and untrained, stretching across a vast spectrum from the staidest community marriage counsellor to the wildest experimentalist. You get some idea of how *that* world is growing when you reflect that enrolment in university psychology departments has increased tenfold since 1970.

"Business is booming," confides one senior member of the Canadian Psychiatric Association. "It seems that one half the country is treating the other half." The Canadian Mental Health Association estimates that one in six children born in 1976 will require hospitalization for emotional disorder at some point. At the moment Canada spends more than $1 billion a year on mental health care.

Why? One Toronto psychiatrist argues that his increasing business is currently due to two major factors: economic insecurity (which may be a temporary problem) and the vacuum left by organized religion (which may not be a temporary problem). "They want me," he says in some puzzlement, "to find meaning for their lives."

A more obvious reason is that now almost everyone can afford a psychiatrist. Medicare pays most psychiatric bills, so what was once the expensive indulgence of the rich can now be the habit of the middle class and the poor as well. Problems that were once worked through privately – or maybe with the help of clergymen – are now taken directly to the shrink. You no longer need to suffer in silence. You can suffer noisily in the shrink's office. Sometimes it's fun: one Toronto matron confided to her friends, with giddy delight, that she was now the member of *two* therapy groups, with two quite different therapists, neither of whom knew about the other. "It's sort of like adultery," she reported. Ontario medicare paid every nickel.

Dr. Don Coates, a B.C. psychiatrist who served on the Hastings Commission on the Healing Arts, doesn't much approve. "The state sanctions, and pays for, long-term techniques such as psychoanalysis to treat 'walking misery' as well as true mental illness." He thinks a lot of that misery should go elsewhere. "I'm convinced there's scope for clergy and community workers to treat the kind of money and marriage problems Canadians are currently taking to high-priced professionals." No doubt about it, there are many people seeing therapists who wouldn't have been classified, in any earlier generation, as mentally ill.

Whatever the causes, the mental health professions are becoming more and more a public – and permanent – part of Canadian life. Therapists turn up everywhere in the media, and lately have become prominent in politics. "Psychiatry is the science of change," says Dr. Camille Laurin, one of the two psychiatrists in the PQ cabinet. Those scientists of change are now also hard at work in the corporations, the courts, and government, and the unseen changes they are bringing about may be even more important than the great political and economic upheavals of these nervous years.

A rich shrink is a happy shrink

The psychiatric Establishment gives its members power, satisfaction and not much else. Usually they're too busy with committees, organizations and departments to make much money as well. The real money-making psychiatrists are outside the Establishment. They follow a different set of guidelines, such as –

• Become the only psychiatrist in a smallish city. Dr. W. P. Kyne reported that he made more than $80,000 a year practising in Prince George, B.C. (On the other hand, shrinks don't like small cities – the isolation sometimes gets to them. Kyne is moving now to Toronto, where he plans to make $250,000 a year shrinking Bay Street tycoons.)

• If you're in a big city, find the right location. In Toronto it's Angst Alley, a stretch of St. Clair Avenue between Spadina Road and Avenue Road, also know as the Mental Block. In Vancouver it's the Fairmont medical building, also known as the Dollar Factory.

• Specialize in group – as opposed to individual – therapy. Charging ten people $20 an hour grosses more than charging one patient $60 or even $70, which is about as high as you can go.

• Open your own centre or institution. Psychologist Dan Hagler is doing well from Ontario government contracts with his highly respected Youthdale Treatment Centre.

• Best of all, invent your own movement, write a best seller about it, and franchise the treatment. Americans like Arthur Janov (primal therapy) have done it, but so far no Canadian has pulled it off. The field is open.

• "Be tall, slim and silver-haired." (This advice is offered by a shrink who is not tall, slim or silver-haired.) For the wise look, grow a beard. (Beards are not, however, worn by the Establishment.)

The Inside Track, *Saturday Night.*

The Cancer Epidemic & How to Stop It

The cancer statistics are bad enough (an 11 percent increase in overall cancer incidence over the past 30 years, in spite of everything medicine can do), but nothing beats your own experience: why are so *many* of your friends dying of cancer these days? There's no mystery – the reason is well known, though the activities of the cancer societies and the U.S. government's multimillion-dollar "war" to find a cancer "virus" have not helped us understand the real problem. But the World Health Organization knows: up to 90 percent of human cancer is "environmentally caused." Other sources are even more precise: the majority of human cancer is caused by the chemicals we breathe, eat and work with. The "cancer maps" prepared for the U.S. and

Canada offer a clear and graphic demonstration: cancer and industry (most notably the petrochemical industry) are clustered together.

The cancer epidemic we're in now should have been prevented. The one we're passing forward to our children is inexcusable. It can easily be prevented – easily in the technical sense, though perhaps not in the political one.

If only cancer-causing chemicals were like cyanide: one whiff and down you go. Unfortunately, cancer usually takes a couple of decades to develop, probably because of a slow and inexorable effect of the chemical poison on the cellular genetic material. One way, therefore, to find out if a chemical causes cancer is to expose a lot of people to it, and wait. Certain sticky questions of medical ethics arise here, however, not to speak of the expense to industry (and society) when the victims and their families get into court. Animal experiments are better, and faster, but they're not cheap. The mouse is a fine experimental animal, generally sensitive to the same chemicals that you are, and develops cancer relatively quickly. Even so, testing a new chemical for cancer-causing potential, according to the U.S. National Cancer Institute protocol, involves some 600 animals (usually rats and mice) and costs at least $150,000. Estimates vary on the number of new chemicals invented every year, but it's probably about 1,000 – not to speak of the number of *old* ones that were never tested to begin with.

That's why the petrochemical, pesticide, food additive, food colouring, pharmaceutical, smelting and plastics industries are not exactly anxious to see laws making pretesting of potentially toxic chemicals mandatory. Another reason involves "false positives" and "false negatives." What this means in the testing business is that your test may not be entirely accurate. It may tell you 95 percent of the time whether the chemical is safe or not, but five percent of the time it may be wrong: a "false positive" means that the test indicates the chemical has an effect that in fact it doesn't have. And if that effect is *cancer,* a potentially valuable and actually harmless product may be shelved unecessarily.

Better to err on the side of caution and set aside a few chemicals now, you say, rather than discover 20 years down the road a spate of liver cancer? Well, consider what's *actually* happening.

Last year the Americans put into effect a Toxic Substances Control Act, which in essence puts the burden on a manufacturer to prove that a new chemical is not carcinogenic. And in May, the U.S. Occupational Safety and Health Administration proposed new regulations that would also shift the burden to employers to prove chemicals used in the workplace were safe. (In the seven years of its existence, OSHA managed to develop controls covering only 20 of the 2,000 suspected carcinogens.) The chemical industry claims that the new procedures would add "billions of dollars" to the cost of production. Well, we have to ask, so what? Is it better *not* to test in advance? The American Industrial Health Council, an *ad hoc* industry group, is said to have raised more than $1 million to contest the OSHA proposals.

Canadian industry has not been galvanized into this kind of action because nothing quite like the U.S. screening tests is required here, nor are there proposals for any under study in Ottawa.

The $150,000 price tag on an animal screening test is a red herring. There's a much cheaper way to screen: a battery of tests are available now that use bacteria instead of rats, and are reliable and remarkably accurate. The best-known of these is called the Ames Test, after Bruce Ames of the University of California. It works like this: a strain of the bacterium *Salmonella* is used, mutated in a way that prevents the organism from growing except in a special nutrient. The *Salmonella* are exposed to the chemical in question, and if the chemical is mutagenic, some of the already mutated *Salmonella* will be kicked back to their normal state, and grow in the midst of their dormant cousins. Because there's a good correlation between mutagenicity and carcinogenicity, the presence of bacterial colonies after chemical exposure is a warning signal. The test, which is still being refined, is imperfect: it identifies some 90 percent of known carcinogens and clears 87 percent of known noncarcinogens. Still, that's a lot better than blind luck. Our government, it seems, would rather count the bodies afterward than count the bacteria before.

The Inside Track, *Saturday Night.*

Great Bores

(This is not in order of preference)

Ted Kennedy: who hopes to ride to presidential power in 1980 on the promise of giving the American people an exact replica of our medicare system which, alas, is already falling apart.

Ayatollah Khomeini: whose hands off (literally chopped off) policy to all offenders against his Grand Islam is boring. Let's face it, there are so many more interesting organs the ayatollah could have focussed his attention on. Modesty prevents me from naming one (it's not my nose).

Harold Ballard: his foul mouth and worse ideas are so nauseating that talking to him is like making love to the back of a bus. It's not the gas fumes that get you with Ballard, it's the way he lands on you when he backs up on anyone or anything that might threaten his pocketbook.

Ayatollah Khomeini of Iran. AP

The Canadian Mafia: not a "Lucky" Luciano, Meyer Lansky, "Bugsy" Siegel or Al Capone among them, yet the CBC has given the Canadian Mafia more air time than the CBC has given all the recorded wars of mankind from Cain and Abel to Vietnam.

Jane Fonda and **Tom Hayden:** the Sidney and Beatrice Webb of American radicalism. Sidney and Beatrice spun their web and came up as the founding Pa and Ma Kettle of British Fabian socialism. Jane and Tom have come up with an American socialism so banal and so devoid of mass appeal that to call it boring would be to debase the coinage of a very useful term. As an actress Jane is superb; as a radical she's so boring she's making Karl Marx's grave turn over and over in ennui. As adult viewing Tom and Jane are as numbingly boring as an adult meeting of Dick and Jane.

Henry Kissinger: Kissinger's love affair with the liberal media and vice versa has turned him from a Dr. Strangelove to a kindly Dr. Jewish Teddy Bear. Kissinger's road to Damascus has certainly been paved with the most boring of intentions. In an age of nonheroes, a nonvillain like Kissinger shines brightly indeed.

Henry Kissinger, then President Nixon's national security advisor, with Le Duc Tho, Hanoi's top Vietnam peace negotiator, 1973. AP

The Rolling Stones: gather all moss; some of it Margaret Trudeau. In an age of musical decadence they are decay itself. In an age of nonheroes and antiromanticism they are the antiheroic killers of the shape and purity of music. If grotesque be boring, put them on the top of the list.

Dr. Benjamin Spock: a classic bore not because Spock was not successful but precisely because he so often was. The Spock Generation is more beautiful, more educated, more happy than mine. Still they are more unemployed than my generation and I'm a Great Depression baby. Also the Spock Generation doesn't sneak into dirty movies, read *Fanny Hill* or remain as content with passionate necking as my teenage generation did. The Spock Generation sex is as up front in a candy store as the Oh Henry chocolate bars I used to eat in my teenage years. Alas, Spock's sex is just as sweet and just as cheap. Spock's generation of sexual clones is far more boring than my generation of ice-cream cones. My generation had more melt downs; the Spock Generation has more auras of bores than the Aurora Bore-alis.

Germaine Greer: she is the Bore of Babylon for reducing all mankind to the level of a pig and all womankind to exploited sainthood. Any woman who believes, as Greer does, that Lucrezia Borgia has more in common with Laura Second than she does with Cesare Borgia, or that Queen Elizabeth has more in common with a sister-wife of a coal miner than a coal miner's wife has with a coal miner or Elizabeth with Philip is more than just boring. Let's face it, Greer's just a silly old yenta.

Larry Zolf, the Mouth that Bores.

Murder

Most killers in Canada are men – nine out of ten – and most murders involve close friends or family. Most occur at night or on weekends and holidays. Most involve drugs or alcohol. Arrests are usually swift, the trials are short, the publicity is brief. Most are soon forgotten by the public.

But some murders, because of the age or identity of the victim, or because of their macabre uniqueness, explode into daily headlines. They captivate the entire nation, sometimes inciting it to anger. The most sensational murders of the 1970s included senseless massacres and the deaths of politicians, Mafia capos and innocent children. Only two were basic, but offbeat, "domestic" cases. But they each, in their own way, became infamous.

On October 10, 1970, Pierre Laporte, 49, Quebec's labour minister, was kidnapped in the Montreal suburb of St. Hubert, by FLQ terrorists. Seven days later his strangled body was found in the trunk of a car only blocks away.

The murder electrified the nation – following, as it did, the kidnapping, five days earlier, of British trade commissioner to Canada, James Cross (who was later released). The government, approaching panic, invoked the emergency War Measures Act, resulting in the arrests of 465 persons in Quebec (of which only 18 were subsequently convicted). But on December 28, two of the kidnappers crawled out of a hidden tunnel beneath a building and surrendered. Terrorists Paul Rose and Francis Simard received life sentences for Laporte's murder. Rose's brother, Jacques, got eight years.

On June 23, 1972, after four teenagers in Don Mills, Ontario, watched a TV horror show in which a woman's body was found in a trunk, they broke open a sealed freezer that had been stored in their living room. Inside, they found the sun-tanned and frozen body of Grace Evelyn Todd, 34, with a 22-calibre bullet in her head, who'd been stashed in the freezer for six months along with vegetables and turkey pies. Grace's husband, David Todd, 38, pleaded guilty to manslaughter and received ten years. The freezer (sans turkey pies *or* Grace Todd) is on display in the Metro Toronto Police Museum.

On July 18, 1973, the body of beautiful former fashion model Christine Demeter, 33, was found bludgeoned to death in the garage of her Mississauga, Ontario home by her wealthy, housebuilding husband, Peter. In December, 1974, after a sensational trial involving ex-mistresses, hired killers and foreign Legionnaries, Demeter, 44, was sentenced to life for hiring someone to kill his wife. After appeals to the Canadian Supreme Court were rejected, Demeter, from his maximum-security cell in Millhaven Penetentiary, is now trying to sue three insurance companies for the $1.1 million insurance on his wife's life. A bad movie, *I Love You, Hugs And Kisses,* and an excellent best seller, *By Persons Unknown,* were both based on the Demeter case. But Christine's actual killer is still unknown.

On December 15, 1974, the bodies of two Moncton, New Brunswick, policemen, Corporal Aurele Bourgeois, 47, father of four, and Constable Michael O'Leary, father of two, were found in shallow, snow-covered graves outside the city. The officers had been searching for the kidnappers of Richard Stein, 14 (who was released after payment of a $15,000 ransom), when they were captured, forced to dig their own graves, handcuffed and shot in the heads from behind. Outraged Maritimers screamed for the death penalty, and raised $380,000 for the two families. Following charges of police bungling and a mass funeral attended by 600 policemen, James Hutchison, 43, and Richard Ambrose, 22, were convicted and sentenced to hang. They are still in prison.

On January 2, 1975, unknown killers walked into the seedy Bar Gargantua in Montreal, herded the staff and customers (ten men and three women, including a cabby, a bus driver, a gambler, a 17-year-old girl and a topless waitress) into a crammed seven-by-eight-foot storeroom, locked it, then set the place on fire. All 13 died. After a massive police hunt for the chief suspect, Richard "The Cat" Blass, 29, an escaped convict wanted for a double murder in the same bar three months before, Blass was blasted to death during a police raid on a Val David mountain-top chalet on January 5. Heading the raid was tough, bald, machine-gun-toting Montreal Sergeant Albert Lisacek, 41, renowned in Montreal by his nickname, "Kojak."

On August 13, 1976, the strangled bodies of four children, aged seven, eight, nine and 12, who'd been missing for three months, were found in shallow graves outside Saskatoon. The fear that had gripped Saskatchewan since June turned into rage – vented against federal MPs who voted to abolish capital punishment. On February 10, bank robber David William Threinen, 27, previously charged with and acquitted for killing a 16-year-old girl, was given four concurrent life sentences after pleading guilty. The judge recommended he never be paroled.

On July 29, 1977, 12-year-old Emanuel Jaques was lured away from his shoeshine spot on Toronto's Yonge Street with the promise of $35 and taken to an apartment above a Yonge Street body-rub parlour, where he was homosexually attacked, tortured and drowned in a kitchen sink. Three days later, police found his body in a green garbage bag on a roof outside. Toronto's consequent fury resulted in swift police and political action that virtually eliminated body-rubs from Yonge Street's downtown "strip." Saul David Betesh, 27, and Robert Wayne Kribs, 29, were convicted of first-degree murder; Josef Woods, 26, was sentenced for second degree; Werner Gruener, 29, to the anger of police, was acquitted. The Crown subsequently appealed his acquittal.

On January 22, 1978, two masked men entered a crowded ice-cream parlour in St. Leonard, Quebec, a notorious mob hangout. They approached a table where Paolo Violi, 46, the capo de capo of Montreal's Mafia, was playing cards with three other men, and shot him twice in the back of the head with a 12-calibre Lupara shotgun imported from Italy. Following a massive Montreal funeral to which floral wreaths were sent from top North American Mafiosi, Giovanni DiMora, 35, Agostino Cuntera, 34, and Dominico Manno, 44, pleaded guilty and were convicated of conspiracy to murder. They got from five to seven years.

British Columbia has led all provinces for bloody massacres in the '70s. On September 5, 1970, eight people, including five children, were shot, stabbed or beaten to death during a rampage by a sole killer in West Creston, B.C. On August 8, 1972, another madman on a shooting spree shot six total strangers, ranging in age from 16 to 71, in the mountains near Oliver, B.C. But the killings that hit headlines across the country were the shootings of four teenagers, aged 16 to 19, on the banks of the Fraser River when, on July 18, 1977, a man wanting to steal a truck for a planned Vancouver kidnapping interrupted a noisy beer party, shot the four kids with a high-powered rifle, and threw the bodies in the river. After an extensive six-week manhunt, Walter Murray Madsen, 24, was arrested and sentenced to life on four counts of first degree murder.

Footnote: No one has been executed for murder in Canada since killers Don Turpin and Arthur Lucas were hanged back-to-back in Toronto's Don Jail in 1962.

Paul King, journalist.

The worst air disaster in history occurred in March, 1977, in the Canary Islands when a Pan-Am jumbo jet-liner collided with a KLM 747 on the airfield of Santa Crucz de Tenerife, killing 582 people.

The worst accident involving a single airliner occurred in March, 1974, when a Turkish DC-10 crashed near Paris, killing 345 people.

The worst crash in U.S. aviation history occurred on May 25, 1979. 271 people died when an American Airlines DC-10 crashed to earth at O'Hare Airport shortly after take-off.

The site of an Air Canada plane crash. The DC-8 was coming in for a landing in Toronto. Ninety-seven passengers and the crew of nine all died. CP

A '70s Quiz

No handbook of a decade is worth anything without a list of the most notable names, slogans and generic terms that will always be associated with it. Barbara Frum, radio/TV star and journalist, chose the following as touchstones of this era, no matter how briefly they affected our lives:

Victor, K-Tel, Rod Stewart, Peter Benchley, Carlos the Jackal, Jeremy Thorpe, Bruce Springsteen, Elizabeth Ray, Wayne Hays, Fanne Fox and Wilbur Mills, Steven Spielberg, Paul Bocuse, Mikhail Baryshnikov, René Simard, Catherine Deneuve, Justin, Sasha and Michel, Yasmin Aga Khan, Julia Child, Adrienne Clarkson, Elisabeth Kübler-Ross, Betty Williams, Dolly Parton, Kunta Kinte, The Weiss Family, Peter Kent, Robert Samson, Mark Fidrych, Billy Martin, Margaux Hemingway, Pete Rose, Small Is Beautiful, Three Mile Island, Greg Joy, John Travolta, Swine Flu, Legionnaires' Disease, Richard Nixon, Claude Wagner, Werner Erhard, Col. Yonatan Netanyahu, Gerald Ford, Diane Jones Konihowski, Jerry Brown, TM, Steve Biko, Cuisine Minceur, The Land is Strong, Gens De L'Air, Keith Davey, SLA, *People*, John Turner, Jim Coutts, Hans Martin Schleyer, You've come a long way, Baby, Emily Harris, Emmylou Harris, Jane Fonda, We do it all for you, Robert Stanfield, Francis Fox, Dave Barrett, Barbra Streisand, Tongsun Park, petrodollars, Congressman Leo Ryan, Lloyd Robertson, Martin Goldfarb, Luciano Pavarotti, Donny & Marie, Margaret Trudeau, Bruce Jenner, Cujo, est, Mork, Christina Onassis, Entebbe, Tania, Jackie O, Fran Lebowitz, Ulrike Meinhof, cellulite, Stephen Lewis, Paul Soles, Gloria Steinem, The Louds, John Le Carré, Olivia Newton-John, Doug Henning, Joe Davidson, Gary Gilmore, Dr. Robert Atkins, Howard Jarvis, Ehrlichman and Haldeman, Son of Sam, Erich Segal, Germaine Greer, David Bowie, Orlando Letelier, Bruce Nevins, Roger Taillibert, Woody Allen, Linus Pauling, Michael Snow, Tom Stoppard, Monty Python, Malcolm Bricklin, The Boat People, David Berkowitz, Frank Stella, Ronald McDonald, E. J. Pratt, Reggie Jackson, Mikhailov and Kharmalov, Cher Bono, Guy Lafleur, Kojak, This Country In The Morning, Yusufu Lule, Margaret Atwood, Dan Hill, Craig Russell, Brian Davies, Lord Ken Thomson, Freddy Laker, Sally Quinn, Peter Lougheed, Evel Knievel, Rachel Zylberg, Robert Altman, Anita Bryant, Peter Bogdanovich, Mike Doonesbury, Karen Silkwood, *The China Syndrome*, *Jaws*, Neil Simon, Dame Janet Baker, *Rhoda*, Archibald Cox, E. Howard Hunt, Bruce Cockburn, George Habash, J. Paul Getty III, Toller Cranston, Steve Martin, Willie Nelson and Waylon Jennings, The Fonz, Idi Amin, An offer you can't refuse, Charles Marion, John Paul I, Bob Marley, John Dean, The Gong Show, Freddy Prinze, Farrah Fawcett-Majors, Bobby Orr, Billy Carter, Scharansky, Ginsberg, Orlov, Bukovsky, Sakharov, Mary Steinhauser, Steven Weed, Maureen Forrester, James McCord, Garth Drabinsky, Willy Brandt, Muhammed Ali, Mary Tyler Moore, Punk Rock, Ken Danby, James Cross, Sam the Record Man, Pierre Laporte, Kain and Augustyn, Deep Throat, Sid Vicious, Andy Bruce, Bay City Rollers, Bee Gees, Cheryl Tiegs, Norman Lear, R2D2, Barbara Walters, Le Duc Tho, Chevy Chase, Robin Phillips, Salt I and II, *Jacob Two-Two*, Howard Hughes, The Gang of Four, Erica Jong, Alexandr Solzhenitsyn, Linda Lovelace, Darth Vader, Harry Brown, Sylvia Fraser, James Fixx, Rev. Sun Myung Moon, Saturday Night Live, Mark Spitz, Henry Kissinger, Fleetwood

Mac, Rev. Jim Jones, Begin-Sadat, Fred Silverman, Morris the Cat, Keith Jarrett, Mason Reese, The Hite Report, The Eagles, Daniel Ellsberg, Seymour Hersh, Black September, Evonne Goolagong, Ritalin, Pele, Gonzo, Martin Hartwell, Steve Cauthen, Uri Geller, Dennis Hills, Roman Polanski, Mel Hurtig, Clay Felker, Tal Zaatar, Mario Puzo, Bill 101, Pol Pot, Bebe Rebozo, Larry Flynt, Greenpeace, Jack Anderson, Bob Woodward and Carl Bernstein, Murray McLauchlan, Jimmy Hoffa, David Crombie, Linda Ronstadt, Mitsubishi, Masters & Johnson, Martha Mitchell, Lynette (Squeaky) Fromme, Zubin Mehta, Michael Pitfield, Sara Jane Moore, Leonard Jones, Robert Lemieux, Deng Xiaoping, Allan J. Hyneck, G. Gordon Liddy, Cosmos 954, Secretariat, Linda Blair, Archie Bunker, George McGovern, Robert Vesco, Warren Beatty, Sam Ervin, Henry Morgentaler, Jimmy Connors, Gordon Pinsent, The IRA, The ETA, Salvador Allende, Chris Evert, Spiro Agnew, The Muppets, Miss Piggy, Paolo Violi, Robert de Niro, Glenda Jackson, Meat Loaf, Cookie Monster, Olaf Palme, Marvin Hamlisch, Aldo Moro, Pierre Juneau, William Obront, Sheik Yamani, Donna Summer, Clifford Irving, Mary Hartman, Burt Reynolds, Bryce Mackasey, Annie Hall, Harry Reems, Ralph Bakshi, Helen Reddy, Barry Manilow, Roddy Llewellyn, Tom Eagleton, Karen Ann Quinlan, Colonel Gaddafi, The Flying Burrito Brothers, Harvey Milk, Betty Ford, Betty Rollins, Happy Rockefeller, Carly Simon, Yukio Michima, Indira Ghandi, Peter Demeter, Isaac Bashevis Singer, Pinochet, Papadopoulos, Irma Bombeck, Costa Gavras, Tretiak and Yakeshev, Jon Voight, John Sirica, Soweto, Ali Bhutto, Marshall Ky, Nadia Comaneci, Alex Comfort, Alex Haley, Ayatollah Khomeini, Anais Nin, Oriana Fallaci, Marjoe, The Pentagon Papers, Robert Redford, Dora Bloch, Airey Neave, Bobby Riggs, Rinka, Anastasio Somoza, Laetrile, Shawn Cassidy, Ultrasuede, Jacuzzis.

Barbara Frum, broadcaster, *As It Happens.*

Divorces

Louise and René Lévesque
Brita and Gordon Lightfoot
Adrienne and Stephen Clarkson
Sophia and Lorne Duguid
Carole and Dr. Bryce Taylor
Sylvia Murphy and Charles Templeton
Dorothy and Frank Duff Moores
Johanna and Tom Cossitt
Joan and Francis Fox
Joan and Bobby Hull
Jean and Jack Kent Cooke
Tammy Grimes and Christopher Plummer
Beverly and Bill Marshall

Sylvia Train, columnist, *Toronto Sun.*

The Most Over & Underrated Things of the Decade

Overrated

Earth shoes
Werner Erhard
Yogurt
Digital anything
Talking to plants
All disco
Mineral water
Designer-labelled anything
Sports instruction
List books
All social events of more than eight people
Woody Allen

Underrated

Touch-tone dialing
Country music
The USA
Reading the "blue news" on TV
Alexander Butterfield
Channel Commander
Francis Ford Coppola's *The Conversation*
Burger King's "Whopper"
Knowlton Nash
Barney Miller
Marriage
The Sunday drive
All social events of less than eight people

Danny Finkleman, broadcaster.

John George Diefenbaker
1895-1979

One of his great contributions was his devotion to human right, the rule of law and the protection of the individual. He had great sympathy for what is usually referred to as "the ordinary Canadian."

Robert Stanfield.

Milestones

People who died during the '70s.

WORLD LEADERS

1970
Charles de Gaulle, 80. The president of France who enraged Canadians with his *"Vive Québec libre"* statement while visiting Expo '67.

1971
Nikita Krushchev, 77. Soviet Communist leader. Deposed 1964 as premier.

1972
Lester Bowles Pearson, 75. Diplomat, politician, writer, Nobel Peace Prize winner and Canada's 14th prime minister.

HRH the Duke of Windsor, 77. King Edward VIII. Came to the throne on January 20, 1936, and abdicated on December 11 of the same year to marry the woman he loved, twice-divorced Wallace Simpson.

1973
David Ben-Gurion, 89. First prime minister of Israel.

1975
General Francisco Franco, 83. Dictator of Spain since 1939. Arranged in 1969 for Prince Juan Carlos of Bourbon to take over on his death.

Chaing Kai-Shek, 88. Leader of China's nationalist forces in the country's long and bloody civil war against China's communists led by Mao Tse-tung.

Mao Tse-tung, 82. Legendary communist leader of the Chinese revolutionary forces and founder of the People's Republic of China in 1949.

1978
President Jomo Kenyatta. Born sometime in the 1890s, he said. The leader who shaped the modern history of Kenya, which emerged as one of black Africa's most notable states.

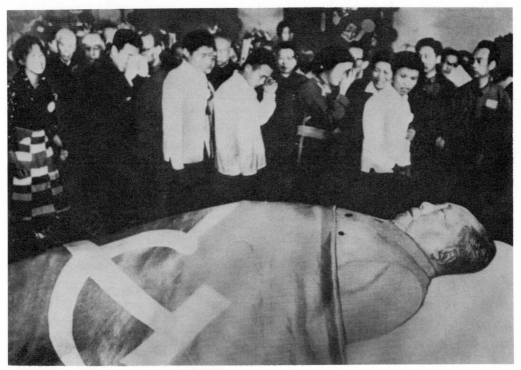

Chairman Mao Tse-tung lying in state as
hundreds of thousands of mourners file
past, 1976. AP

The last photo of General Francisco
Franco, Spanish chief of state, before he
died in 1974. AP

The late Pope John Paul I greeting Polish
Cardinal Karol Wojtyla, Archbishop of
Krakow, who became Pope John Paul II in
1978. AP

Golda Meir, 80. One of the generation of pioneers who built Israel and was prime minister from 1969 to 1974.

Pope Paul VI, after a 15-year reign over a church torn between excessive expectations for change and equally excessive resistance to change.

Pope John Paul I, 65. Died of a heart attack after a 33-day reign.

1979
Ali Bhutto, 52. Former prime minister of Pakistan. Hanged by the revolutionary government that overthrew him, for his attempt to murder a political opponent.

BUSINESS LEADERS

1972
Colonel R. S. McLaughlin, 100. Put Oshawa on the map with his auto manufacturing.

1973
John David Eaton, 63. Fourth president of the T. Eaton Co. Ltd., a post he held for 27 years.

1975
Howard Hughes, 71. One of the world's richest, most eccentric and most secretive men. Hughes is reputed to have left an estate of $2.3 billion.

Aristotle Onassis, 69. Greek shipping magnate who won world attention by marrying Jacqueline Kennedy.

1976
Lord Thomson of Fleet, 82. Multimillionaire newspaper and television magnate who made his fortune after 60.

H. R. MacMillan, 90. Millionaire industrialist and philanthropist in Vancouver, whose company formed the basis of the giant MacMillan Bloedel Ltd.

1978
John Angus "Bud" McDougald, 70. The archetype of financial tycoons and chairman of the powerful Argus Corporation.

W. Garfield Weston, 80. The baker's son from Toronto who stamped a multi-million dollar financial empire out of his father's bread and pastry business.

1979
Nelson Davis, 73. Canadian businessman.

Cyrus S. Eaton, 95. Multimillionaire industrialist born in Pugwash, Nova Scotia. Winner of the Lenin Peace Prize in 1960.

Jean Monet, 80. The founding father of the European Common Market.

CANADIAN POLITICIANS

1970
Pierre Laporte, 47. Quebec labour minister murdered by the FLQ on Saturday, October 17, 1970.

1973
George Drew. Former premier of Ontario and national conservative leader from 1948 to 1956.

1975
Charlotte Whitton, 79. Controversial mayor of Ottawa.

1979
W. A. C. "Wacky" Bennett, 78. B.C.'s most durable premier and father of its present premier, Bill Bennett.

ENTERTAINERS

1972
Maurice Chevalier, 84. French actor.

1977
Elvis Presley, 42. The King of Rock who's immortalized as much for his erotic hip gyrations, sexy snarl and long sideburns as his music.

Charlie Chaplin, 88. Whose roles in silent movies have become part of the world's comic folklore.

Guy Lombardo, 75. Speed-boat cham-

The Presley family burial plot at Forest Hills Cemetery in Memphis, Tennessee. AP

pion and bandleader whose Royal Canadians became a trademark of New Year's Eve.

Bing Crosby, 73. The first real crooner. Crosby's popularity continues today with songs like *White Christmas*.

Groucho Marx, 86. One of the legendary Marx Brothers.

1978
Edgar Bergen, 75. The ventriloquist who brought the wooden dummy "Charley McCarthy" to life for millions on Sunday-night radio.

Charles Boyer, 78. French-born leading man of the '30s and '40s.

1979
Mary Pickford, 86. Born in Toronto (Gladys Smith), immortalized in silent films as a young innocent.

John Wayne, 72. The "Duke" beloved by generations of movie-goers.

ARTISTS, WRITERS, MUSICIANS

1970
Jimi Hendrix, 27. Rock singer who died of an overdose, shocking dope addicts.

Janis Joplin, 27. Famous rock singer, *Me and Bobby McGee*, who died of drugs and alcohol.

Lawren Harris, 85. One of the last of the Group of Seven.

1971
Sir Tyrone Guthrie, 70. Playwrite, director and producer. First artistic director of Stratford.

Nathan Cohen, 48. Theatre critic whose tough reviews gained him an international reputation and frequently caused productions to stay clear of Toronto.

1972
A. M. Klein, 64. One of Canada's best-known poets.

1973
Sir Ernest MacMillan, 80. Conductor and composer. Sir Ernest was the first person to be knighted outside the United Kingdom.

1974
A. Y. Jackson, 91. Member of the Group of Seven.

1976
Benjamin Brittain, 63. One of the 20th century's leading composers and regarded as England's greatest composer since Henry Purcell in the 17th century.

Alexander Calder. Famous for his "mobile" sculptures and monumental iron and steel motionless structures.

Andre Malraux, 75. Writer, war hero, de Gaulle's aide – and an intellectual and a man of action.

1977
Edwin Headley Holgate, 85. Group of Seven.

William Kurelek, 50. Canadian artist lauded for his paintings of everyday life on the prairies.

Jack Bush, 68. One of the few home-based Canadian painters to be recognized internationally.

William Arthur Deacon, 87. Book critic for the Toronto *Globe and Mail* and pioneer in a wave of cultural nationalism that swept English Canada in the 1920s.

1978
Jack Chambers, 47. Canadian artist who directed our attention to the significance of everyday experience.

1979
Dora Mavor Moore, 91. A dominant force in English Canadian theatre.

SPORTS

1970
Terry Sawchuk, 41. Detroit goalie.

Vince Lombardi, 57. Green Bay Packers'

coach whose famous line was "Winning isn't everything: it's the only thing."

1971
Bobby Jones, 69. One of the world's greatest golfers. A founder of the Master's Gold Tournament and the Augusta Golf Club.

1972
Turk Broda, 58. Longtime NHL goalie. Had 13 shutouts in 101 playoff games, which was a Stanley Cup record.

Bill Durnan, 52. Montreal goalie.

Doug Bentley, 56. Chicago Black Hawk star.

Roberto Clemente, 38. An outstanding baseball player who was killed in a plane crash.

1973
Abebe Bikila, 46. Ethiopian marathon racer and two-time winner at the Olympics.

Gil Boa, 49. Canadian Gold Medal shooter.

Ada Mackenzie, 80. Outstanding women's golfer and sportswoman.

1974
Lloyd Percival, 61. Canadian fitness expert.

Peter Revson, 33. Heir to Revlon fortune and Formula I car racer.

Tim Horton, 44. Hockey star for Toronto Maple Leafs and later played for Rangers, Penguins and Sabres.

1976
Bobby Pearce, 76. Famous oarsman.

1977
Frank Boucher, 76. Played with the New York Rangers, from 1926 to 1938, before retiring to coach.

1978
Dit Clapper, 70. First NHL player to play 20 years with the same club (Boston).

Gene Tunney, 81. Former World Heavyweight Champion. Lost only once in 76 bouts.

Lyman Bostock, 27. One of the highest-paid players in major league baseball.

PIONEERS

1972
Charles Lindberg, 72. First man to fly solo across the Atlantic.

1976
Dr. Wilder Penfield, 85. Noted Canadian neurologist.

1978
Dr. Charles Best, 79. Coworker with Sir Frederick Banting in the discovery of insulin.

Margaret Mead, 77. Noted anthropologist.

Isabel Bassett, reporter on *Hourlong*.

The '80s Memorandum: The Future's Not What It Used to Be

"Come, it's pleased so far," thought Alice, and she went on. "Would you tell me, please, which way I ought to go from here?" "That depends a good deal on where you want to get to," said the Cat.

Lewis Carroll,

So we bid farewell, with a sense of perverse nostalgia or good riddance, to the past ten years. An uneasy transition is presently underway: *Maclean's* magazine has already waved good-bye, likening the '70s to a thief in the night, absconding with our fondest hopes and dreams. The '80s are almost upon us, particularized and made urgent by the fearful connotations of 1984. (Now's a good time to tackle this, since Orwell published 30 years ago, and since his name is already being taken in vain. A current advertisement for Datsun automobiles is addressed to George himself, urging him to smile, wherever he is, at the prospect of far-sighted purchasers motoring happily through, and beyond, that dire year. We will see more of this as the turning point draws nigh.) And now's as good a time as any, given our ritual deliniation by decade, to repeat those perplexing and seemingly timeless questions: Where are we supposed to go from here? And what, in heaven's name, is about to happen next?

The future affords a false assurance because it hasn't happened yet. Its cutting edges are readily discernible: in the form of social phenomena (women's liberation, fragmentation of the family); global crises (energy, pollution and population); and national trends (inflation, unemployment, an aging population). But we tend to isolate such unwelcome harbingers into manageable lumps, to be considered and rejected at will, or dealt with piecemeal. This is a natural defence mechanism, but it no longer works – we are busily plugging holes in the dike, oblivious to an impending tidal wave. In the words of Don Toppin, chairman of the Toronto branch of the World Future Society, "So much time has to be given to the important and the urgent that no one has time for the critical." What appears to be a multiplicity of choice is proscribed first by *ideological* fragmentation. We identify a given problem with ease – everybody knows that inflation will ruin us all – and then sit bickering over possible cures. Focussing our energies may advance a particular cause, but this, too, puts on the blinkers; the passionate advocate of (say) Equal Pay has little time for, or knowledge of, the ecological horrors of Acid Rain. One nonstop urban activist nicely summarized this most galling aspect of the humanist dilemma: "You can only attend so many meetings."

This is why many people have given up, presuming the future to be something that will arrive, to be met when the time comes, thus absenting themselves from a process of change. If we presume tomorrow to be inevitable – beyond our control – we may succumb to either unreasoning dread (the sky's got to fall sooner or later) or to a sort of nostalgia for the *present* – hoping that things are going to be the same, only different. Such an attitude merely assures they'll be *worse*. Architect Martin Pawley, in *The Private Future*, explores the perils of this peculiar apathy: "Western society is on the brink of collapse – not into crime, violence, madness or redeeming revolution, as many would believe, but into *withdrawal* – not from an assault on their most cherished values, but from a voluntary, almost enthusiastic *abandonment*." Pawley is right: It's a whole lot easier to get up and boogie than to get out and vote, so why not accept whatever life slaps upon your plate? We aren't doing all that bad. But if the city – like the Cheshire Cat – seems relatively benevolent, offering an existential choice (Where do we *want* to go?) then our actions, decisions and aspirations shape the course of things to come. Someone else will assume the responsibility you so blithely abdicate; you may not like the results, but they'll be the product of your own benign neglect. Trite, but true: The future is *now*, and we are its architects.

Perhaps this is why the future is hard to grasp and why it is hard to *think* about, as opposed to worry. Barring a nuclear holocaust or the Second Coming, the '80s will represent a stream of ongoing change rooted in the present. Its pace may accelerate, but the ways in which we act and react (contrary to the fevered expectations of the utopian community, which tends to yearn for world government) are unlikely to dramatically alter. There will be ebbs and flows within ethical and moral frameworks, and refinements and redefinitions of positions. We may postulate an all-pervasive swing to the right, but people with new modes of thought (the infamous television generation) are about to enter the decision-making process, and influence its course. We, the momentary powers that be, move from the cumulative experience of a lifetime; we will not move very far in five or ten years, except under the greatest duress.

There are dangers here – among them, a certain blasé attitude toward early warnings of every kind. The sky has refused to fall on schedule; by the '60s we were *supposed* to have a helicopter on every roof. Moral: We can cope with change, some of which won't even come about. Secondly, we respond to a crisis by invoking the Level Crossing Solution – you wait till there's an appropriately crucial body count before installing an underpass. The British economist Robert Theobald views this as yet another symptom of incipient collapse: "We are coming to accept things that are intolerable." But what to do? Out of necessity we delegate authority, placing some degree of faith in institutions, systems, elected leaders. How much information can we absorb – how much responsibility can we assume for society at large? We have our own lives to lead, and they impose restrictions. Example: Unless you work with computers, you will be hard-pressed to define the term "software," yet self-preservation would seem to demand at least a nodding acquaintance with these new technologies. Our response is passive acceptance, or the purchase of a digital watch. (Or maybe not. The wearing of an old-fashioned watch, with hands, may become the mark of a neoLuddite, like a refusal to learn metric, let alone Fortran and Cobol.)

But institutions are themselves changing daily – subverted by technology. Witness the politician, struggling to fathom the meaning of a silicone chip the size of a ball-point tip, containing 40,000 bits of information. The hapless leader doesn't know what a bit of information *is*, or how 40,000 of them managed to get inside this tiny *thing*. This does not aid the formulation of policy – but it *does* illustrate the unpleasant fact that *each* of us is a yahoo, functionally illiterate outside our sheltered expertise. One highly intelligent man, amazed by his child playing binary games in the kitchen with a deck of cards, a transit punch and a knitting needle, summed up this yawning (generational) gap: "My wife thinks it's magic. Our kid is thinking like a machine – a tacitly accepted extension of himself. He's been marinated in electronic sauce, and machines are simply tools to him. We invented them, but we can't understand their implications. Kids deal with them directly, as we did with cars and the times table. It's sociological and technological imprinting – things as they *are*. There's no magic; no mythology. The kids are going to put these things to *use*. Of course, McLuhan was right. He just didn't go far enough."

PostMcLuhanism! That's all we need to brighten up the day. But let's admit, at least, that times *do* change. It is unwise in the extreme to assume that *anything* is irrevocable – for confirmation, apply to the Shah of Iran, somewhere west of the Peacock Throne. His epitaph: He didn't see it coming. Neither, with any degree of clarity, do we. The annoying thing is that with all the skills at our command – divination by computer, prophesy by poll, an absolute plethora of informational experts and middlemen – the future *ought* to be foreseeable. But this is fallacy. Nothing is written: Nobody knows.

"Oh, I'm not particular as to size," Alice hastily replied; "only one doesn't like changing so often, you know." "I don't know," said the Caterpillar.

Futurists are a strange breed, and unassailable: You can't prove them wrong. It's like arguing theology with a priest. There are enough of them around to sink ships, and their activities command your attention.

First come the extrapolationists, who thrive on data, arguing from the present. But this is risky: John Kettle, a Toronto practitioner, exhorts his many clients in government and industry to remake their forecasts constantly, never letting, say, a five-year projection go full term, by which time the trends may have reversed. For a society that loves to study things and postpone decisions, futurism is obviously a growth industry – though an imperfect science. Kettle is the author of a pamphlet called *Hindsight on the Future*, which contains a devastating scenario for the year 2001, featuring (among other horrible prospects) the virtual depopulation of Saskatchewan. This is not going to be the case – but it *was* indicated by StatsCan data available at Kettle's time of writing in 1976. Plainly, to be at all relevant, these investigations ought to proceed nonstop; and Kettle is the first to admit that a given conclusion – be it computerized or intuitive – is subject to an endearing variety of errors.

Witness the remarkable boondoggle that enjoyed brief notoriety during early 1979 in the Toronto *Star*. The *Star*, ever vigilant, got hold of a study warning that Toronto's population, far from mushrooming away as everybody had assumed, was in fact declining and would continue to do so. This was announced in ringing tones on a quick succession of editorial pages, accompanied by calls for a crisis debate in council, and grim visions of a city occupied solely by the old, jobless and poor – in short, everything but a leper colony in the Eaton Centre – and went on for the better part of a week, until someone contacted the planners responsible. They admitted, with chagrin, that the gloom-and-doom scenario was, in fact, a low-ball figure, presuming a combination of heinous factors. They were understandably miffed that it was snatched out of context and given so much play. "There is a difference," remarked one irate fact-finder,

"between projection and prediction."

Very well. Ill-founded alarms are one thing. Nobody is guiltless here; we all make mistakes. But mistakes in the accumulation and propagation of data that affect matters of public policy can lead to awful results, as students of Ontario Hydro's grand-scale shooting in the dark will attest. We will shortly be paying for that one, in convenient monthly installments; but you can think of 100 other vital issues on which our elected representatives and business leaders are deluged with wildly conflicting facts and figures. The wonder is that anybody gets anything done. All this is equally applicable to our private lives, and lends eerie credence to the thought that *any* plan is outmoded before it can be adopted, let alone put into practice – if indeed it was sensible in the first place. Under these circumstances, enlightened debate becomes a guessing game, with no prizes given.

Nonetheless, such lapses do not prohibit the futurists from making a good thing of it, as may be gathered from the list of clients serviced by Ruben Nelson, the author of an imperative text entitled *The Illusions of Urban Man*. He pictures us "agonizing over which 19th-century system to impose on the *21st*," and suggests the only way out is to face the anguish of introspection and *inter*personal responsibility: "To presume we stop at our skins is, I think, insane." He also charges $425 a head – excluding meals and accommodation – for a three-day seminar that promises a "sweeping, fundamental and integrated analysis of the Canadian condition," and has advised the Economic Council of Canada, the Department of Consumer and Corporate Affairs, Ontario's Ministry of Culture and Recreation, a gaggle of insurance companies and the Privy Council Office. (No doubt this intimate acquaintance with the mandarins has led to his conclusion that, in terms of aberrant lifestyles, "politicians are the worst offenders – engaging publically in behaviour which, if undertaken personally, would be certifiably mad." Apply this where you will, and if you dare.)

Nelson is an interesting man, and his views ought not to be trivialized. The point is that next time a bureaucrat is up and musing, his or her thoughts may well have been instigated, perhaps *penned*, by Nelson or one of his ilk. The rest of us, short the $425 necessary to getting our horizons broadened in a hotel, are too busy facing the anguish of a mortgage payment to assume the keeping of our brothers on a cosmic scale. Unlike the government, we can go broke. Our activities are properly channelled toward avoiding such a fate, leaving little time to engage in a crablike motion beloved of Nelson's disciples – the Paradigm Shift.

As defined by Don Toppin, paradigms are deeply ingrained value systems, or modes of thinking, that must be corrected if we are to survive. His assessment is that less than 10 percent of the population is aware of a process of change, while approximately one-tenth of one percent can define its nature. Those chosen few are the folk who will usher in a better world, since *we* show neither the inclination nor the capacity to shift in time. Shame on us. Our undue recalcitrance in this regard permits the best and brightest in every field you care to name to couple biweekly calls for drastic action ("Attitudes must change! A basic overhaul is long overdue!") with superficial tinkering that wouldn't fool a child. *This* is unlikely to change in the near or distant future. In all, beware of insights filtered downward from above, snap-judgement headlines, and the computer print-out as deus ex machina. Our capacity for transformation may well be finite, but it's all we've got – and tomorrow, in all its warlike aspects, is far too important to be left to the futuristic generals.

"I could tell you my adventures, beginning from this morning," said Alice, a little timidly; "but it's no use going back to yesterday, because I was a different person then."

The question remains: What kind of trouble are we in? An example springs to mind; call it a Baby House. For many years, June Callwood, Toronto broadcaster and long-time espouser of Worthy Causes, has been proposing that every community or neighbourhood ought to have one – a place that would offer prenatal and pediatric treatment, babysitting and day care, a toy exchange, a public-health nurse, birth-control information and a 24-hour emergency service staffed by professional workers with the help of parents, senior citizens and kids themselves. It would be like a firehall (for which nobody questions the need) – simply a place to take the pressure off familial relationships. "It would recognize that *all* infants and parents need to be seen as vulnerable – not just the poor, or teenage mothers. If we started to provide for those infants in a non-interfering and totally supportive way, we'd have fewer casualties." That's the trouble. We've got the casualties – but the Baby House, despite Callwood's prodigious energies, does not exist.

Perhaps it never will. Our attempts to contain a burgeoning chaos may constitute interference, no matter how you phrase it. Those who come after us may not wish to provide their fellows with total support, from cradle unto grave. That is a long-term commitment; John Kettle, asked to identify the most likely fundamental change in our way of life, promptly named *disorder*: "I don't mean riots. I mean *absence of order*. It's very hard for people brought up on *self* to be interested in complex systems – you won't find people to *run* things."

If Kettle is correct, the '80s may witness the final bankruptcy of liberal good intentions – with each of us engrossed in pulling our own, highly selfish, strings.

And yet, this very selfishness *ought* to

produce, at least, a sense of anger – often a spur to change. In another context (the prospect of salvaging what's left of our somewhat illusory civil liberties) Callwood perceives a degree of hope. "Surely," she says, "we know enough by now to be able to *act*." Maybe *that*'s the trouble. Of course we know our rights are largely fiction, but scandals and improprieties serve only to numb the mind, trailing off into a larger, nonspecific malaise. Such abuse is *not* overt, and tends to happen to somebody else. The Mounties aren't knocking on *your* door in the dead of night; they might be tapping your phone, but you've got nothing to hide. And besides – what *can* one person do.

The trouble may be that an individual is, in fact, powerless, alone or within a chosen group. But having argued your way down to the bottom of that particular barrel, it is difficult to resurface. The complexity of our problems is overwhelming; conflicts and contradictions abound. Witness our responses. First is a longing to apportion *blame*, pinning our woes on the poor, the immigrants, the welfare cheaters, our political opponents, government in general, developers or suburbia. Pick a bogey. Next is passivity – waiting for life to be delivered, like the mail, holding our breath to see what tomorrow brings. Then comes the desire for simplistic solutions – Proposition 13 writ large and various. So it goes. We may not drop off the edge into quasifascism – if a dictator arose next week, our first move would be to commission an impact study – but we may succumb to the attractions of retreat. In fact, that option remains forever closed. There is no going back.

Indeed, there is no standing still. Perhaps our ability to set change in motion and live with it when it comes will prove unequal to the challenge. In this case we *will* be doomed to sudden or gradual decline, manipulated from every side, dragged down by the sheer weight of the incapable. We will live out the seige as best we can, grown soft and fatalistic, burdened by trinkets. Pogo's definition of the enemy holds true, and nobody is about to save us from ourselves. We will survive, but we will be different people – unadventurous and afraid.

Or perhaps not. We can court the apocalyptic muse because we are possessed of reason and cursed with imagination. We are the literate elite, free to indulge our angst to the full, our dissatisfactions bordered only by desire. It is very tempting to stand pat, hoping for the best or fearing for the worst, rather than move toward a potentially unpleasant surprise, lurking just around the corner. But if we undertake the journey, we may discover, en route, a certain resilience. We may surprise *ourselves* at last.

Where do we go from here? Northrop Frye, in his search for our elusive identity, posed another question: *Where* is here? Until we find that answer – until we begin to take our presence seriously – the future will remain intangible, beyond our reach and understanding. There is ample cause for despair, and only one slim hope: That we, who have the luxury of choice, will choose wisely, and soon.

Ed Hailwood and **Janet Enright**, journalists, *Toronto Life*.

Miss Piggy takes a break from filming of *The Muppet Movie.* AP

Index of Contributors